# LOVE AND WAR IN THE PYRENEES

# LOVE AND WAR
# IN THE PYRENEES

A Story of Courage, Fear and Hope,
1939–1944

ROSEMARY BAILEY

Weidenfeld & Nicolson
LONDON

First published in Great Britain in 2008
by Weidenfeld & Nicolson

1 3 5 7 9 10 8 6 4 2

A CIP catalogue record for this book
is available from the British Library.

ISBN 13 978 0 297 85127 1

Typeset at The Spartan Press Ltd,
Lymington, Hants

Printed and bound at Mackays of Chatham,
Chatham, Kent

The Orion publishing group's policy is to use papers that
are natural, renewable and recyclable products and made
from wood grown in sustainable forests. The logging and
manufacturing processes are expected to conform to the
environmental regulations of the country of origin.

www.orionbooks.co.uk

For Martha Stevns

# CONTENTS

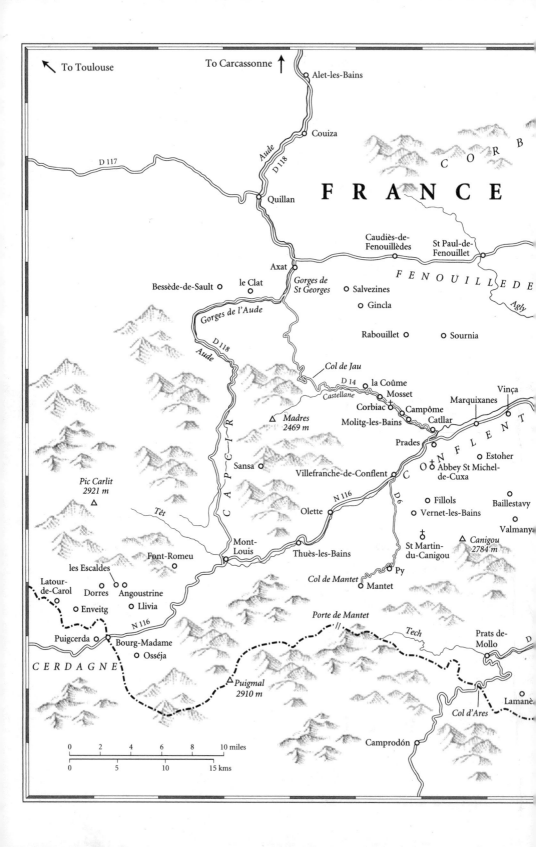

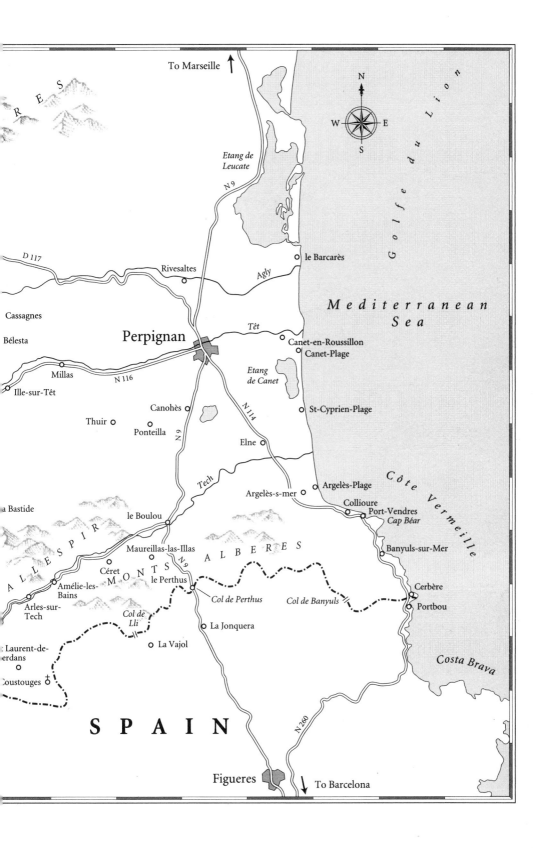

# PROLOGUE

Better to light one single candle than to curse the darkness.
Confucius

The places in which any significant event occurred become
embedded with some of that emotion, and so to recover the
memory of the place is to recover the emotion, and sometimes to revisit the place uncovers the emotion. Every love
has its landscape.

Rebecca Solnit, *A Field Guide to Getting Lost*

It began with a pair of shoes, worn espadrilles, the canvas faded,
the ribbons twisted and frayed, the rope soles shredded and dirty. I
saw them in the tiny museum of St-Laurent-de-Cerdans, a French
Pyrenean village near the Spanish frontier where espadrilles and the
traditional striped cotton Catalan fabric are still made. The espadrilles,
along with a battered old canvas rucksack, were evidence of the
*passeurs*, illicit frontier guides, who had criss-crossed the rugged border
paths here, helping refugees to escape during the Second World War.
The village of St-Laurent is tucked beneath the mountain, and looking
upwards from the street the hillside is incredibly steep. Anyone anxious to escape would certainly have needed a guide.

I began to wonder what had happened in this region, my adopted
second home, a magical land of sea and mountains and two countries
(three if you count Catalonia). This eastern corner of the Pyrenees,
where the mountains meet the Mediterranean, had been no great
theatre of war. There were no films about dramatic Allied landings
and no bloodied battlefields to see. But by 1939 the Pyrenees stood at
the frontier of two wars, with refugees escaping in both directions. I
was sure that the war had marked these people deeply, that the
landscape held many memories.

I had already written two books about the Pyrenees, trying to put the
places I lived and visited in historical context. I never had any problem
finding people to talk – about the Cathars, the Romanesque abbeys and
their monks, the Romantic poets and mountaineers of the nineteenth
century. But underlying all this distant history there was always a

closer past that few wanted to recall, a more sombre history of these beautiful green mountains and blue sea.

The more I discovered the more I realised I didn't know, and many did not want me to know, about the French during the Occupation, the real role of the Resistance, the level of collaboration, the concentration camps in the Pyrenees and the treatment of Jews and other refugees. People were evasive. I was treading on delicate ground. But over the years I have been visiting and living in this region of the Pyrenees, the Pyrénées-Orientales, I have begun to feel a shift in attitude towards the war. There is a thawing; among people of a certain age, in their sixties and seventies, reaching retirement, whose parents are growing old and dying, who feel it is time to lift the veil. A few of the older folk seemed willing to talk while they still could, to resolve their history, to clarify the past for the next generation.

It is still very much a veiled history. Though now the French acknowledge that the role of the Resistance in winning the war has been glorified way beyond its actual numbers or achievements, few even now are willing to admit the level of outright acceptance of the German occupation, of the fascist ideals of the Vichy government, and the degree of collaboration, passive or active, that went on throughout the war years. Most of the archives remain firmly closed or have been doctored; dossiers have disappeared, pages gone missing, letters and names have been removed. But since the 1970s there has been a steady stream of books in French and English about the *années noires* (the black years) of the war, trying to peel back the layers of silence and get at the truth of what really happened.

Slowly though, as I visited small villages, talked to elderly survivors, read local histories and looked at old photos, it all began to come into focus. There were so many scattered stories, it was like a jigsaw puzzle in different languages: the story of La Coûme, the school run by German pacifists; the exile of the great cellist Pablo Casals; the Jews shipped off to Auschwitz; the strange death of the priest in our village of Mosset; the terrible fate of the village of Valmanya; and the Spanish refugees in camps on the beaches where we swam and picnicked in summer.

I began to appreciate the importance of the Spanish connection to the war here, the flood of Spanish Republicans who had fled to France and whose commitment to fighting fascism and hope for their own future liberation made them the driving force behind the local Resistance. In this frontier region it was clearly vital to grasp what was happening on both sides of the border.

I wanted to understand the choices people made between compromise, acceptance and resistance, and why some at least became 'single candles in the darkness'; the early Resistants in France, the Germans who struggled against the rise of fascism; the Swiss nurses in the concentration camps, the refugee work of the pacifist English Quakers; all those who risked their own lives helping others to escape. I have no desire or competence to judge. I just want to begin to understand.

# CHAPTER 1

# RETURN TO THE LAND

It is really beautiful here, the sky is blue, without any mist, and the mountains look so strong and so calm, it makes you think the world must be mad. It seems impossible we could lose so much beauty.

You know what I'm thinking about . . . of that rainy morning when we were out walking and took shelter in an abandoned farm and you talked to me about the life we would lead together. What it would be like in such weather if we had been peasants on the farm . . . It was so beautiful, all the details, the dog with wet hair, who pressed his nose against your corduroy trousers, the animals in the stable, the leather smock spattered with rain, me in the kitchen, the fire, the clogs . . . It feels as it if really happened, and I am nostalgic for that period of our life, that we have never lived . . .

The story starts as so many of my stories have with Corbiac, the abbey my husband and I bought in the Pyrenees many years ago. I sat by the log fire with a faded blue folder of love letters, written by Pierre and Amélie, a newly married couple who lived there fifty years before us, at the start of the Second World War. Their letters had been given to me by their daughter, who had heard our own story and thought I might find another tale to tell. Their correspondence captures a brief intense period during their relationship, with the young husband at the front in eastern France, waiting out the Phoney War – the French called it *la drôle de guerre* – and his new wife is struggling to hold on to their dream. Corbiac had been our dream too: to live in the peace of the mountains, grow our own food, escape from the world, an adventure I had already written about.

At first I felt voyeuristic as I opened the tightly folded yellowing pages, edges blurred with repeated readings, and began to absorb their intimate contents. But as I sat by the same fireside reading of their hopes and dreams I started to feel a connection. Their experience seemed to offer a key to understanding what had happened in this region during the war. They wrote of their own dreams for Corbiac, how they would live from the land, and the work of their hands, try to live a pure simple life far from the world, bring up healthy children in the fresh air, eat home-grown vegetables, raise pigs and chickens, walk in the mountains and glory in the beauty and inspiration of nature. It sounded familiar.

In the summer of 1939, just before war was declared, they too had spent an idyllic summer camping out in this semi-ruined old monastery, washing in the river, lying under the stars and listening to the birds. They too waited for a baby here. They too planted an olive tree, for their marriage and for peace.

Their story seemed to have a universal significance, as their plans for the future were to be shattered along with millions of others as the war took its pitiless course. Although I had only fragments of their story, this glimpse of their particular lives helped me discover what else had happened in this region. I found a tangled knot to unravel, a history sometimes forgotten, often deliberately suppressed, of concentration camps and mountain escape routes, of collaborators and Resistance fighters, of cruelty and self-sacrifice. Most of all I learned the history of the ordinary folk who had waited out the Second World War, as they had waited out so many wars in this frontier land. Gradually the war in this farthest corner of southern France began to take on a reality.

Pierre and Amélie's chosen kingdom seemed then to be far from the war. The monastery of Corbiac lay 2 kilometres from Mosset, a small village in the foothills of the eastern Pyrenees, 40 kilometres from the Mediterranean, not far from the border with Spain, a frontier that has long been disputed, a mountainous no man's land that submitted reluctantly to the yoke of distant kings. It had always been a place of refuge and escape, and its particular geography was the key to its fate during the Second World War.

I found a book about the region, written just before the war, a classic old-fashioned English travel book illustrated with sketches of happy smiling peasants. But apart from occasional whimsical lapses, 'the young girls trembling with desire in summer groves', *Catalan France* by Basil Collier, published in 1939, offered an excellent portrait of what was then and to some extent still remains a little-known corner of France. It has only been French since the treaty of the Pyrenees in 1659, before which it was ruled either by Spain (when there was a united Spain) or the kingdom of Aragon. It is the Roussillon, roughly (though not exactly) equivalent to the modern department of the Pyrénées-Orientales. It is often known as French Catalonia and still has more cultural allegiance to Barcelona than to Paris. Even today many people converse in Catalan. Before the war it was the common language, and though French had been compulsory in schools since the beginning of the twentieth century, most people still spoke Catalan as their first language.

Basil Collier wrote then:

> This is a book about a tract of country which has existed as a recognizable entity, and whose soil has been tilled by men acknowledged to be not very different from its present cultivators, for the best part of three thousand years. It has been invaded, conquered, ravaged and laid waste not once, but many times within that period. Its people have been by turns oppressed, made much of, killed, ignored; and it is doubtful whether these experiences have changed them much. They have gone on tilling the soil and speaking their obstinate, uncouth language for the last eight hundred years at least. That language is being corrupted, habits are changing; but at bottom there is in these people, as there is in all peoples rooted in the soil, something eternal and indestructible which will not change.

The region forms a rough triangle bordered by the Pyrenees to the south, where the main range meets the Mediterranean, the hilly spur of the Corbières to the north, and the coast to the east. It combines extremes of landscape, from some of the highest and coldest pasture land in Europe, to the vines, palms and lemon trees on the coastal plain. The climate is harsh and dry, with brilliant sunshine, azure skies and wild winds. Over all stands the regal bulk of Canigou, the mountain that affects all who live in its compass, giving a permanence and security to the landscape, inspiring awe in the valley dwellers clustered at its foot.

There are few large towns. Perpignan is a modest capital, its old medieval centre feeling more like a village than an urban metropolis even today. There are small market towns like Céret, Elne and Prades, and on the coast several fishing ports; Collioure, Banyuls and Port-Vendres, which attract crowds in the summer to the seafront restaurants and pebbly beaches. Since the 1960s there has been substantial coastal development, with resorts and camp sites along the flat golden beaches of the Golfe du Lion.

But mostly the Roussillon is its villages. There are the wine villages of the plain, with their roofs of terracotta tiles, and the arched entrances of ground-floor wine *caves*, the streets pungent with the smell of new wine when the grapes are harvested. In the mountains defensive hamlets built of locally hewn granite and slate huddle in the valleys or cling like limpets to the hillside.

The village of Mosset is typical, built on an outcrop halfway up the Castellane valley, the dwellings stacked like a rocky Cubist pyramid around the stronghold of the original thirteenth-century château. Austere, defensive, more Spanish than French, it faces downstream towards the peak of Canigou and a verdant valley of pastures and orchards, the river Castellane cutting its winding inexorable course down the valley. It is a landscape that seems little changed since the Middle Ages. There are more trees now as the steeper pastures are abandoned, and the stone walls terracing the hillside have crumbled as the population has diminished; people no longer need to farm the steep hillsides to support their families. Soon the terraces will crumble away completely, return to the land whence they came.

Of course Mosset has changed – these days it boasts of its international population, calls itself *village du monde*. Before the war they had rarely seen a foreigner, *les gavatchs* as they called anyone from outside, French or any other. But there are many respects in which it has stayed the same. For a start the centre of gossip has not changed. It used to be the village blacksmith, the forge just down from the church on the main street; here people gathered, especially in winter when the blacksmith's fire would warm them. In the 1950s the forge became an *épicerie*; here you can buy coffee, ham, cheese, vegetables and pinafores. (The potatoes are packed in commercial-looking mesh bags, but they really come from Yvette's own garden.) The formidable Yvette, daughter of the blacksmith, presides here, and though past retirement age (and still grumbling about the euro) she has remained, cherished as an essential part of the village.

I waited in the shop one day as Yvette served her finest Roquefort to some summer visitors. (They say they come specially from Perpignan to buy it, and it is so good because she stores it in the church crypt.) Yvette is a tall, still handsome woman, disguised in her traditional flowered pinafore and slippers, her grey hair knotted in an old-fashioned bun. She looked beautiful in her wedding photo, coming out of the church. Once I had tried to talk to her husband, Joseph, the child of Spanish refugees who came to France after the Spanish Civil War. His father, a Republican soldier, had come to Mosset in 1939 and worked in the mountains as a charcoal-burner during the war. His family, including Joseph, had to wait seven years until they could join him. Joseph is solid, stocky, mustachioed, well built from years of hunting and carrying heavy butane gas tanks up the rickety stairs for the old ladies of the village. He is always ready with a warm *bonjour*, and sometimes a bullfighter's flourish when I pass him in the street. But when I asked him to tell me more about his childhood, he refused.

'I can't talk about it,' he said. He shook his head slowly and tapped his breast. 'But it is all in here for ever.'

People didn't want to talk about the war, even now. But the women at least would talk about the village in the past – when it was still alive, when all the fields were farmed, before all the foreigners came. 'Now it is dying,' says Yvette, nodding at the diminishing stock on her shelves.

'There used to be three *épiceries* in the village,' she told me, in her strong Catalan accent. 'You could get anything you needed here.' They stocked essentials they could not produce themselves: salt, pepper, cheese, oil, sweets, biscuits, chocolate, espadrilles – and aprons, of course. As well as the baker there was a butcher, a cobbler, a *bureau de tabac* and a coffee-grinder, who sat on the street with his coffee mill. But the forge was the centre of the village. 'People loved to come here, especially when it was cold.' They would stand around the fire, as the blacksmith in his leather apron wielded his hammer, the sparks flying. Out in the street, the mules or donkeys waited, attached by iron rings to the wall, the cows in harness, and he nailed the new shoes to the animals' hoofs with a red-hot iron, the acrid smell of burning horn permeating the air.

'He knew all the animals of the village,' said Yvette proudly, 'what size shoe each of them took.' In those days the blacksmith was one of the most important people in the village, since they were entirely dependent on animals for working the fields and for transport, usually carts pulled by oxen. He also made and repaired all their tools for agriculture and building.

'Is there any evidence of the forge still here?' I asked hopefully.

'No,' she said with a gesture of disdain. 'We threw it all out.'

Life was still dominated by the seasons, by agriculture, the weather, the lack of rain, the wind that might damage the crops. It was the land, the mystique of the land that the French so cherished, that had brought Pierre and Amélie here. Mosset was one of thousands of French villages that followed the same pattern of life, close-knit communities depending on each other for survival, working every daylight hour to grow enough food to eat and to store for the winter. Despite the hardship of such a life, it was considered somehow virtuous, to have a moral dimension that was inevitably dissipated and lost in the cities. To this day the word peasant has a hallowed quality in France. It was here that Pierre and Amélie believed they could find the new life they so desired.

As I sat on the wall outside the *épicerie* with Louisette, older than Yvette, a petite woman, with smartly permed hair, still sharp and busy, always involved in village events, selling raffle tickets, serving pizza or Muscat at the village fête, I asked her if she could remember Corbiac in those days. 'Oh, yes, my mother worked in the potato fields there,' she said. 'We used to take her lunch.' There is a faded photo of several women with aprons and baskets digging potatoes in the field in front of the abbey, one of whom is Louisette's mother. 'I can just remember the chapel full of cows – how dark and scary it was.' Her elder sister had worked there too, helping with baby care and housework. Louisette remembered the young doctor and his new wife. 'They say he bought Corbiac for a song.'

The abbey had been sold in 1936 by a family who had owned it almost since the Revolution when the monks left, but had no more sons willing to farm the land. It was a substantial farm in those days, worked by the peasants who came down every day from the village. It had been a monastery, with a small number of monks ministering to the needs of the local population, until the Revolution. Then the monks were thrown out and the abbey turned into a farm. The cloisters were turned into stables, their lovely stone arches blocked up with smashed stones and boulders. The chapel was equipped with mangers made of long planks of chestnut hung at an angle from the walls, their edges smoothed by the animals' necks as they munched their hay. Beams were slung under the great barrel vault to create a hayloft and one of the deep round windows was enlarged to tip in the hay. The huge fresco of Mary and the infant Jesus painted in the apse was rubbed away on one side by the constant passage of men doubled over with hay bales. Henceforth the sacred space was filled with the lowing of cattle in place of liturgical chant.

Apart from the occasional whispers about ghosts and hidden treasure, the peasants saw only the fields and the stables. They did not see the architecture of the abbey, the carved stone arches and columns, the Gothic tracery, the frescoes painted on the apse and walls. Pierre was unusual in appreciating the potential of the building as well as the land, realising the spiritual element that was obscured by a century and a half of cow muck.

Basil Collier spotted the old chapel on his travels round the region in the 1930s:

In spring the road along the valley of the Castellane is lined with wild columbine, snapdragon and convolvulus and anchusa; iris, eglantine and daisy; sun rose and veronica and pimpernel. Flowers which in England one cultivates with jealous patience in a garden grow here

unregarded in the roadside waste . . . The road goes through Campôme, near which there is a farm-house with a private chapel. It leads
to Mosset, a large boldly situated village which was once a stronghold
of some importance. Its streets are narrow, steep, and rather dirty, but
here and there, in a fragment of carving or a moulding round a door,
are signs of former grandeur.

From the kitchen of the *mas*, on the first floor as is traditional, I
could open the window to see the same view, the fields around, the
road passing by, the peak of Canigou in the distance. I could hear the
same river, the cow bells, feel the same wind on my face, smell newly
cut grass. I wanted to know what attracted this particular couple to this
particular place.

They had met in Arles-sur-Tech, a small village in the Vallespir, the
valley of the Tech, on the southern side of Canigou. Amélie had been
visiting her grandmother there, and fell straight away for the young
doctor attending her. She remembers the meeting in one of her first
letters:

> I will never forget seeing you for the first time, in grandmother's
> bedroom. How you made the poor woman shiver with fright at your
> adventures, the mountains you climbed, the great rivers and gorges
> you crossed, the narrow paths you discovered, and the man you met
> who had such a sinister look you hid your money in your shoe!

They seemed so different. Pierre was not yet thirty, idealistic, deeply
religious, a young doctor dedicated to his patients, passionate about the
land and the mountains, his great dream to become a farmer and live
off the land. Amélie was thirty-four, a city girl, and despite her family
roots and summer vacations, she had grown up in Marseille, in the
heart of a big, pulsating, colourful port. In the faded photos given me
by the family, Pierre looks small and intense, with a shock of curly
hair. Amélie looks more languorous, with dark eyes, brown hair
and expressive mouth. She worked as a civil servant for the Colonial
Service; well educated, she loved the cinema, books and music. For
her the country was a romantic notion, the sunlit hills of Provence
visited for summer picnics. But she was deeply drawn to the young
doctor and his dreams and tried hard to share his faith and learn to love
the country.

The prospect of Mosset, however, clearly filled her with doubts, and
she was not entirely enthralled by the village when she first saw it. A
place where a stranger was anyone who did not come from the village,
did not speak Catalan. They even called her *l'anglaise*. It all seemed very

primitive. The streets were full of cattle, pigs and goats. Women had a hard life, working in the fields swathed in black (they even got married in black), their feet shod in espadrilles or clogs. They could be seen descending the hillside, bent double with bundles of kindling as big as themselves on their backs. Electricity was limited to a few hours a day (none at all at Corbiac). They still washed clothes in the river, bleaching them with cinders and spreading the sheets on the rocks to dry. Amélie would get to know traditional village life better than she ever expected.

At the beginning of 1939, they decided to marry and Amélie wrote almost daily from Marseille, in a beautiful clear script, honed by years of French bureaucracy, anticipating their future and the practical details of their life together, so excited about their prospects she can hardly believe her good fortune. Only Amélie's letters survive from this period, but she wrote in such detail, describing her own life and responding to Pierre, that it is not difficult to reconstruct their communication.

While Amélie went to the office, met friends for lunch in quayside restaurants or visited the cinema, Pierre was struggling through the winter as a country doctor. Many of his patients lived in remote villages and he was called to deliver babies in primitive cottages with no running water or electricity, or to attend to ghastly agricultural accidents, struggling to reach them by motorbike, sometimes by car, as often as not on foot when the weather made driving impossible.

They only called the doctor in extremis. He would have to be paid after all, even if only in bags of vegetables or bottles of wine. Mostly they took care of their own. A favourite remedy for flu or bronchitis was two or three kilos of boiling hot potatoes padded around the patient to produce a sweat, with a tisane of camomile or lime blossom afterwards. It was in everyone's interest to get them back to work in the fields as soon as possible. (And I expect they ate the potatoes.)

The first bundle of letters from Amélie gives a brief glimpse of life before the war, when the conflict was a rumour most preferred to ignore. A brief glimpse of what might have been . . . Amélie had been to visit Prades, where Pierre was starting his new practice. She had met his parents and Pierre and Amélie had spent a day together in the mountains. He had taken her to see Corbiac, the half-ruined abbey they would try to make their home, where he was already planting vegetables and fruit trees. They went to La Bastide, the little stone shepherd's hut in the hills high above Mosset which became their secret romantic hideaway. I like to think they enjoyed one of those magical midwinter days when the low sun warms the garrigue and draws out the aromatic fragrance of the plants and the herbs, so that it smells like the month of May. 'We had such marvellous days,' she wrote, 'and the country was so beautiful. Canigou . . . I see it always, and I hear you offering me all the splendour of the world.' Amélie uses the familiar form of '*tu*' for the first time, perhaps because their marriage has been officially approved by his parents. 'I will never exhaust the joy of the days spent with you, the memory of the mountains, the trees, your songs on the path.'

Already she is concerned about how she is going to manage her rustic responsibilities:

> I am glad you want me to share the work on the land, but aren't you worried that I will prune the wrong plants? Will I have the strength and you the patience to teach me? The lambs must have grown – perhaps they have already gone . . . I know nothing of country life . . . The violets, are there any left? I think of the river, as well. Are there are any holes there where we can bathe?

Amélie was preoccupied with the wedding plans, the marriage formalities, reminding Pierre to send his birth and baptism certificates. She described the wedding gifts they had been given, the sets of table linen, glasses, a set of cake plates, a Lalique oil jar. 'We will unwrap them together and the house will be full of straw. Perhaps we need to find a cupboard to keep them all in, in the *cave* perhaps?'

Meanwhile Pierre was busy with his patients, struggling through the snow to remote mountain villages like Valmanya and Mantet. (Even today Mantet is very inaccessible, with a steep, precipitous road better to walk than to drive.)

'What worries you have!' wrote Amélie, often mentioning his motor-bike on the mountain roads. 'Don't try to break the speed record, unless the quarter hour you gain is essential for your patients. How is the typhoid? Is it the fault of the water?'

She was concerned about her elderly grandmother in Arles:

> Have you seen *grand-mère*? How is she? It's several days since we had any news. Tell me if there is more snow up there. It would not be surprising if she was ill . . .
>
> How nice of you to suggest visiting her on our first outing together. But I will have to inspect myself from head to toe because so often I have irritated her with my country look . . . espadrilles, no gloves, no hat . . . And then when we go to La Bastide we can be comfortable, I can just wear a light dress and you can wear your collarless shirt.

They discussed their household arrangements for Corbiac:

I got your letter about housekeeping this morning. Let's talk about the maid when I come, the hours she needs to come, so the house is not left empty – I am sure you will want me to get out in the fresh air sometimes!

More wedding presents arrived:

Lily has given me a coffee service and I have asked for towels and napkins and knives and forks and coffee spoons. We've also been given some crystal knife-rests. How pretty our table will be! Is there really nothing that you want?

While she blithely planned table settings for a house with no electricity, Pierre was chopping wood for winter.

You know I had already got used to thinking of you as a farmer, and now I must add the image of a woodcutter. I'm sure you were right to fell the acacia, but please don't tackle the cedars on your own, you will damage your hands.

I think and talk house, saucepans, trees, when I know that really it is all nothing, nothing . . . I am waiting for you, that is all.

But the prospect of war was there always in the background. 'All the talk around me is of war. I'm writing this in the office and all they talk about is cannons, bullets, aeroplanes . . . All we need is for this horror to extend to the entire world . . .'

Pierre wrote about his fear of being called up and asked whether they might get married sooner, but Amélie insisted they must have all the family there. 'Tell me where you will have to go if you are called up. But no, mon chéri, it is not possible, women must be very weak if they can't prevent this happening! Surely even if you are called up, you will be allowed twenty-four hours to get married? Perhaps being newly married will delay your mobilisation a bit . . . ?' she added, hopefully.

Occasionally they managed to talk by telephone.

You can call me from 1.15 to 2 o'clock at my neighbours. 34 30 Marseille. It was wonderful to hear your father on the telephone, it was as if I had him in front of my eyes!

We talked in the office of wedding bouquets, and I said: 'I have even better, an olive, and blue sky, and the snow.'

I hope you are not too tired now, and I am so sorry that the baby did not survive . . . What disappointment and suffering for the poor mother. Does she have other children?

Were you able to go by car to Valmanya, or did you have to go part of the way on foot?

I have left the world and its problems at the door, to spend a
moment with you. (Though I can still hear the neighbour's radio,
which reminds me of all one wishes to forget . . .)

Today the sky is blue and there is sunshine. It seems impossible to
me that I am going to the real country!

After their marriage they spent an idyllic summer together at
Corbiac. Soon Amélie was pregnant – at thirty-four, old for a first
baby in those days. I wonder if they slept in the same bedroom, looking
out to the same view as ours, the window framing a green vista of trees
on the other side of the valley, the air so clear it seems you could touch
them. Taking siestas on drowsy afternoons, sunlight piercing the half-
closed shutters, dreaming of the baby to come, just as I did. Even their
wedding day was the same as ours, April the 11th. It was exactly fifty
years before we spent our first summer there, dreamers like them,
planning impossible things. City escapees as she was, revelling in
rustic pleasures, with no idea of the harsh realities to come. Maybe
their joy was made more poignant as rumours of war came closer. They
were not ignorant peasants, they must have been aware how soon their
peace would be disturbed, felt the approaching shadow that would
darken them all.

Even while they were making their marriage plans in early 1939, a
great catastrophe was already unfolding across the Spanish border.
In February 1939 Amélie had observed the disaster from her grandmother's house in Arles. She wrote:

> Grand-mère was so happy to see us, but she is terribly distressed by the
> sad sight from her window, all these wounded and starving men, so
> thin, looking for food. Apparently the delivery wagon has not appeared,
> and no bread will be distributed till tomorrow.
>
> The countryside is so beautiful . . . but it is hard to enjoy it when one
> sees such misery, such suffering. I want to wish for some hours of
> absolute happiness, but inevitably our joy will be mingled with tears.

As I held her letter, and reread her careful, exquisite script, I huddled a
little closer to the fire I felt I was already sharing with these Corbiac
ghosts. It was all there in that early letter: the suffering to come, the
Spanish refugees already pouring over the frontier, escaping Franco in
the final appalling weeks of the Spanish Civil War.

While Amélie was planning her wedding and her future, many
thousands on the other side of the border were leaving their homes,
not knowing if they would ever see them again. She wrote to Pierre:

Do you know what Pilar, our friend from Barcelona, saved in her flight? Two little lace baby dresses, a present for a future mother of France, she said. All the rest was stolen from her. We wept together for a long time, her shoulder on mine, with this little sign of hope on her knees.

# CHAPTER 2

# THE SPANISH RETIRADA

'Better to die on your feet than to live on your knees.'
Dolores Ibárruri ('La Pasionaria')

We are walking up a steep mountain path on the Spanish side of the border, into the Pyrenees. It is a glorious day, as winter often is in these mountains, cold with limpid blue skies and clear refreshing air. But even at a relatively low altitude the atmosphere grows noticeably cooler as we climb. There is a fresh wind whipping round us, lifting the dry brown leaves that fill the ruts in the path. There are perhaps a hundred people stretching in a ribbon along the track, young and old, a few children, held firmly by the hand. Ahead of us marches an elderly man, white-haired under his peaked black cap, hoisting proudly on his shoulder the Republican flag, a tricolour of yellow, red and purple. Behind him a smartly dressed woman walks alone, softly singing a song about her mother.

Snug in my warm anorak, stout boots and gloves, I am trying to imagine the snow and rain that descended on the heavily burdened Spanish refugees who took this route to the frontier in February 1939. Desperate families, carrying children, dragging animals and carts, struggling to hang on to precious bags and suitcases, casks of oil and blankets. Some were wounded, some pregnant, many fell by the way-side. Most wore only espadrilles of rope-soled canvas on their feet. Some carried a fistful of Spanish soil.

It was February 2002, the first time the Retirada – the retreat – was officially commemorated, with a symbolic walk over one of the routes into France which had been followed by many thousands of the refu-gees. It had been planned by a new organisation, formed by the children of refugees exiled in France, called FFREE (Fils et filles de Républicains espagnols et enfants de l'exode – pronounced 'Free'). After the fall of Barcelona to Franco's forces at the end of January 1939, almost half a million Spanish Republicans, civilians and soldiers, struggled across the eastern Pyrenees into France, one of the greatest exoduses of modern times. Finding the main frontier posts at Cerbère and Le Perthus blocked by the French, many had headed for the many smaller paths that snaked over the hilly frontier. The little village of La Vajol, from where we began our walk, now only a few kilometres' drive from the main international truck-stop at La Jonquera, gave access to one of them.

We went on up the zigzagging path, paved with large uneven stones and flanked by a forest of chestnuts, moss-covered boulders and spiky undergrowth, until we reached the Col de Lli. From the crest we could catch a glimpse of the Mediterranean, glinting below us. How often the refugees recall with irony the beauty of the landscape that unfolded before them in their flight, the blue line of the Pyrenees on one side, stretching into the far distance, the horizon of the sea to the other, and the peak of Canigou, the Catalans' holy mountain, a remote deity presiding over all.

At the Col we gathered around a statue erected in memory of the Retirada. On a great outcrop of granite stands a man with a blanket round his shoulders, holding by the hand a little girl aged seven or eight, with only one leg and a wooden crutch. The statue, modelled on a photo, was the first memorial to the Retirada in the whole of Spain.

The flag was raised and speeches delivered. One elderly man spoke in passionate Spanish about his childhood in Andalucia, his experience of escape and exile. There were many tears and prayers. It was only when I developed my photos later that I saw that for a moment a stormy cloud had passed over the sun and the statue was rendered in a dark dramatic silhouette against the sky.

We crossed the frontier into France, by simply opening a wooden barred gate in the fence, and continued our pilgrimage, down through the chestnut and cork oak forests of the Albères. When my dodgy hip started to ache, I thought of the child with one leg, and did not complain.

We arrived at the little whitewashed village of Las Illas, where on the façade of the Hostal dels Trabucayres there is a plaque to the four presidents who escaped this way. Manuel Azaña, president of the Spanish Republic, Martinez Barrio, president of the Cortes (Parliament) José Aguirre, the Basque president, who had retreated to Catalonia, and Luis Companys, president of the Catalan generalitat. On the Col de Manrell, further down the ridge of the frontier, is another monument, dedicated to Companys. After Germany invaded France the Vichy government handed him over to Franco. He was executed in 1940 in the moat of the prison of Montjuich in Barcelona. They say that at the end he removed his shoes and socks to die with his feet on the soil of Catalonia. The Olympic stadium in Barcelona was named in his honour.

We all sat down to lunch together, at wooden tables and benches in a small park. There was a heightened atmosphere, tense and emotional, but with a warmth that seemed to me particularly Spanish, as they shared the food and wine they had brought along with their memories. I spoke to some, asked about the past, what their parents had told them. Most said that their parents would never talk, that the memories were too painful, but one remembered being greeted by the priest of Las Illas, who lifted him and his grandmother into a truck, a great surprise for an anticlerical Republican child bred on tales of the corruption of the clergy. Another described to me how after his parents' death, in Toulouse, he had found a big suitcase full of letters, photos and family mementoes. It had never been opened since the day they left Spain in 1939.

I talked to one of the organisers of FFREE, Sonia, who told me she was the daughter of two refugees, a Jewish mother and a Spanish Republican communist, who had met working for the Resistance in the South of France. Also seated at the table was Acracia (the name derives from democracy, she explained), who said that her father had arrived in France to hear that his father and brother, whom he had last seen in a Spanish village not far from the frontier, had both been killed. Her mother had been put on a train after crossing the frontier, and been sent to the Vosges in north-east France. But when I asked if their parents would be willing to talk to me, they were doubtful.

Acracia's father was dead, she said, and he had never talked to her.

'It is so hard. I try to imagine it now. There are so many things I wish I had asked him.'

Sonia said: 'My parents are both still alive, but I have never talked to them either. It is too hard, it is not just the suffering, and the memories, but they felt humiliated. They lost the war.'

Acracia said: 'My father always blamed the communists for losing the war.'

Sonia responded grimly: 'And my father always blamed the anarchists!'

There were more ceremonies that weekend; at Argelès-sur-Mer in memory of the concentration camps on the beaches where the refugees were accommodated. Survivors bore witness – one who had been born in the camp, another who had been a soldier, had later volunteered to fight for France, and been sent to a concentration camp in Germany. The following day there was a memorial ceremony under the palm

trees in the cemetery of Collioure, in honour of the poet Antonio
Machado. He had arrived in Cerbère by train from Port Bou on 28
January, exhausted and sick, accompanied by his mother. They had
found lodging in a pension hotel in the little seaside port of Collioure,
but there Machado died, aged sixty-four. His mother died three days
later and was buried next to her son.

Poems were read around the tomb, in particular Machado's famous
poem, 'The Crime was in Granada' about his friend Federico García
Lorca, written after Lorca's brutal murder in 1936 at the beginning of
the Civil War:

Federico fell,
Lead in his stomach, blood on his face.
And Granada was the scene of the crime.

(Lorca's death remained a taboo subject in Spain until Franco's death
in 1975 and no one is sure to this day where his body lies.)

For the Spanish during the Franco years, Machado became a symbol
of liberty, and more than 300,000 visit the tomb every year. They send
poems and letters, some simply addressed to Antonio Machado,
Cimetière, Collioure. I had visited the tomb once before, touched to
see it so covered in flowers and offerings, with my Spanish friend
Clara. She grew up in Valencia under Franco's rule, and had heard her
grandmother's memories of offering soup to the troops as they left for
war. Clara wept as she stood at the tomb, the first time I had ever seen
anyone weep for a poet, ever really understood the privilege of the
liberty I took for granted.

The Spanish Civil War has been the subject of many thousands of
books and films. Seventy years on we are still trying to understand the
politics and the passions that led to it, and how the outcome affected
the Second World War to come. Gerald Brenan's book *The Spanish
Labyrinth*, written in 1942 after many years of living in Spain, remains
the oft-cited classic. Brenan seems to understand the spirit of Spain, its
unique position beyond the Pyrenees, between Europe and Africa,
between the Atlantic and the Mediterranean, perhaps most of all
between Islam and Christianity. He said that the overwhelming cataclysm of the war was characteristic of the Spanish, to want nothing less
than the moral overhaul of society, to insist on the need for inner faith
or ideology, to fight with more nobility and courage than strategy. He
attributes this to the influence of Muslim ideas upon a Christian

community: 'The deeper layers of Spanish thought and feeling are Oriental.'

The war devastated Spain between 1936 and 1939, resulting in half a million deaths. The slaughter and bloodshed were horrifying, as two sides fought to the death for Spain and their beliefs. There is a painting by Salvador Dali which expresses it. In *Autumnal Cannibalism 1936*, two intimately entwined figures are consuming each other with knives and forks. Even the weather was extreme, with battles taking place in such Siberian cold that troops suffered as much from frostbite as gunshots, or in searing heat surrounded by corpses blackened by the sun. Revolutionary anger and fascist cruelty resulted in appalling atrocities on both sides. Peasants were brutally murdered (that was how they would get their own bit of ground, said one of the Andalucian landowners), thousands of monks, nuns and priests were killed and hundreds of churches and monasteries burnt or pillaged. Bodies were exposed to view everywhere. The memory remains traumatic, and only now are many of the mass graves of the postwar reprisals being investigated.

As Brenan explains it, the war began as a class struggle between reactionary landowners, supported by the Church, army officers and most of the middle class, on the one hand, and on the other, revolutionary peasants and factory workers, supported by the petite bourgeoisie and intellectuals. The gulf was enormous. The rich owned vast tracts of land, while in some of the pueblos in the south men were unemployed for nine tenths of the year. Some agricultural workers owned only a cooking pot.

The divisions were further complicated by vast cultural differences between the regions, with Catalonia and the Basques particularly resentful of rule from Madrid. While Catalonia had undergone an industrial revolution, and was the centre of a flourishing textile industry, the rest of Spain was a throwback to the eighteenth century. Literacy was a luxury.

Two Spains found themselves face to face. Photos of election queues in 1936 tell it all. One shows the poor, old women wrapped in shawls and headscarves, young women in skimpy coats and worn-down boots, their faces grim and worn, clutching their ballot papers. The other is of men in smart suits and ties or heavy overcoats, hats and plus fours, with highly polished shoes and hair en brosse, women in fur coats, high-heeled shoes and stockings, a priest wrapped in his soutane, nose in the air.

Spanish fascism, says Brenan, was 'an exuberant creed drunk on

fantastic dreams of empire and glory in the future'. The left represented a wide spectrum of ideologies, though all were lumped
together as 'Reds'. There were social democrats, anarchists and communists, and various shadings in between, an alphabet spaghetti of
acronyms. All had very different ideas as to how the war should be
played out, and they were just as likely to quarrel with each other as
with the enemy, a legacy of strife that carried on long after the war
ended. Anarchists wanted to make revolution at the same time as war,
the socialists and communists argued that it was necessary to win the
war first. The communists wanted political power for the proletariat.
The anarchists rejected all authority and wanted to destroy the state,
believing that absolute liberty was essential for everyone. They saw the
war not just as defence against fascism but as the opportunity to create
a new type of society. Rural anarchists dreamed of collective independence, free of landowners, lawyers, priests and even money. 'We are not
afraid of ruins, we are going to inherit the earth,' said the anarchist
leader Buenaventura Durruti.

The second Spanish Republic was elected in 1931 to great rejoicing
on the left. A Republican constitution established freedom of speech,
separation between Church and state, and gave women the right to
divorce and to vote. Key attempts at land reform soon foundered,
however, and the removal of state subsidies for the Church backfired,
since they had been largely responsible for any education available.
Nevertheless the Republic made great efforts at reducing illiteracy,
claiming to have built 7,000 schools, and there were many imaginative
educational projects. During the war foreign visitors often noted the
earnest reading of the ordinary Republican soldiers.

The Second Republic was soon in trouble, with strong opposition
from the old order and violent political disagreement within the
government, exacerbated by worldwide economic recession. There
were riots, strikes, shootings and uprisings, and the forces of the right
readied themselves for intervention, gaining power in 1933. When the
Catalans declared independence, the president Luis Companys was
imprisoned with several of his ministers. Further elections in February
1936 resulted in a narrow victory for the aligned left of the Popular
Front. But it had only 48 per cent of the votes (the right had 43 per
cent, the centre 8 per cent) and the country began to splinter. In July
the army rose in Spanish Morocco and the war was on. African troops
were airlifted into Spain by German and Italian planes.

The following day the government agreed to distribute arms to trade
union militias to defend the Republic. They had been reluctant to arm

the anarchists in particular, a delay that cost them dear. Twenty-nine provincial capitals fell into the hands of the Nationalist forces, but twenty-one major cities remained under government control. Barcelona and Madrid held out almost till the end.

Foreign intervention – the Soviet Union on one side and the Germans and Italians on the other – made Spain in Brenan's words, 'the scene of a drama in which it seemed as if the fortunes of the civilised world were being played out in miniature'. Many have called the confrontation a rehearsal for the Second World War. Hitler, Mussolini and Stalin tested weapons, especially aeroplanes, on Spain, most famously at Guernica, a scene of horror and destruction recorded for ever in Picasso's famous painting. Günter Grass recalls the celebrations in Germany at their successes: 'The newsreels showed our Condor Legion helping to free Spain from the Red menace with the most up-to-date weapons. Americans contributed petrol and trucks to Franco's side.'

Only the brave or desperate volunteers of the International Brigade arrived to support the beleaguered government, some idealistically inspired to fight the growth of fascism, others already on the run from the fascist reality elsewhere in Europe. Many arrived in Perpignan to be smuggled across the frontier of the Pyrenees. There were about 40,000 volunteers; at least 20 per cent of them died. The rest of Europe, already struggling on the verge of war, signed a non-intervention treaty (adhered to with timorous scrupulosity by the French and British and not at all by the Germans and Italians). As part of the non-intervention treaty the surviving International Brigaders had to leave Spain, their ideals in shreds.

Women too threw themselves into the battle, determined to defend their recent emancipation. Their great heroine was La Pasionaria, Dolores Ibárruri, a charismatic leader of the Spanish Communist Party, whose passionate speeches inspired many to fight. There are compelling photographs of women in trousers, boots and combat gear, carrying guns and ammunition belts, their sleeves rolled up, some faces worn and lined, some youthful and fresh, all with shining eyes, glowing with nothing but hope.

After two years of fighting Franco had gained control of most of the west and north of the country, while the Republicans held out in the east and in Madrid. But Franco's troops arrived at Tarragona on the Mediterranean coast in April 1938, cutting the Republican zone in two. The most bitter battle was fought on the Ebro front as the Republicans made a final desperate offensive, calling up sixteen-year-olds to replenish their dwindling troops. (Actually many of those fighting were even

younger, mere children.) They tried to push back across the broad river
Ebro and reconnect the Republican forces, but after appalling casualties they were defeated. The greatest air battle of the war took place over
the Ebro front (Amélie said that autumn they could hear the roar of the
planes from Corbiac). By the end of 1938 the Nationalist forces had
entered Catalonia and finally Barcelona fell on 26 January 1939. Many
Republicans had already fled, but still ten thousand people were killed
in Barcelona.

Basil Collier was just finishing the research for his travel book as the
war drew closer and closer to France. He wrote in his introduction:

> At the time when the material for this book was being gathered, one
> saw in the Roussillon surprisingly little evidence of the Spanish War.
> The roads near the frontier were patrolled by gardes mobiles; an anti-
> aircraft battery, hastily installed in the meadows of Mahjua, fired a
> warning round when an alien plane flew overhead. One was awakened
> at Collioure, on a shiningly peaceful morning in spring, by the alarm-
> ing sound of gun-fire echoing across the bay. There were some
> incidents. A few bombs fell in France . . . From the heights of Font-
> Romeu I saw an aerial bombardment of Puigcerda, whose roofs and
> towers glittered in the high plain of the Cerdagne. Appalling detona-
> tions rumbled out of their Alexandrine length; great columns of inky
> smoke rose slowly through the shining air. An old woman ran out of a
> house, asked what was the matter, and was told. 'They are mad!' she
> said. She poured the fire of her criticism impartially on both factions.

Collier concludes: 'No mention of these things will be found in the
body of this book.'

As Franco's forces closed in, controlling all but the corridor of the
eastern Pyrenees, the Republicans fled before them. There were
already many refugees from all over Spain, some of whom had been
en route for weeks. Children had been sent to 'safety' from the south of
Spain, and many of them died in the bombardment of Catalonia by
Italians and Germans. The population abandoned their towns and
villages, even the hospitals were evacuated, with the sick and wounded
loaded onto trucks or forced to walk. One witness recalled the evacuation of the hospital in the coastal village of Blanes on the Costa Brava,
during a bombardment. He saw a line of blind people leading each
other, marching into the forest towards France, tripping and falling
over each other, clinging to tree branches, like Bruegel's painting of the
blind leading the blind.

The roads were crammed with vehicles of all descriptions from
trucks to wheelbarrows, people were sleeping in ditches, struggling to

care for children, the old and the wounded. Women clung on to their dead babies. Some gave birth in the midst of it all. Many refugees had not eaten for days, many were ill. As they trudged along, increasingly exhausted, they were forced to abandon their meagre belongings along the roadside. First the carts, then the animals, then the suitcases. To feed themselves some carried dead animals on their shoulders, geese, sheep, and goats. Bread trucks were besieged, and arriving at a fountain there were fights for water. The horror was compounded by bomb attacks from low-flying planes.

Herbert L. Matthews reported the disaster for the *New York Times*:

> There are not ten square yards anywhere near roads that have not their refugees. Every side road, every field, and even the hills are swarming with unhappy thousands who are gradually finding their way to La Junquera. It was not just an army fleeing, not only families, but entire villages, complete cities with everything they could take, an entire people, one was surprised the earth itself did not follow them.

Matthews was apparently subsequently told by his editor, not to 'send in any sentimental stuff about the refugee camps'.

But when they arrived at the main frontier posts of La Jonquera/Le Perthus and Cerbère, the border was closed, and crowds of refugees waited for days in pouring rain. The French government, worried as to how it would cope with such a massive influx, waited till the last minute to let them through. On 29 January the French finally relented.

The English Quaker Edith Pye, who had been working with refugees since the First World War, was running frontier relief operations for the International Commission for the Assistance of Child Refugees. From Perpignan she telephoned the Commission office in Paris to announce: 'They have opened the border!' She reported the massive influx of civilian refugees and soldiers, and the immediate response they had made. 'Four canteens on lorries were organised by us, each having a boiler to provide hot drinks, and these followed the streams of refugees, giving hot milk and bread, and in some cases cheese or chocolate.' Howard Kershner, the new director of the Commission, freshly arrived from New York, took the night train from Paris to Perpignan, and they set off next day to see what could be done in Spain.

As the refugees poured through the open barriers any attempt at quotas was soon overwhelmed. Women and children were evacuated as fast as possible all over France, the rest were accommodated in make-shift camps.

Nowadays we would watch television reports of the columns of refugees in fascinated horror. From that time we have the reports of a few journalists, the powerful, unflinching photos of Robert Capa, and the observations of aid workers like Edith Pye. This was her report to the International Commission:

The immensity of the tragedy of the flight from Spain must have been seen at first hand to be believed. The bombardments from the air forced the inhabitants to leave the ruins of their houses, and the descent of the aeroplanes almost to roof level to machine gun the fleeing inhabitants left them no choice.

For days while only a meagre trickle of civilians were allowed to pass the frontier, there were literally hundreds standing in queues between one village and another, or camped without any shelter on the hillsides on each side of the roads to the frontier in deadly fear of bombardment from the air . . .

Of these frontier posts there are three in which there is a road through – Port-Bou/Cerbère, Puigcerda/Bourg Madame, La Junquera/ Le Perthus. There is also a road on the Spanish side but only mountain paths at Prats de Mollo which is above the snow line, and there were pitiful cases of women and children lost in a snowstorm and being picked up half frozen. Intellectuals and peasants suffered alike, the latter perhaps less since many of them brought their mules and bread with them. Some had a sheep or two tied by a string, here and there one saw a cow or goats, and even hens carried by their legs, as uncomplaining as their owners. The first 3 nights there was heavy cold rain in which it was stated there were many deaths from exposure, especially among the children and the wounded.

There was no shelter of any kind available. The French authorities by a tremendous feat of organisation succeeded in getting 45,000 women and children sent into the interior in the first 3 days. They were brought down, after several days on the frontier with no possibility of washing or of proper food, in lorries and buses, vaccinated, and sent off in trainloads to destinations unknown. The separation from their menfolk produced despair among the refugees.

But many thousands more spent another 5 nights on the hillsides on the French side. The misery and helplessness of these crowds, harried by French cavalry to keep them from straying, is indescribable.

Le Perthus today is a thriving mass of bodegas and supermarkets selling cheap Spanish wine, cheese, olives, ham, dried sausages and baskets; now the only delay is honking traffic and roads full of bargain-hunting shoppers. But it has always been a place of passage and invasion – even Hannibal passed this way – and the people are inured to it. The photos of 1939 show the streets a solid mass of desperate people. Federica Montseny, who had been the only woman minister in the history of the Spanish government, arrived there on foot with her daughter of six, a baby of seven months and her dying mother. She remembered banging on the doors of the houses in Le Perthus, to no avail. They remained firmly closed.

José Sangenis was there as a child of twelve. 'My father, mother, my sister a year older than me, we left on foot, with the planes behind us, flying at low altitude, shooting unarmed civilians. I will never, never forget it.'

Sonia had put me in touch with José, who had experienced the Retirada as a child and was willing to share his memories. We arranged to meet in Perpignan ouside the new FNAC store, and his instructions sounded like someone well used to clandestine assignations. 'I will be wearing a brown leather jacket,' he said, 'and carrying a copy of the *Combat Syndicaliste.' Syndicaliste* is the French for trade unionist, and José was still, at seventy-nine, faithful to the political struggle to which he had devoted his entire life. I knew him at once, a short, stocky man with thick grey hair and neat moustache, and deeply etched smile lines around his eyes. A man who, despite all the suffering – or maybe because of it – has laughed often. We found a quiet corner in a nearby café and ordered coffee, and José began to tell me his life story, his French still musically accented with Spanish.

'I lived in Spain till I was twelve, in a small village near Barcelona. My parents were anarchists, involved in organising the collectives in Catalonia,' he explained. 'The important thing about the Spanish revolution was not the weapons and the guns, but how they transformed society. They believed that a new society would sweep away the injustices of the past. From my child's viewpoint, it was like a permanent fête, despite all the hard work involved.' He described the peasants working together to reclaim land and plant gardens – 'the joy on the faces of people working together. That is what we were fighting for . . . what we are still fighting for.' His strong mason's hands gripped the tiny espresso cup as he spoke.

It did not last long however, and they had to escape with all the rest. 'We had nothing but turnips to eat, food for animals. But we had to go on, in the cold, sleeping on the ground. My poor mother, trying to look after us.' And all those years later, his eyes began to fill with tears at the thought of his mother.

They arrived at Le Perthus, where along with thousands of others they were obliged to wait several days until the frontier was opened.

Then they were directed to Le Boulou, where they camped beside the river. 'It was snowing, and we had only one blanket each to protect us from the cold. I still remember it now whenever it snows, I feel those tears of cold again.' José produced a photocopy of the account he had written, and indicated some of the photos, the women carrying babies, clutching small children, some with suitcases on their heads, old men hunched in blankets by the side of the road, the wounded lying in a ditch among their crutches, a little girl in a buttoned-up coat already too small for her, carrying a well-dressed doll in her arms like her own baby, the soldiers guarding them.

Le Boulou, a sedate little spa town, was invaded by the refugees, who camped in the fields, collected wood and lit fires, while the women washed clothes in the river and tried to dry them in the sun. José recalled being assisted by nurses – presumably the Quakers, perhaps Edith Pye herself – who were distributing powdered milk for the children. 'Then the gendarmes came and separated the men from the women and children – when I say children, they took young boys aged thirteen to fifteen with the men. My father managed to escape and find us again. But they returned the next day and this time he did not come back to us.'

On 10 February 1939 the upper-class English writer and left-wing activist Nancy Cunard was at the frontier, reporting for the *Manchester Guardian*:

At the great central camp at Le Boulou are thousands of men, women, and children. On one side of the road is an enclosure with wire fencing. On the other the refugees who walked down from Le Perthus yesterday are lying, sitting, standing, doing nothing this cold end of a February afternoon. It is a horrible sight, and all of them, men, women and children, are in the utmost depression. This 'camp' is a large, flat, bare area, the grass trodden down into a sort of grey compost. They sleep here, in the open. A few have rigged up some vague kind of shelter.

As for medical aid – just one case I saw will show the state of things. A woman lamented that she could do nothing for her child. She took off the little girl's bonnet and said: 'These dreadful sores are the result of typhus.' They come and stand around you and talk; they argue among themselves in front of you: 'Are we worse off here today than we might be in Spain?' Then a woman cries out, 'I shall never get into a train without knowing where it is going, for I have heard that they want to send us back to Franco.' Other voices broke out: 'Ninety-five per cent of us want to go to anything rather than return to Spain as it will be under the fascists.'

Refugees continued to enter until mid-February by every possible route. From Cerbère to Andorra a great wave of misery poured into the sleepy agricultural region of the Pyrénées-Orientales, with its population of fishermen, winemakers and farmers. The refugees came by road and footpath along the coast and over the mountains, or by fishing boats to the little ports of the Côte Vermeille. Cerbère was besieged, with refugees camped in their thousands on the platforms of the international rail station, and waiting to cross at the frontier post at the col overlooking the town.

The local population watched silently from their doorsteps. Most of them knew the Spanish only as poor, illiterate peasants who came to France as seasonal agricultural labourers, or as Reds who wanted to kill all the priests. They were sympathetic to the misery they could see, but also appalled by the demands they would make.

The French government was grudging in its reception of the refugees (the interior minister proposed preparation for 20,000 refugees; there would be over 500,000), and there are many reports of the brutality of the soldiers. The Spanish bitterly resented the black Senegalese troops, then stationed in Perpignan, because they reminded them of the African troops that had fought for Franco with such brutal success. But the initial reaction of most of the Catalan people seems to have been genuinely humane. After all a lot of the refugees were also Catalan, and many people were naturally sympathetic to fellow human beings in such a plight. At Port-Vendres, on the coast, the refugees were welcomed by the fishermen, and a group of local schoolchildren came to offer them sweets and chocolate. The population of Cerbère gave accommodation to families from Port Bou, just the other side of the coastal border.

Two years after the first commemorative walk, I had planned to join another, to make the crossing over the headland from Port Bou to Cerbère. That year, though, the weather was atrocious. There had been violent storms the day before, and the concrete walls of the sea defences at Cerbère had been smashed by the wild seas. It was so bad that the coast road we were to take to the starting point for our walk had been closed, and so instead we walked up the steep road to the frontier from Cerbère. There in the wind and rain a new memorial stone was inaugurated. As we shivered under our umbrellas it somehow seemed more appropriate to be there in such weather, and we could feel a deeper sympathy with the refugees who had waited here.

All along the frontier small mountain villages, like Arles-sur-Tech, where Amélie's grandmother lived, tried to cope with the sudden influx of these miserable, exhausted, hungry people. The arrival of a column of refugees at the tiny village of Lamanère, the most southern village in France, on the frontier high above the Vallespir, was described by Francine Mach, then a child of eight. She had watched them from the school yard.

'A solemn file appeared over the horizon. I had never even heard of refugees. Everybody went to meet them. My mother and her neighbours put their pots on the fire to make soup from vegetables picked in the garden, with lots of vermicelli, while the men organised houses. The wounded and sick were sheltered from the cold, in the school. One man was dead on the path. The villagers went to get the body and buried him in the municipal cemetery. Soon the Senegalese soldiers arrived to take the refugees, willing or not. They gave them the choice of a camp or returning to Franco.'

Prats-de-Mollo, high above the Vallespir valley, was the first town to receive refugees, 100,000 of whom struggled over the Col d'Ares by the mule path from the town of Camprodon. There the road ended and they had to abandon their vehicles. From the Col at 1,200 metres altitude you can see both sides of the frontier, and mountains in every direction, austere purple folds darkened by forests of pine trees and beyond distant peaks covered in a veil of snow. The first time I drove through to Spain along that route, in 1998, the border had only recently been opened. It had once been a heavily guarded border post, but as a result of the Schengen Agreement of 1985 and the subsequent opening of European frontiers, it had been abandoned, the barriers torn down and left lying by the road, the searchlight towers fallen, and graffiti scrawled over the guard houses.

By 2006 it had been cleaned up. There was no sign of its former role, other than the new plaque erected in memory of the refugees. Below me I could see a steep narrow path snaking down the hillside to Prats-de-Mollo, the first French town they would come to, far below.

Prats was a garrison town, reinforced by Vauban, Louis XIV's military architect, still with stone walls and gateway intact. Within it, stepped cobbled streets rise up to the thirteenth-century church. There I searched the graveyard for Republican graves, but I could find only a single stone stele emblazoned with the yellow, red and purple flag. Austere as it is, Prats must have been a welcome sight to the refugees coming down from the mountain.

Between 27 January and 14 March, under cold, rain and snow, more than 100,000 refugees crossed the frontier above Prats-de-Mollo. In a few days the population rose from 3,000 to 30,000. Among them were the originals of the statue we had seen, the father, Père Gracia, hollow-eyed, clasping the hand of his crippled daughter. Behind them is her younger brother, also on crutches, aided by a French First World War veteran and inhabitant of Prats, Thomas Coll, who unbelievably is also one-legged. Another older brother walks unaided but with a pack on his back, and an expression of such harrowing exhaustion, one wants to weep.

The mayor recorded the arrival of the refugees:

> It is raining and snowing on the mountain. The Spanish refugees are soaked and chilled to the bone. It is urgent to find shelter for these poor people. They are squeezed together in the classrooms and stair-ways of the school, women with babies, and young children, and are shivering all over, despite constant supplies of hot drinks and blankets. It is a truly lamentable sight to see and tears fall from our eyes seeing the little kids, half naked, often covered in vermin, trying in vain to suck the dry breast of their young mother and crying with rage to find nothing available from this source of life.

Daily deliveries of thousands of kilos of bread from Perpignan and Arles-sur-Tech were necessary to feed everybody. The situation was further complicated by the number of animals the refugees had brought with them, mules, sheep, goats and cows, estimated at 25,000. They too needed feeding.

One day I met Dr Bouchey, now retired, who had been a nine-year-old child in Prats-de-Mollo then, where his parents were teachers. He remembered it well. 'From the school on the river bank you could see the stream of refugees, women dragging suitcases through the snow. They were all starving. They put women and children in the school, the men on the other side of the river in a camp. The villagers gave what they could to feed them, but it was so difficult to divide it up, every-thing, rice, pasta, even chocolate, was all thrown into a big cauldron outside and cooked together.'

When the Republican soldiers began to arrive, they were relieved of all their weapons. 'It was great for us, me and my brother who was sixteen, we had no school, and great piles of weapons everywhere! We found guns, and rifles, they had even dragged machine guns through the snow.' In the makeshift camp the soldiers were fighting each other in bitter recrimination for their defeat. 'We could hear explosions as grenades were thrown in the camp, and after the great flood in 1940 buried bodies were revealed with gunshot wounds to the head.' The Senegalese troops arrived to remove the refugees. 'The women and children were separated and put into trucks – I remember them shouting to us, "It will happen to you soon!" '

If possible the plight and reception of the Republican soldiers, whose misery was compounded by defeat, was worse than the civilians'. Though the frontier had been opened to civilians it remained closed to the soldiers until finally, after the fall of Figueres, the frontier posts at Cerbère, Le Perthus, and Bourg-Madame lifted their barriers on 5 February. Thousands of soldiers poured through, many of them severely wounded, all in a lamentable state of exhaustion and despair. They were searched by the French troops and gendarmes, and made to surrender their arms. Huge piles of precious guns accumulated, many of which were destroyed (much regretted later by the Resistance). Photos of the Republican soldiers show them giving their famous clenched-fist salute. (The French rather objected to them singing the Internationale as well.) The Republican gesture of the fist of solidarity is said to have originated in the Spanish Civil War. One member of the International Brigades remembered being greeted by old women on the doorsteps in Madrid with a clenched-fist salute of encouragement. Typically though, the Anarchists used the right arm and the Marxists used the left.

Only three days later the Francoist troops arrived at the frontier, giving their own open-palm fascist salute (not quite Heil Hitler but nearly, and derived from the salute of the Romans). They blew their bugles in triumph, and the French and Spanish generals shook hands across the border at Le Perthus. The British and French governments recognised the Nationalist government of General Franco on 27 February. Marshal Philippe Pétain, who called Franco 'the cleanest sword in the Western world', was appointed French ambassador to Spain.

Nancy Cunard watched the soldiers arrive, and wrote in the *Manchester Guardian:*

Le Perthus, 9 February 1939
From nine o'clock this morning until 4.30, I have been watching soldiers pass between the two stone posts that are actually the frontier-line. They have come by in thousands and thousands, in groups, singly, and in numberless lorries. At the posts stand the French soldiers, who immediately search them for arms. The Spanish soldiers give up their arms in an orderly fashion. The pile of rifles, revolvers, cartridge belts, dirks, and even a knife or two grow throughout the day. Two machine-guns have been brought in; farther up, an armoured car.

But all this is only the beginning; we are told: 'Tomorrow the rearguard of the army, and afterwards – the army that has fought.' On the mountains each side they come, so that the whole landscape seems to be moving. Soldiers on horseback, wounded men, women, children, a whole population, and cars and ambulances.

I met one of those soldiers, Cristobal Robles, a friend of José Sangenis. At the age of eighty-six, he could still recall his experience in all its bitter detail. I drove up to the smart new bungalow in Bas-Elne, down on the plain, on a sunny day with clouds scudding above the vineyards and fruit orchards. He was waiting at the door, a big broad-shouldered man, now leaning heavily on a cane. While we sat at the table his tiny wife Maria made us coffee, and waited quietly in the background while her husband did the talking. When I asked if they were happy there, Robles sighed. 'We have had a good life here – we are grateful to France. We have been able to integrate, to educate our children . . . Would it have been so good in Spain? I don't know.'

He came from Barcelona, and stressed that he was a socialist, not a communist. He volunteered for the Republican army at the age of sixteen. After the collapse of the Ebro front in 1938 he had fled up the Segre valley to cross the frontier at Osseja, high in the snow above Puigcerda and Bourg-Madame on the flanks of the Puigmal, one of the high peaks of the Pyrenees. 'There were about six hundred of us, soldiers and civilians. We inspected the crossing the night before and when we discovered we would have to surrender our arms we destroyed them instead.

'We were put in a cow field. In forty centimetres of snow. We had only the food we had brought with us, the army had supplied us with bread, sardines and corned beef for three or four days. But we had no water, we had to dig up the snow and melt it in a cup. It was minus seven or eight degrees and we had no fire. We just huddled together, body against body.' He pauses to remember, passing his hand over his face as if to suppress tears. 'We were there for about a week.'

Then he looks at me, holding my gaze as if to make me understand. 'All war is dirty. Though we were fighters we didn't like war. We were trying to improve the world!'

They were sent on to a camp at Latour-de-Carol, the railway junction at 1,248 metres altitude between Barcelona and Toulouse. 'We were not allowed to leave the field. It was so cold that we burnt all the wood we could find, posts, fences – we demolished everything to warm ourselves. The peasants surrounded us with guns.' After that they were sent to Perpignan. 'Fortunately at eighteen I was strong, but for the old people . . .' He ended up in the notorious camp of Le Vernet in the

Ariège, where they had to construct barracks for themselves. It was to be nineteen years before he saw his mother again.

By 14 February about 500,000 refugees had arrived in France. The population of the Pyrénées-Orientales was doubled at a stroke. The desire to help the refugees gave way to fear. After their initial sympathy the local people became worried about their farms as the large numbers of Spanish livestock, herded over the frontier by the refugees, roamed their land, eating all the crops. The right-wing press denounced all the refugees as Reds, dangerous dirty revolutionaries invading France, and complained about the escalating expense needed to support them. More troops and police were mobilised to control them. Thousands died, including many children, after a week or more waiting in freezing rain at the frontier. The estimate of deaths is 4,700, but nobody really knows.

Among those who fled from Catalonia to France was the Catalan cellist Pablo Casals, sadly abandoning his beloved region and his fine villa at San Salvador on the coast south of Barcelona. Casals, then sixty-two years old, one of the great cultural icons of the twentieth century, was already celebrated the world over for his extraordinary musical talent. But he was as committed to peace and justice as he was to music, and said that the years he was involved with the young Spanish Republic were among the most meaningful of his life.

As the fascist troops closed on Barcelona at the end of 1938, he was giving a concert in the city. During the rehearsal there was a bombing raid and all the musicians dived for cover. When it was over Casals quietly picked up his cello and began to play a Bach suite. The concert was broadcast. During the intermission Casals sent a message to the world in English and French. 'Do not commit the crime of letting the Spanish Republic be murdered,' he begged. 'If you allow Hitler to win in Spain, you will be the next victims of his madness. The war will spread to all Europe, to the whole world.' It was the last time he would play in Spain, and he swore never to set foot there again while Franco was in power. For their part one of Franco's generals said: 'Pablo Casals! If I ever catch him I will cut off his arms – both of them – at the elbow!'

Casals eventually found refuge in Prades, where he was to be based for the next seventeen years. He often visited Mosset, to play at La Coûme, the school that had been set up by the Quakers as a refugee centre high in the hills above the village. A favourite (apocryphal) local story describes a piano being taken up there for him on the back of a donkey. I had been to La Coûme to find out more about the history of that time, and when I talked about the Retirada to Olivier Bétoin, director of La Coûme and also mayor of Mosset, he said immediately; 'You must go to Barcelona and see Madame Alavedra! But you need to hurry. She is hundred years old now. But she was in the Retirada, and came here to Prades with Pablo Casals. She was the first piano teacher here at La Coûme.'

It wasn't long since he had seen her. 'She was sitting on her balcony enjoying a glass of cognac – she can still talk for hours!' He gave me a contact number for Alavedra's granddaughter Gemma Chaix-Durand, in Montpellier, and I made haste, travelling to Barcelona as soon as we could arrange a mutually convenient time to visit.

The apartment of Montserrat Alavedra was high above one of the wide avenues in Barcelona, with a balcony overlooking the church domes and streets below. I was welcomed by Gemma, who is devoted to her grandmother and has written a book about her grandfather, the distinguished Catalan poet Joan Alavedra. Madame Alavedra was sitting upright in a small chair next to her grand piano. A small, plump, vivacious woman with a soft cloud of white hair beneath a turban, sparkling earrings and a beatific smile that seemed permanently fixed on her face. Her green eyes regarded me quizzically as I fumbled with my glasses, and she commented crisply that her own eyesight was still perfect. She spoke French at first, but soon slipped into Catalan and Gemma patiently translated.

I looked at her sitting room, the walls hung with paintings, and the piano and every polished table covered in framed photos, portraits of her husband, her children, photos of Madame Alavedra next to Casals and his cello, a room full of memories. 'That is why I am still alive!' she exclaimed. 'The exile that brought so much suffering is a happy memory for me. With music, and poetry, we transformed suffering into happiness.'

She met the young poet Joan Alavedra on a mountain ramble, when he noticed her, a young girl with swinging plaits and clear green eyes, singing Schubert as she marched along. It was an enduring love, and Gemma is bidden to find the poem he dedicated to her. Joan Alavedra had been part of the Republican government of Luis Companys in 1931, and was both poet, politician, journalist and translator. This was not an untypical combination in the heady days of the Spanish Republic, which pursued its lofty ideals with a government composed of scholars, scientists and university professors as well as poets.

Alavedra had been imprisoned with Companys in 1934 after an ill-judged declaration of Catalan independence. After three months' imprisonment he returned home on Christmas Eve to find his family preparing the traditional *pessebre*, crib, the nativity scene of terracotta figures representing the Christmas story. Their daughter Maria (Gemma's mother), then aged five, asked: 'Papa, please tell me what the animals are saying.' This became a poem, which Alavedra spent a week writing in a notebook, and then presented to his daughter. Now Gemma opens the book, and reads from the poem, translating from Catalan into French, while Madame Alavedra nods with pleasure.

When the Spanish Civil War broke out Montserrat and her young children, Maria and her brother Macia, aged five, took refuge in her maternal village outside Barcelona, but when the city finally fell to the fascists, they too had to run.

'We suffered terribly,' says Madame Alavedra, shaking her head as if to eliminate the memory. They piled as much as they could into a truck, but as they joined the enormous wave of refugees it became clear they would have to go up into the mountains. Soon the steep roads thick with snow meant they had to abandon the vehicles and walk, taking with them only what they could carry. They marched all night in the long line of refugees, Joan carrying his small son on his shoulders, holding his daughter by the hand. As they walked, they were gradually forced to jettison almost all their belongings, though nine-year-old Maria trudged along clutching a little black case of treasures, firmly refusing to abandon it.

They arrived in Prats-de-Mollo on 29 January, among the first refugees to cross the frontier. There families were separated, men to one side, women on the other, all behind barbed wire. Alavedra fortunately managed to exert some influence (as did many government officials), and after a matter of days they were released, and made their way eventually to Paris. There they met up with Casals, who had shut himself in a dark room, sunk in a deep depression at the collapse of all their great dreams.

From Paris Casals and the Alavedras came to Prades, the nearest they could get to Spain. 'Prades felt like my own country,' explained Alavedra. 'It was still Catalonia.' At first Casals was warmly received, and they took rooms in the Grand Hotel (Prades is a modest town, so it was probably not all that grand, but it did have a magnificent lobby of the local red-veined marble, all ripped out now and replaced by a Maison de la Presse). For the proprietors, Raymonde and Nicolas Salètes, it was an honour to have Casals as a guest, and everyone would stop whatever they were doing when they heard the maestro playing music. In Prades Casals and his companions would do what they could to help their compatriots, and set about trying to alert the world to what was happening. But as Robert Capa wrote, 'The newspapermen wrote their story and I took their pictures. But the world was not interested, and in a few short years there were many other people on many other roads, running and falling before the same troops and the very same swastikas.'

# CHAPTER 3

# THE CAMPS OF SCORN

'For now, we are inside and you are outside. Soon we will
all be imprisoned together.'

The Pyrénées-Orientales has magnificent beaches, the small pebbly
coves of the fishing ports on the Côte Vermeille, and the broad golden
sands of Argelès, St-Cyprien and Canet. In the summer they are packed
with visitors. Mothers gossip under the parasols and rub cream on their
children's sunburned shoulders; fathers help dig sandcastles, or carry
fat babies into shallow waves. Gangly dark-skinned boys sing out their
litany of candied nuts and cool drinks.

It is hard to imagine these beaches as scenes of horror. You get
closer in winter on the empty stretch between Canet and St-Cyprien,
when the beach is deserted, and the harsh Tramontane wind whips up
the sand on the dunes. Beyond the beach is the saltwater lagoon, with a
cluster of primitive fishing huts built of reeds, and in the distance
Canigou seems to float like a snowy mirage on the horizon. If you sit
on the sand, plunge your hands into it and feel the deep cold beneath
the surface, then you can get a sense of what it must have been like to
sleep here in winter, with no shelter, a blanket perhaps or an overcoat,
without food or fresh water, after days or weeks of trudging down
ruined roads.

Nothing was prepared, despite all the warnings of the wave of
refugees that would pour into France as Franco's victory became more
and more inevitable. The first main camp was hurriedly set up at
Argelès, then just a small fishing village bordered by swamps and
mosquito-infested beaches. A few shuttered seaside villas presaged
the beginnings of summer tourism. (It now has the most camping
accommodation in Europe.) On 25 January Pierre Izard, deputy mayor
of Argelès, was instructed: 'Faites un camp, urgence!' He was ordered
by the local army commander to construct barracks with whatever
labour was available, which was to say the wounded and even amputee
Spanish refugees already huddled on the beach. Then a few days later
the barracks were cancelled, and instead Izard was ordered to drive
stakes into the ground to form rectangles of one hectare each to be

enclosed with barbed wire. An official visit was due from the interior minister, and he was apparently more concerned with security than shelter. The minister was satisfied.

Some of the refugees simply dropped dead of exhaustion when they arrived. The rest had to make shelter as best they could, burrowing into the sand, creating crude tents of branches, blankets, and whatever driftwood and detritus they could find on the beach.

José Sangenis still remembered it sixty-seven years later, as we talked that day in Perpignan. He and his family had to walk from Le Boulou to Argelès. 'I remember two posts and the sign, "Camp de concentration d'Argelès". Now they say there was no such sign, but I know it was there.' He insisted on this fiercely, calling me the next day to offer proof. There is still argument about the use of the term concentration camp, which has since become so loaded with horror. But it was indeed used by the French for the first camps they set up.

'I was terrified, being put inside the fence.' José shuddered. 'There was nothing there, no shelter of any kind, just the bare sand. We dug a big furrow in the sand to shelter from the wind. It was about forty centimetres deep, so it was really damp. Even in summer, as you know, at twenty centimetres the sand is wet. For all our needs, including the most basic, we had to go down to the sea. At first the women had to go in front of the men and soldiers. We were treated like beasts.'

Photos bear out José's memory of men naked except for bandaged limbs, trying to wash in the sea, and of women trying to bathe and dress their children, watched over by armed guards.

After a week the camp at Argelès was hopelessly overcrowded, with 20,000 more refugees arriving daily. Another camp was opened at St-Cyprien a few kilometres along the coast, but soon this too was crammed with 95,000 people. A third camp was set up at Barcarès, 15 kilometres further north, where 300 barracks intended to accommodate about 13,000 people were soon overflowing with 50,000.

By March there were over 100,000 in Argelès, and the camps at St-Cyprien and Barcarès were still growing rapidly. The big open-air camps in the mountains had to be abandoned because of the bitter weather, but by March there were still more than 50,000 soldiers camped outside between Arles and Prats-de-Mollo in the Vallespir.

Conditions in the camps were appalling. Some said they were being treated worse than German prisoners in the First World War. Every day a military truck arrived and loaves of bread were thrown over the barbed wire, where a great crowd would gather to fight over it. Sanitation was primitive or non-existent, disease was rife, dysentery common. There was not enough water for drinking, let alone washing, and medical facilities were almost non-existent. The lack of hygiene was one of the worst things. The smell of shit pervaded. One woman described the lack of sanitary towels. The women watched the gendarmes go to the toilet with newspapers, and afterwards they would collect them, rub them clean and dry them to use again.

Pablo Casals and the Alavedras were in Prades, trying to help their suffering compatriots. They wrote hundreds of letters appealing for help, and communicated regularly with the refugees themselves. Gifts of clothing, medical supplies and money poured into Prades, boxes of supplies were loaded into trucks and taken to the camps. After visiting the camps in early February, Casals wrote to a friend:

> There are no words to describe the horror of what is going on here. The scenes I witnessed might have been from Dante's Inferno. Tens of thousands of men and women and children were herded together like animals, penned in by barbed wire, housed – if one can call it that – in tents and crumbling shacks. There were no sanitation facilities or provisions for medical care. There was little water and barely enough food to keep the inmates from starvation. The camp at Argelès was typical. Here more than a hundred thousand refugees had been massed in open areas among sand dunes along the seashore. Though it was winter they had been provided with no shelter whatsoever – many had burrowed holes in the wet sand to protect themselves from the pelting rains and bitter winds. The driftwood they gathered for fires to warm themselves was soon exhausted. Scores had perished from exposure, hunger and disease. At the time of my arrival the hospitals at Perpignan still overflowed with the sick and dying.

Seeing the camps became something of a family outing for the Roussillonnais. My friend Dr Henri Goujon, now eighty and living in Prades, was fourteen and living in Perpignan with his family. He was taken to the camps at Argelès and Barcarès by his father, an unforgettable history lesson. Young Henri took photos, and though the handful that he copied for me are blurred and amateur they have a personal authenticity that makes them all the more real. Henri and his father must have been standing just a few yards from the barbed-wire fence, in the scrub and sand of the beach, beyond which they could see a mass of men standing, huddled in blankets against the wind, or lying on the bare sand.

The men and women were soon separated into different camps, and had to get permits to see their families. José remembers: 'We managed to see our fathers, imprisoned in the soldiers' camp, by digging a hole under the barbed wire to get through. The men were so pleased to see us, giving us bits of bread they had saved. It was only later that I understood what a sacrifice this was. I was able to hug my father a couple of times, but I didn't know it was the last time I would see him for many years.'

The refugees had doubled the population of the Pyrénées-Orientales, and the costs were immense. The French were keen to send as many back to Spain as possible. Loudspeakers urged the internees to volunteer for repatriation, and many did return. Others feared the kind of reception that might await them in Franco's Spain.

The Spanish were profoundly disappointed by the reception they received in France, a place they had considered the land of liberty, and they were deeply cynical about the treatment they received. Many of them were highly politicised young people, far from ready to abandon their political struggle or submit to the repressive regime imposed by the French authorities. They were guarded by French troops and gendarmes, who had orders to shoot anyone trying to escape. Punishment consisted of being tied upright to a pole in a small barbed-wire enclosure, exposed to the elements. They called them 'Camps du Mépris' – camps of scorn. Political infighting continued and scores were settled here. Hugh Thomas in his book on the Spanish Civil War describes an incident when one of the leaders of the hated Republican secret police was greeted by old war comrades who took him to an unfrequented part of the camp where a deep trench was dug ready. There they buried him alive.

Gradually, grudgingly, conditions improved, though no proper barracks were constructed until July. The internees became involved in the camp organisation, and soon they began to resemble refugee tent cities the world over. They had street names, a flea market, hairdressers, even a brothel. Among the internees were many intellectuals, teachers and students, and continuing education was important. They arranged classes, produced newspapers, organised football matches and choirs. They even found a sense of humour: when a sand sculpture competition was organised in July, among the castles and personalities represented was a bust of Franco that they covered in a sugary syrup. Soon it was swarming with flies. A scene worthy of Buñuel.

Refugees were sent to other camps, of which there were a number in the south, including Gurs, near Pau, Bram, near Carcassonne, Les Milles, near Marseille, Agde, and Le Vernet in the Ariège. Particularly undesirable internees – communists and the like – were sent to secure camps or prisons: Le Vernet or the château at Collioure. The great impenetrable stone walls of the château still dominate the little harbour of Collioure, though now they are more likely to shelter art exhibitions than 'dangerous anarchists'. About 400 men including boys as young as fourteen were subjected to a harrowing regime of forced labour, breaking stones, from 6 a.m. to 7 p.m. They were lodged in underground cells, with one huge trough for washing, and one latrine that they had to fight with each other to get to in the morning. Federica Montseny remarked on the contrast in Collioure: 'Its smiling beaches, its golden coast, its marvellous steepness can never be detached from the sinister and evil silhouette of the castle.'

Some of the soldiers, like Cristobal Robles, were sent to Le Vernet, a harsh camp in the Ariège, originally set up for First World War German prisoners. It was used for political prisoners, and many members of the International Brigade ended up there. At one stage there were five thousand political prisoners, of thirty different nationalities, especially Spanish, living in terrible conditions, in bitter mountain cold, with no blankets, subjected to forced labour by brutal guards. The Hungarian writer Arthur Koestler was interned there in 1940. His account of his experience, *Scum of the Earth*, was written directly after his escape to England in 1941, and is a powerful, bitter, contemporary account. He compares Vernet with Dachau, already familiar to other inmates of Le Vernet. 'In Vernet beating-up was a regular occurrence; in Dachau it was prolonged until death ensued. In Vernet people were killed for lack of medical attention; in Dachau they were killed on purpose. In Vernet half the prisoners had to sleep without blankets in 20 degrees of frost; in Dachau they were put in irons and exposed to the frost.'

There were major problems looking after the sick and wounded in the camps, who often lay untended in the open. Two hospital ships anchored at Port-Vendres held over 3,000 patients. All the hospital facilities in Perpignan were overflowing. Nurses and doctors worked round the clock. A nurse at the Hospital St-Louis in Perpignan remembered: 'They came walking, all the way from Argelès, some of them, with all kinds of terrible wounds. They had cut branches off the trees and improvised splints. Many of them were gangrenous, all of them were emaciated, hungry and exhausted.' In one temporary medical barracks in St-Cyprien the patients had to sleep on the sand and share their quarters with the coffins that were delivered every evening.

There is no knowing the total toll of deaths in the camps, but estimates (based on cemetery counts: they had to build new ones) suggest there may have been as many as 15,000 who died between

February and September 1939 in grievous conditions. There were twenty-five or thirty deaths a day at St-Cyprien alone. Most of the inmates suffered from some sort of malady, with conjunctivitis, throat irritations and skin problems resulting from violent wind and driving sand, and the constant irritation of fleas, lice and sheer dirt. Dysentery, tuberculosis and pneumonia were frequent, malaria and even leprosy made their appearance.

In July 1939 Philippe Pétain came to visit the camps. He had been French ambassador to Franco since 2 March, and wished to reassure himself that all the criticism of the camps was no more than propaganda against France. He said he was satisfied that they were doing all that was humanly possibly to give asylum to the refugees.

There was a strong inclination to repatriate them, whatever their fate, and it was suggested that conditions in the camps were kept deliberately bad to encourage the refugees to go home 'voluntarily'. In some of the camps they were harried night and day by a barrage of Franco propaganda. Some were repatriated, though numbers are uncertain, but probably around 200,000. Life became even more difficult when the non-aggression pact was signed between Hitler and Stalin in August, and all Spanish Republicans were automatically assumed to be Reds. Hundreds of communists and anarchists were hunted down and imprisoned.

As war drew closer, the French realised that the skills of the Spanish could be mobilised. After April 1939 thousands were contracted out to farmers; others went to work as miners, or for industrial enterprises in the north. Many were recruited for labour companies erecting fortifications in the north. Some joined the Foreign Legion or the French army.

Eventually those left in the camps were mainly the old, the sick, women and children. It laid a heavy burden on the French, and there were not many other countries willing to take the refugees. Mexico welcomed about 15,000, who were shipped out from the port of Sète by the Quakers. About 4,000 communists went off to the Soviet Union. Britain and America took very few.

Thousands of women and children were sent off to other parts of France. José was one of them. 'We stayed in Argelès for about three months, then at the end of April we were mustered together and selected for another destination. The men were to stay at Argelès. We went on foot to Elne [about 10 kilometres away], where we were put on a train to Clermont-Ferrand. They put us in a barn full of straw, we slept well, and were well fed too, at least to begin with. Our mothers even organised a school for us, so we could continue our education and above all learn French.'

International relief efforts for the camps had been quickly mobilised. Among those trying help the refugees were a British contingent that would have been at home in an Evelyn Waugh novel. Nancy Mitford was one of them. She went to Perpignan in May 1939 to join her husband, Peter Rodd, who was working with the refugees as a volunteer in an office surrounded by a mass of refugees with cardboard suitcases, dogs, donkeys and goats. He had written to Nancy: 'The thing that is happening is so appalling it amounts to the cold blooded murder of thousands of chaps. It is impossible to get at the mortality figures but the dying has not even properly begun.'

Nancy spent most of her time driving a dilapidated Ford van, wearing a large straw hat, delivering supplies and taking a group of expectant mothers to embark from Sète for Mexico. (When not looking after refugees the Brits went for picnics in the mountains or swimming at Collioure.) Other British volunteers included General Murgatroyd, who, Nancy wrote to her mother, 'speaks no French or Spanish but bursts into fluent Hindustani at the sight of a foreigner', and the writer Humphrey Hare, a South of France playboy who had gone to join the International Brigade. All were working fourteen hours a day. Nancy at least was under the impression that her husband was running the whole show, though she does acknowledge that the French seemed to resent this a bit.

The Mitford family were famously divided politically, with half of them left-wing, the other half favouring the fascists (Nancy's sister Unity was madly in love with Hitler). In another letter to her mother Nancy writes: 'Darling Muv, If you could have a look, as I have, at some of the less agreeable results of fascism in a country I think you would be less anxious for the swastika to become a flag on which the sun never sets.' (Muv had been taking tea with Hitler, 'such a nice man', not long before.)

Most significant among the relief workers were the Quakers – often the refugees are quoted as saying they seemed to be the only ones there to help. Since their foundation as a dissident religious movement in Britain in the seventeenth century, the Quakers have dedicated themselves to non-violence, and have been in the forefront of humanitarian relief efforts. Worshipping in silent meetings, rejecting the outward ritual and priestly intermediaries of the established Church, they emphasise inner spirituality and express their faith through their lives in practical action. Increasingly this has meant campaigning for peace.

The Quakers came to international attention for their humanitarian work during the First World War, and they continued their relief work afterwards, in the devastated countries of Europe. During the Spanish Civil War they provided relief to both sides, a decision that caused controversy and heart-searching amongst many of the Quakers working in Spain, some of whom decided to leave after Franco's victory. Howard Kershner, the American director of the International Commission for Child Refugees, who was responsible for these operations, asked 'how far one should cooperate with those who are doing evil', and answered: 'Surely it is possible to denounce evil deeds, yet preserve good will towards the evil doer. He is one of the persons whom we are trying to help.' He also noted that preserving the good will of the Spanish Nationalists meant that a key channel for relief workers and supplies through Spain to France remained open – even after war had been declared – in 1940.

Already weary from the conflict in Spain the Quakers continued their work with the refugees in France, helping with food distribution and medical assistance and finding sanctuary for many. They seemed to be everywhere, discreetly offering care where it was needed, and, even more discreetly, escape to thousands of desperate people.

The relief effort in France in 1939 included American Friends, the British and a small group of French Quakers, and was coordinated by Kershner. Relief teams were organised to work in the camps, travelling in light trucks loaded with supplies. They tried to reunite divided families, caring for and identifying lost children. They brought clothing and extra food to the camps. Later they opened schools, and organised holiday camps for the children. Kershner notes that such care was relatively easy at first, since supplies were plentiful and cheap. Later on in the war they would be trying to do the same for entire populations with such scarce supplies that there was little they could do to alleviate the suffering.

What I notice though is the number of women who are there, modest, hard-working, self-sacrificing, 'doing their duty' – and escaping the stifling confines of a traditional women's role in Britain. I wanted to know more about these women, and went to the Quaker library in the Society of Friends meeting house in central London, opposite Euston station. There amongst the tall wooden shelves, the balcony with its portraits of severely benign past Quakers like prison reformer Elizabeth Fry, and the fridge full of water bottles, paid for on the honour system, I found a connection.

The Quakers do not go in for glorifying their own deeds. They have no desire to be famous. But eventually the library archives yielded several brown cardboard folders tied up with ribbon. Within were the diligent reports of meetings and conferences about the refugee problem, the official letters pleading for support, endless blurred and flimsy carbon copies. There were reports from the field, some typed, many handwritten, sometimes in pencil, one written on HMS *Queen Mary* notepaper, headed with a picture of an incongruously jolly ship.

Certain names recur, Edith Pye for one, and her friend Dr Hilda Clark. They had both been working with refugees since the First World War. There was Mary Elmes, who first appears working in Spain during the Civil War, then caring for refugees in the camps in France, and later helping refugees to escape over the Pyrenees.

Another was Francesca Wilson, who was a Quaker from Newcastle, and after graduating from Oxford had been working as a history teacher in Birmingham in 1912. She began relief work with the Quakers in the First World War in Belgium and Serbia and was in Russia during the famine of the early 1920s. During the Spanish Civil War she took leave from her job to join the relief committee in Spain, working with displaced children in southern Spain. She returned to Birmingham in January 1939, but appalled by the stories of the refugees, came to France in her Easter holidays. In her book *In the Margins of Chaos*, she recalled her first reaction. 'I had read such terrible accounts of the camp at Argelès that I dreaded seeing it,' she wrote. But with Dr Audrey Russell, another Quaker, she visited the camps and helped to arrange supplies of tools, books, paper, pencils, blankets and shoes. They tried to set up a welfare centre for women and a school for children (much to the disdain of the French commandant, who seemed to think it was a waste of time trying to educate Spanish children). The Quakers helped establish a *Université des Sables*, to teach the inmates French, and this developed into education in a wide range of subjects for children and adults.

During the spring of 1939 the Quakers turned their energies to organising transport and refuge, including the ship that sailed to Mexico from Sète, with Nancy Mitford's passengers aboard. They tried to find local accommodation, in the hotels of spa towns like Vernet-les-Bains and Molitg-les-Bains in the Castellane valley, down the valley from Mosset. And some of the Spanish children were sent by Edith Pye to Mosset, to La Coûme, a place that was to become a haven and refuge for many.

# CHAPTER 4

# A QUAKER REFUGE

One day in early spring I walked up to La Coûme from Mosset, past the schoolhouse with its signs for *Filles* and *Garçons* still over separate doors, past the last houses of the village, the spring, where villagers used to come to fetch their water, and then the old forge on the other side of the river. The road winds steeply up to the Col de Jau, one of the high cols of the Pyrenees at 1,500 metres, and the border with the Aude department and the Pyrénées-Orientales. Occasionally a car or a tractor passed, but mostly it was very quiet, plenty of space for birds to sing, for dogs to wander across the road. There was a freshness in the air, the river was full, pounding over the rocks below, a light wind stirred the trees just beginning to bud, here and there white clouds of almond blossom, and irises thrusting out of the ground like green blades, a typical spring.

I thought of those refugees, most of them children, walking this way in 1939, carrying their meagre possessions, separated from their parents, perhaps not knowing where they were. Some of them were injured, traumatised by their experiences of the war, all of them fearful of what was to come. A sharp turn leads to the road up to La Coûme, now tarmacked after a fashion, then just a rough track. A further two, even steeper, kilometres brought me to the farm, sheltered in a cradle of woodland, 'la coûme', the coomb, the end of the valley, a safe retreat. Beyond lay only forested valleys folding into each other, and the distant blue mountains, clouds hovering over them like haloes.

From the upper windows of the old farmhouse I could hear the faint chords of a guitar, one of the current pupils practising. I saw José, a refugee from Pinochet's Chile, who works here now, chopping logs for firewood. After the war La Coûme became a school and now it runs holiday courses in pottery, music, and languages. It is still a special place, retaining something of its original ideals, a cherished spirit of cooperation and fellowship. The original farmhouse is virtually unchanged, a stuccoed façade with sturdy wooden shutters on the windows. Behind the farm is a large barn, and a further scattering of houses and dormitories accommodate the guests. At its heart is a communal dining hall and kitchen with an open fireplace and big windows.

Olivier Bétoin was fixing a tractor beside the barn. Olivier, eldest son of one of the original group of volunteers who helped La Coûme during the war, is now mayor of Mosset. He has the clear-eyed direct gaze that characterises all his family, as if they have kept something of childhood lost to most of us. He was once asked who his heroes were. 'I don't have heroes,' he replied. 'I respect those who do good without any need for recognition.' It reflected an altruism and humanity learned growing up at La Coûme.

Olivier's wife Marta, who shares the running of La Coûme, appeared in the doorway of the farmhouse in jeans and rolled-up shirtsleeves carrying an armful of laundry, the wind whipping strands of black hair around her delicate pale face. Her fragile appearance belies her strong character, not least her passionate Catalanism, a fierce commitment to the preservation of Catalan culture and language. She can remember the Franco years in Barcelona, when Catalan was banned, the constant fear, the special secret rings on the doorbell. Her grandfather's experience typified the crazy political atmosphere of the war. 'At the start of the war he was imprisoned for helping the nuns . . . when Franco came he was imprisoned again for being an anarchist.'

Olivier came over to shake hands, and as I murmur feebly about the cold wind, he laughs.

'There's more to come,' and he indicates the chainsaw with which he is about to cut more wood supplies.

'You should have been here last winter,' adds Martha. 'There was so much snow we had to go on foot for a month, it was impossible to get up the road here.' They invited me into the farmhouse. On the wall of the whitewashed entrance hall was a large photo of Edith Pye and Hilda Clark, visiting La Coûme together in 1935, belted firmly into thick overcoats against the chilly mountain air.

In the archives of the Quaker library I had found a few personal letters, fragments of correspondence between Edith Pye and her companion Hilda Clark, and began to piece together their story. Some were handwritten letters on good-quality headed notepaper, some brief notes on hotel stationery, others typewritten screeds on onionskin airmail paper.

Both Edith Pye and Hilda Clark were deeply involved in anti-war and refugee work during both world wars. Hilda Clark came from an old Quaker family, the manufacturers of Clark's shoes. Her sister was

Alice Clark, a pioneering feminist historian, and Hilda herself took part in suffragette actions, riding on horseback in the great Pilgrimage of Women protest march to London in 1913. She remembered going to suffragette meetings in Bath where boys pelted the women with ashes and stinking fish heads.

Hilda became a doctor, and in 1907, when she was twenty-six she met Edith Pye, a trained nurse and midwife six years older. Hilda must immediately have taken her new friend to a Quaker meeting because Edith also joined the Society of Friends in 1908. From then they were passionately committed to their work and to each other.

Their activities meant they were often apart, Hilda in Vienna, Switzerland or Greece working with refugees, Edith on a trip to China in 1927 for the Women's International League. They exchanged news of refugees and bureaucracy on the one hand, of kittens, gardens and sick relatives on the other. I imagine them sitting in drafty cold hotel rooms, banging away at huge old typewriters, wearing coats and fingerless mittens, or close by the fireside with tea and buttered toast.

Though I found only one side of their personal correspondence, fragmentary at that, in a box full of Hilda's papers there was enough to suggest a moving love story. They addressed each other as dearest love, and dear one, and in 1910 Hilda wrote to Edith from the Lake District:

> I long to feel your arms about me, twin-soul. I do long for thee so precious sweetheart, my whole being craves to feel thee in my arms. I think that love is the only thing that carries one beyond the boundary of life.

For Hilda there was no contradiction in their love for each other and their spiritual commitment:

> No. I can't separate it from the joy of 'doing right' they are two wonderful fundamental essentials of the soul's existence. Thou and I can have and will one day perfect, the true spirit love.

(I had always thought that addressing each other as thee and thou was a peculiar biblical affectation, but in fact it stems from the seventeenth century, when English still had a form of *tu* and *vous*. 'You' was for addressing your betters, 'thee' and 'thou' for familiars, as well as for children and servants. The Quakers' habit of addressing everyone equally as 'thee' was thus quite shocking.)

From the moment war broke out in 1914, Hilda and Edith saw the need for action, and they joined the relief operation in the devastated region of the Marne valley after the German invasion in 1917. Edith Pye worked as a nurse behind the lines, setting up a desperately needed maternity hospital at Châlons-sur-Marne. Both women continued to be involved in the relief work in Germany after the war. The Quakers sent workers and food to centres all over the country, and for several years they fed a million children daily. In many German cities, the streets where their Child Feeding Centres were established are still affectionately referred to as 'Quakerstrasse'.

During the early years of the Third Reich the Quakers established a reputation for their willingness to assist Jews or anyone else who sought refuge from Nazi Germany. Thus it was that they came to rescue the Krüger family and establish the refuge at La Coûme.

In the photo with Edith Pye and Hilda Clark are Yvès and Pitt Krüger, the refugees from Germany who arrived at La Coûme in 1934. Pitt, thin and wiry, with spectacles, his hair brushed back from a domed forehead, looks gentle and reserved. He is standing a little apart from the women, in what looks like a new suit he has just been given. Yvès, wrapped in a loose trench coat, is smiling, petite, gamine. Even in a photo you get a sense of her vitality and presence.

Alongside the photo was a summary of the story of La Coûme. The farm had been acquired by the Quakers in 1933 as part of a scheme by the Friends Committee for Refugees and Aliens to resettle young German refugees on land in France. As Hitler rose to power in the early 1930s in Germany, the Quakers had intensified their efforts to protect opponents of his regime, who were increasingly vilified and persecuted.

Pitt Krüger and his Swiss wife Yvès had been living in Potsdam just outside Berlin. They were both teachers, inspired by the progressive educational ideas of Montessori and Piaget, teaching children self-rule and freedom, ideas that were anathema to the growing fascist tendency in Germany. They were intellectuals, cultured people with a shared love of art and music. Yvès had grown up in Geneva, and as companion and governess to the Hungarian family of Baron Podmaniczky (whose ancestor was responsible for uniting Buda and Pest in the nineteenth century) had travelled frequently between Germany, Italy and Hungary. The Krügers participated in the cultural life of Berlin throughout the 1920s Weimar Republic, when Germany's brief liberal democracy led to a great flowering of culture and intellectual and critical thought. But the couple were socialists and pacifists, and immediately after Hitler came to power Pitt Krüger lost his job, the first teacher to be dismissed under the new fascist regime in East Prussia.

'Two days after the elections in January 1933, they came to the school and threw me out, without even time to get my hat and coat from the classroom,' Pitt recalled in an interview, not long before he died, for a book about anti-fascist German refugees. He had been denounced by Nazi colleagues for his politics and his anti-militarism. The burning of the Reichstag in February 1933 was blamed on the communists and Hitler seized the opportunity to outlaw all other political parties. As goose-stepping stormtroopers terrorised the streets, smashing Jewish shops and working-class bars, arresting and torturing anti-fascists, the Krüger family were given a month's notice to leave their home. 'We sold our furniture and bought a tent, and we camped out beside the lakes in the Wannsee forest until autumn came.' It began to rain incessantly and their two-year-old daughter, Jamine, fell ill. As winter set in, they were finally rescued by a member of the police, the father of a former pupil, who helped them to obtain an exit visa. 'I used to go to Potsdam by bike every week to see what was happening. I was spotted by a policeman whose son I'd helped at school. He said to me: "You are still here? They are looking for you! Have you got a passport? Give it to me – in two days everything will be in order." '

In their desperate need for sanctuary the Krügers turned to the Quakers. Pitt had been involved with the Quakers in Berlin for several years, working with them for peace and disarmament between France and Germany. He had met Corder Catchpool, the British Quaker representative in Berlin, a man of extraordinary courage and charisma who had been working for peace between Britain and Germany since the end of the First World War. Catchpool had volunteered in the early years of the First World War as an ambulance man at the Front, but when he was conscripted he refused to fight. He was sent to prison for eighteen months as a conscientious objector, and there he learned German in order to work for Anglo-German reconciliation. He was tireless both in his efforts for rapprochement with the Germans and in helping those suffering under the increasingly harsh Nazi regime. His Berlin home was always full of people, refugees and orphans, attracting peace workers, students, and anti-Nazi activists. After 1933 Catchpool intensified his efforts to protect political victims, pacifists and Jews, struggling always with the challenge to Quakers of pursuing peace in the light of Nazi warmongering. Many of the German Quakers provided hiding places for Jews and many who refused to fight died in concentration camps.

The Quakers were looking for land in France for refugees, and Edith Pye had spent a holiday in the Pyrenees, visiting a German friend in

Prades, the niece of Alphonse Paquet, a German poet and journalist. He had been an early convert to Quakerism in the 1920s – when he first came across the Quakers in Russia, he described them as 'an order of kind human beings, making no fuss about themselves'. While walking in the mountains Edith had been struck by the number of abandoned farms, a legacy of the peasant flight from the land after the First World War.

Equipped with the essential papers, Pitt Krüger escaped from Germany via Switzerland and arrived in Perpignan in October 1933. When Yvès, his wife, applied to leave Germany herself, along with her daughter Jamine, the authorities already knew where Krüger was – it transpired much later that he had been denounced by the hotel-keeper in Perpignan, a Nazi sympathiser. (The Resistance blew up his hotel in 1943, Pitt noted with satisfaction in the interview.) Pitt Krüger was one of many thousand anti-Nazi Germans who took refuge in France at that time, believing they would be safe from fascism.

Pitt Krüger and Edith Pye had looked at several properties in the region, one of which was Corbiac, but with foresight, Pitt decided it was too exposed and visible, close to the main road up to Mosset. There would be no chance of escape. (And in the end it was Pierre who bought the abbey.)

A few kilometres above Mosset they discovered the small derelict farm of La Coûme, unoccupied and available at a modest rent, partly because it was difficult to irrigate with only a small stream running through it. It was at 800 metres altitude, with only a few acres truly suitable for cultivation. In November Pitt was joined by Yvès, Jamine and five other refugees.

'We had no idea of our future,' said Pitt, 'but I thought, here at least we have wood to keep warm, we can grow potatoes, kill rabbits to eat, we are far from Nazi Germany and we have the Pyrenees behind us.' Still, he stressed, 'I had no desire to retire from the world.' Already he had the idea of a community of like-minded people, devoted to peace and cooperation. They had very little money, just a small grant from the Quakers, and overnight had to turn themselves from teachers into peasants, farmers and woodcutters.

I had heard that their daughter Jamine had returned to Prades after living most of her life in Germany, and Olivier Bétoin introduced us one day at a concert in Mosset. Eventually she agreed to talk to me, and I went to see Jamine Noack in Prades. We shook hands and she ushered me formally into her house, to a table in the window, framing a fine view of Canigou. I was struck by her resemblance to her mother's photos. She is petite, elegant, with an upright posture, smoothly cut silver hair springing from a high forehead. Her manner was almost severe until she smiled, rather shyly.

She had married a German musician, Rainer Noack, met while he was studying the cello with Pablo Casals in Prades. She went with him to Germany, where she became a teacher, and had two sons, both highly accomplished musicians. La Coûme remained a place close to her heart, and after her husband died she chose to return to live nearby.

She offered tea in the German style, a small pewter teapot kept warm on a tealight, served with milk in delicate porcelain cups and saucers.

'I've found some photos to show you,' she said, spreading out on the table a selection of early black and white photos of the Krügers and the farm. 'Here is La Coûme when my parents first arrived. The farm was a ruin, there was manure everywhere, the rooms were all full of hay. It was like a barn.' At first they had to live in the village, where they were given lodging by the priest, Benjamin Vernet. 'Every Saturday the curé invited us to lunch, even though he knew we were not Catholics. I can just remember him in his black soutane, giving me chocolates.'

Jamine showed me another photo, the Krügers at the village carnival, in February. 'We even joined in the village festivities.' Yvès is clutching her small daughter, clad in a short dress and laced black boots; Pitt, wearing the corduroy jacket and checked shirt of the *paysans*, looks slightly ill at ease. Behind them a row of village girls pose in men's suits and ties and hats, one with a jaunty straw hat and a banjo.

Jamine talked passionately about the village and the support they received. 'We would never have survived without them,' she said firmly. The villagers looked after them, gave them food, and helped out with their agricultural efforts, no doubt astonished at their incompetence. Pitt always talked with reverence of the Spanish shepherd, the *berger* Santos, who helped him so much. 'He was an illiterate *berger*, but Pitt always said he taught him everything,' said Jamine.

Pitt himself observed: 'Until the Nazis occupied France in 1942, I think the villagers of Mosset believed all Germans were nice people, and that like me, they all wore glasses!'

Mosset could hardly have been more of a contrast with 1930s Berlin. For most villagers life had changed little since the Middle Ages. The population, which had dwindled after the death toll of the First World War, and the flight to the towns, numbered about 700. But it was still a busy village, more so in winter than summer, when everyone went up to the summer cortals (rough stone barns) to pasture the animals, only returning once a week for supplies. Although education had become compulsory in 1906, most of the village children only went to school in winter, spending their summers in the fields or barefoot in the mountains with the animals. They learned French at school but still spoke Catalan at home.

There are few people in Mosset now who remember, but Louisette was happy to tell me more and I went to see her in her house on the main street with a balcony and view of the valley. Now it is completely renovated with a smart modern formica kitchen and a large television in the corner.

'It wasn't like this at all,' she said, describing her family's home before the war, when she was a young girl, a village house laid out in the traditional manner. 'There were the animals on the ground floor in the *cave* – it was just beaten earth, there we kept the pig, goats, chickens and rabbits. We kept all the tools there too.' The family lived on the first floor, the centre of action the fireplace, high enough to do all the cooking. They slept in bedrooms or alcoves off the kitchen. On the second floor was the *grenier* where the hay was kept to feed the animals. The arrangement worked admirably, the animals below keeping them warm, the hay providing insulation.

'We had to fetch water every day from the *fontaines*, the village pumps.' There were no inside toilets – 'We emptied the buckets in the river!' There was electricity from a small generating station for a few hours a day but only enough for lighting, and the village was not connected to the EDF network till 1960. Laundry was a complicated task, heating water on the fire and using cinders for cleansing. 'We rinsed the clothes in the river and dried them on the rocks.'

'It was a hard life.' Louisette shook her head. Perhaps it was not so surprising that so few of the old folk really wanted to remember it. No one had cars, and most still depended on animals for transport. Or else they walked. To go to Prades there was the bus, whose arrival with the post was a daily event. The road was tarmac as far as Mosset, but the peasants had even complained about that, since their oxen and horses could no longer get a firm grip on the surface.

They were virtually self-sufficient in food, what with the animals they kept, the fruit and vegetables they grew in their fields, and the vegetable gardens that surrounded the village, watered by irrigation canals. At least it would have made sense to them that the Krügers wanted to grow their own food, however ignorant they seemed about the process.

There was a baker by then, though many families still made their own bread weekly in the great bread ovens that hang suspended like giant stone beehives from the outside walls of the houses. There were no telephones, and only a handful of radios in the village. Information was still relayed by the public crier who went round at the end of the day with essential news, or to announce the arrival of the knife-grinder, the chair-mender or the barber. (The barber still came and cut all the men's hair when we first came in the 1990s.)

There were three cafés at that time, frequented by the men in the evening for cards and company. (The women stayed at home, knitting and sewing.) Most of the real conversation happened among the old men sitting on the stone parapet of the main street with its steep drop to the vegetable gardens below and its view of Canigou at the end of the valley.

After six months of gruelling labour, clearing scrub, ploughing, and planting seeds, the farm at La Coûme was finally considered habitable and they moved in April. They bought four cows and fifteen goats for milk they hoped to sell, and a mule for transport. But survival was hard, and the other refugees hated the work – one of them said he would rather starve on a grand Parisian boulevard than have enough to eat in the country. Soon the other pioneers left and the Krügers were alone. They began a new scheme to cultivate hundreds of fruit trees, planting the first apple and pear trees in the Castellane valley.

The Quakers continued to support them and Hilda Clark bought the farm outright in 1934. She refers to the purchase in one of her regular letters to her beloved Edith. After details of the cats, the garden, anxious talk of disarmament and rescuing Jews from Vienna, she expresses her concern for Edith's welfare in the primitive conditions of Mosset:

> Thy long and interesting letter from Mosset came just after I had posted yesterday. I can let thou have the money whenever thou wants it. I do hope thy lodgings are not too Spartan. I am afraid it may be uncomfortable in wet weather and I am anxious lest thou should feel the cold at that height . . .

It was not long before the Krügers found a role better suited to their talents, as the Quakers began sending convalescent refugees for Yvès and Pitt to care for. A community began to emerge. Everyone was expected to share in the work. Groups of English students visited in the summer, and helped on the farm, chopping wood for winter, and building a bridge over the river. Students came from Germany to support their former teachers.

A second daughter, Veronica, was born in 1936, and there is a photo

of the family perched on an ox cart, Pitt looking irredeemably intellectual in such bucolic surroundings, Yvès laughing, the children un-
encumbered by clothes. Nature, fresh air and hiking were then all the
rage, and Krüger had been involved with the German youth movement
Quickborn, the Catholic equivalent of the Protestant Wandervogel,
romantic back-to-nature movements, attractive to both sides of the
political spectrum (later hijacked by the Hitler Youth). In 1936 when
the Popular Front government introduced paid holidays for workers, La
Coûme had become one of the first youth hostels in France, appealing
to a prewar generation reacting against the bourgeois restrictions of
society.

Olivier and Marta Bétoin had searched through a big cupboard full
of yellowing newspapers and tattered school books for any remaining
material from that period, and among the accounts books listing
purchases of cabbage, books, sugar, bread, wine, stamps, eggs, potatoes, the repair of a lamp and the cost of a telegram, they found one of
the first visitors' books from 1937. I leafed through the notebook with
its marbled cover and faded brown pages inscribed in ink, looking with
curiosity at the names – Patience Scott, Winifred Smith, Patricia
Walker. They came from Oxford colleges, from Yorkshire, from the
Welsh valleys. There were German names too, Polish and Jewish,
Swedish and Dutch, arriving on foot, by bicycle and by car. It was
already an international community.

On the first page was the name of Denis Healey, the bushy-
eyebrowed English Labour politician and peer, sometimes described
as 'the best prime minister Britain never had'. He visited La Coûme
twice in the Thirties (24 June to 5 July 1937, Balliol, he had inscribed,
when he arrived).

In his autobiography, *The Time of My Life*, Healey writes with
enormous respect about the Krügers and their work, creating a picture
of a lost prewar world of hope and idealism. Of the Krügers he wrote:
'they represented all that was best in the Germany of the Weimar
Republic'.

In response to a letter Lord Healey agreed to talk to me on the
telephone about his memories. 'La Coûme certainly made a deep
impression on me,' he said in his distinctive gruff voice. 'I had gone
there on my first trip to France via a Quaker friend – I will never forget
the time I spent with them, gathering crops, tiling the roof, improving
that dangerous track up from the road.' He recalled climbing trees to
pick the cherries – 'bottled sunshine Pitt used to call them'.

'They grew their own food, and got water from the stream, there was no electricity then of course.' But they enjoyed good simple food, fruit, local wine, sweet wine from Banyuls. 'We would talk for hours far into the night, on everything from Bach to psychoanalysis.'

Healey and his friend stayed in a hut a hundred yards from the farmhouse. He writes of those clear Pyrenean nights: 'a brilliant incandescent moon lit the valley, its contours broken by the black trees which rose above it as we advanced, while the snow-capped peaks of the Canigou glistened on the horizon, emerging above a wreath of cloud.' He spent two days climbing Canigou alone, sleeping out in the forest below the summit. The next year he returned with his girlfriend to spend another week with the Krügers. But by 1938 the world was changing fast. It was to be a long time before Healey returned to La Coûme. 'Do send my love to Jamine,' he added as we ended our conversation.

World events eclipsed the nascent Youth Hostel movement and by 1939 La Coûme was full of refugees, providing sanctuary for Spanish children who had fled across the frontier from Franco's forces. Pitt remembered: 'That was really when our house of children began, with first four, then six, then twenty Spanish children. We fed them, dressed them and taught them. I remember a family of four from Malaga, completely traumatised after the death of their father in the war. The youngest was only eighteen months old and I will never forget when Yvès went to collect him from Perpignan – when she got back to Mosset, people said he would never make it here alive. But he did survive and so did his sister, who was mute with shock after being bombed. After a year my wife had got her to talk and even to sing.'

Pitt recalled going to the village one day to collect the bread, and encountering the new village curé, a young Spanish priest, a supporter of Franco. 'He stopped me in the boulangerie and asked me why I didn't bring the Spanish children to catechism. I answered him: "Listen, monsieur, we have children with us whose father was killed by the priests in Teruel during the war. These children would not want to set foot in a church." He was furious and accused me of being a communist, so then I told him that he should go and see what it was like on the other side of the frontier if he was really for Franco.' It was an encounter that was to have far-reaching consequences for them both.

La Coûme became virtually a community of children, who from economic necessity as well as educational theory had to learn to be self-sufficient and take part in the life and work of the farm. They did laundry, and cooking and gardening, chopped wood, looked after animals, carried water and churns of milk from the road below. Jamine remembers picking off the *doryphores*, Colorado beetles, before school to stop them eating the potatoes.

Yet there was culture as well as potatoes. Art, literature, drama and especially music were equally essential to life. In Germany Pitt had a music room with piano, violin, cello and wind instruments. He was able to bring only two flutes with him to France, but they always sang and played music together. Denis Healey recalls Yvès singing Bach and Schubert as she did the farmyard chores.

Jamine recalls her childhood there with joy, no matter that they were so poor. 'It was life in the open air, with the animals, collecting wood, working in the garden. We shared everything. If someone brought a box of Spanish oranges we shared them out. We all had one pair of trousers and an anorak and shoes. We were treated the same as the others so we always called them Yvès and Pitt so as not to differentiate us from the children who had no parents.'

All ate together round an enormous wooden table in the big farm-house kitchen. Despite their rustic existence, Yvès expected proper behaviour. 'It was always a struggle for her – my mother was not from the country, and she had grown up in a Geneva orphanage, educated according to strict Calvinist principles. She insisted on good manners, the table properly laid, the napkins ironed. You might have to cook over a wood fire but you could eat from good plates.'

The days were carefully disciplined, with hours for work, meals, and rest all allocated. Sunday was a special day, with clean clothes, and though La Coûme had no specific religious affiliation (the Quakers would not require it) they held an Hour of Unity together, celebrating the idea of fellowship, reading aloud, singing together and listening to music. It all sounds so unfashionable today, along with the ideals they cherished of pacifism, anti-materialism, cooperation and friendship.

But in 1939 their fragile future had been threatened like so many others. Edith Pye reported: 'In June 39 Pitt asked for proper legal standing for the farm as he hoped to be able to pay rent for it. They were so happy and proud about it. The war has destroyed their hopes for the present.' During the summer of 1939 prospects were looking increasingly grim, especially for exiles. The Nazi–Soviet pact in August meant that the Communist Party was outlawed and many French and Spanish communists were imprisoned. In the camps the position of the Spanish communists became even more untenable.

On 3 September, after the invasion of Poland, Britain declared war on Germany. France followed a few hours later. The war had different meanings for everyone. For the Brits it was a straightforward battle with the Boche. The French had no great desire for war but they felt they were secure behind the massive static defences of the Maginot Line, and confident in their great army that had defeated the Germans in the First World War. For the Spanish in the camps there was a wind of hope. Perhaps an Allied victory over the Reich would mean reconquest of their own land. If France and Britain were willing to fight against the fascist Hitler, they would finally liberate Spain too.

At La Coûme on the night war was declared there was a rainbow of different nationalities taking refuge: Russians, Germans, French, English, Italians, Belgians and Spanish. Suddenly many of them were technically enemies. They faced an uncertain future and sat silently together and listened to Beethoven's Ninth Symphony on a wind-up gramophone. No one knew what would befall them all.

In Mosset there must have been many sad faces and grim talk at the forge, or on the parapet, the high stone wall looking down the valley to Canigou, which was always a gathering place for the villagers. Opposite at the bottom of a steep flight of steps was the *Monument aux Morts*, the memorial for those who died fighting the First World War. Every French town and village has one, erected during the 1920s to the memory of the millions who went to the Front in 1914, in their bright uniforms of blue tunics and scarlet trousers, their heads full of sacrifice and heroism.

Always it is impossible to believe the numbers of names of those who died. From the tiny village of Mosset there are thirty-seven names carved into the granite, thirty-seven husbands, sons, fathers, brothers, dead in that awful war. No family can have been unaffected. One in every six men enlisted was killed, 1.3 million, including a quarter of those sent to the Front. A million survivors were left invalids. Many bodies were never recovered.

In 1939 all that was only twenty years ago. Not surprising then that there was little enthusiasm for war again. But however terrible the Great War, they had finally won. And their victory was popularly attributed to the legendary figure of Marshal Pétain, the hero of Verdun.

The siege of Verdun in 1916 came to epitomise the French at war, the final triumph after appalling bloodshed. Five months of carnage in flooded trenches had left hundreds of thousands dead, bodies strewn in all directions, gassed and asphyxiated, some men buried alive. Pétain became known for his sensitivity to the *poilu*, the ordinary soldier, after he had realised that the troops could only survive by limiting their time at the Front. Almost three-quarters of the French army had been sent to Verdun at some time. Eventually the siege was lifted. Verdun did not fall and the Germans gained nothing.

One particular book had been a bestseller at that time, *Le Feu* (Under Fire), by Henri Barbusse, a socialist and pacifist before the war, who had volunteered as a simple soldier. While in Picardy he wrote a guts-and-all description of life in the trenches, which had sold a quarter of a million copies by 1918. He concluded with a plea for pacifism. Barbusse emphasised that teachers had a mission to regenerate France in a pacifist and revolutionary direction. But despite Barbusse most people were still unaware of the true numbers of dead and remained ignorant of the horrors of front-line warfare.

As well as the legendary Pétain there was a more local hero for the people of Mosset, Colonel Jean-Jacques Ruffiandis, a teacher and musician. In the First World War he had been wounded three times and decorated six times. He was captain of the 53rd Roussillon regiment, who suffered bitterly in the trenches of the Western Front. They were miserably cold, so far from the warmth of the South. Looking at their photos I had been struck by how Catalan they looked. Here were the farmers I had met, the hard, stocky bodies and short muscular legs like Picasso, intense dark eyes under black brows. They looked Spanish but earthier, more bullish.

There is a photo of Ruffiandis himself, dancing the sardana in the trenches, just a few metres from the enemy, knees lifted high, while a comrade wearing the Catalan baratina, the floppy red cap they still wear for traditional festivals and dancing, plays a flute. In a second-hand bookstore in Perpignan I had found a book, *Mosset: Vieille Cité*, with an ivory cover and a black and white line drawing of the village on the cover, written by Ruffiandis himself. The Ruffiandis family, it turned out, had owned Corbiac almost since the Revolution, only selling it in 1936. Ruffiandis had spent all his holidays in Mosset, visiting his grandparents, looking after the animals in the summer pastures, eating meals *en famille* around the big kitchen table. It was his childhood paradise and he writes with misty-eyed nostalgia about the village, working the land, bemoaning the loss of traditional rural values. Like so many others, he too set off to fight for France again in 1939.

# CHAPTER 5

# THE PHONEY WAR

A strange peace descends on the Castellane valley at the end of August. It is calm, somnolent. Even the wasps are lazy. The scent of pines is almost narcotic. The notes of thyme, rosemary and lavender on the breeze are pungent after the dry weeks of summer. When the wind drops the only sound is the clicking of cicadas. It is so still, it is like being a fly caught in amber.

From the east window of the monastery I can see Canigou, flanked by lower hills, 17 kilometres distant, hear the water bubbling along the irrigation canal beside the field, see fat round golden haystacks drying in the sun. I imagine Amélie coming in here to write her first letters from Corbiac, sitting at the big kitchen table beside the curved white plaster fireplace, wondering where her new husband might be, hugging the growing roundness of her belly for comfort. Waiting. Wondering too how she is to follow all the instructions Pierre has given her, about how to look after the farm. How she is to harvest the ripening beans, the potatoes, apples and pears.

Now their bucolic dream was about to become reality as the crops they had so idealistically planted were calculated as essential provisions. Life had assumed its most basic aspect. For men war, for women feeding their families. It was as if the whole of France had returned to the Middle Ages.

On 3 September 1939, only six months after their marriage, war was declared on Germany. Despite many months of negotiation and appeasement, Hitler had continued his policy of *Lebensraum*, more room for the German people, annexing Austria in March 1938 (the Anschluss) and the Sudetenland in October. Despite his agreement with British prime minister Neville Chamberlain and French prime minister Edouard Daladier for 'Peace in our Time', Czechoslovakia was invaded in March 1939. Confident that France and Britain would never go to war to defend their ally, Hitler invaded Poland. The cynical non-aggression pact signed between Moscow and Berlin on 23 August meant Hitler had nothing to fear from the Russians. The declaration of war led to general mobilisation in France, and Pierre was called up at once. Later Amélie remembered:

I'm thinking about the evening we parted. You packed your suitcase, we bought bread, wine and fruit, and in the evening I watched the barber shave your neck and cut your hair. How we went to Corbiac and arrived at the beehives at the turn in the road and I said to myself, 'Next spring you will be here, with Pierre, and a child in your arms and you will breathe freely and all will be beautiful.' But next spring perhaps the entire world will be in agony and sadness . . .

Though nobody was surprised by war, it still turned life upside down. From Saturday the 2nd of September passive defence measures were introduced. At nightfall, public and vehicle lighting was forbidden, curtains and shutters had to be closed. The normally animated streets of Perpignan and other small towns, where the citizens were accustomed to take a promenade in the cool of the evening, took on a feverish, anxious atmosphere. On Place Jean Jaurès in Perpignan people would gather to listen to the loudspeakers broadcasting the latest news from L'Indépendant, the local newspaper.

Pierre was garrisoned for several weeks in the South. Then he was sent to the Marne valley in eastern France, as a medical lieutenant attached to the 9th army, based south of the Maginot Line and the Belgian border. Amélie wrote almost daily in her tidy elegant script, Pierre more erratically, snatching a moment to scribble a postcard on top of his kitbag while waiting for a train, or dash off a pencilled note as he collapsed exhausted into bed in whatever billet he found himself.

Sometimes the letters cross, often they go missing or turn up weeks later. The writer never knows if the information in the previous letter has been received. Amélie's letters survive in excellent condition: he must have gone to such lengths to preserve them carefully in all his movements. But his letters are more difficult, hard to read, written in doctor's handwriting, often in pencil, creased and tattered, smudged with rain. When he writes it is a respite from the war, and he is almost entirely preoccupied with the small beloved universe he has left behind; he rarely volunteers very much about his experience as a soldier or a doctor.

Marching to Captivity, the diaries of Private Gustave Folcher, a wine-maker from the Languedoc, help fill in the details. Folcher bemoans the sudden shift from the shirts and sandals of the southern summer to greatcoats and military boots, the burden of 40 kilos of kit and weapons, and feet soon blistered by new boots. He describes the new recruits crossing Avignon being given buckets of water to drink and baskets of grapes, finding the train supplied with stores of tinned food, tuna, bully beef, sardines, chocolate, cheese and loaves of bread. He sighs with relief at meeting a Catalan with a good bottle of wine in his pack.

As they head north, Folcher observes the changes in landscape, the lush meadows, flowers and cattle: 'For me, who have never been outside Bas-Gard, I can't settle down, for these are not at all the same views as at home, where at this time of year we only see vines and the fields are roasted by the sun.' Folcher had been obliged to leave his grapes, almost ready to harvest – it was a particularly good harvest that year and the tension of waiting for the grapes to ripen had mingled with the anxiety of approaching war. He sniffs disdainfully at the meagre Alsace grape yield when he sees it, and wonders how those left behind will get the vendange in.

Amélie stayed in the house of her new parents-in-law in Prades, a world where the family still sat by the fire in the evening, sewing and reading aloud to each other, while the maid washed the dishes in the kitchen. She went up to Corbiac as often as she could and made occasional visits to her grandmother's home in Arles-sur-Tech in the Vallespir valley south of Canigou, where her mother also visited from Marseille.

In one of her first letters she describes Pierre's parents trying to cheer her up: 'Your mother bought four little trout from the lake of Nohèdes, wishing to please me.' And I am reminded of the same blue trout we used to buy from the market in Prades; they were so fresh they were still alive, swimming around in a tank – you chose the ones you wanted and the *marchand* banged them on the head and popped them in a bag. They were delicious. 'Each name in this country is a part of you, and to see the mountain now, makes me feel terrible.'

The beauty of it all makes her sad:

> The weather is radiant, with a light mist over Canigou. Suddenly everything is ripening, the figs, the melons, the tomatoes and aubergines. I am sitting under the fig tree in the garden. The birds fill the tree and all is calm and beautiful. It is impossible to believe the world is so vile.
>
> Yesterday was market day, but what a sad market, with no stalls, no customers. You remember the queue of country people you always had in your surgery, and how we laughed that they took advantage of market day to feel ill! I must console all your patients in your absence. It makes me feel better to hear them talking about you. We will go to Corbiac tomorrow for a few days to take care of the beans and pick the vegetables. We must hurry to do as much work as possible in the fields.

In the Castellane valley the fields were full of haricots, the beans that, once dried, were a staple of the local diet. Women, and children taken out of school, had to replace the men in the fields. The comforting round of the seasons became a tyrannical imperative, without their menfolk to bring in the crops. While soldiers at the front remembered country life nostalgically, the women had to live the reality.

From a farmer's point of view the war could not have been more badly timed. Men were called up, horses and transport requisitioned, just as the *vignerons* down on the plain were about to bring in the harvest, fruit of a whole year's labour in the vineyards.

Amélie, with Finette, the maid from Prades, arrived at Mosset in time to save the beans:

> They were about to die they were so dry. We have not finished yet. Nobody seems to be using the irrigation water. The roads are empty. This morning we finished watering the haricots. Tomorrow we will pick what plants we can. We will keep most of them to dry. We ate the first red haricots at noon.
>
> The weather is perfect for drying the lucerne, lots of sun and a bit of wind. Some of the older folk came to help today. Me, I can only think of you and how you would have enjoyed the dawn on Canigou, and washing at the pump. Big hug in haste, we are harnessing the horse for Prades.

She took a photo of the farmers who were helping work the land at Corbiac, a Spanish couple named Riu, who stand each end of a large muddy cow, harnessed to a crude wooden plough, still the traditional method of working the land. The women too worked hard in the fields. All were accustomed to begin work before dawn and finish after sunset, which in the long days of summer often meant fifteen-hour days.

Amélie began to value the peasants' relationship with the land:

> It amuses me when I'm working that a whole lot of poems about the land come to memory. But Madame Riu has fresher images than mine. She told me the origin of all the names of the haricots. When some seeds fall on the ground she collects them and sings their praises.

One of Amélie's important new responsibilities was to clear the irrigation canals and dig new channels for the precious water across the fields. The irrigation system was an ancient and precious resource, with a system of canals feeding both village gardens and the fields in the valley. This was strictly controlled, especially in summer, so that proprietors did not steal each other's allotted supply. To this day it is an arcane system to an outsider, but its apparent complexity makes perfect sense. The water is used twenty-four hours a day and everybody has a designated time, with eight hours tacked on each time, so that all benefit from the water at different hours of the day. This meant that sometimes it was necessary to water in the middle of the night to get your portion – not a prospect that appealed much to Amélie (or to me).

The irrigated land could be used to grow potatoes, haricots, maize, beetroot and salads, and sometimes could be stretched to two harvests. The crops after all had to feed not only the family for the whole year but all their animals as well.

They put the haricots to dry in the sun.

We've been podding them all day. It's a good thing we are here because there is lots to pick and the apples might get stolen. All is calm here, so calm. The four cows are good company, at night we can hear the bells.

I think constantly of you. I spent several hours in the night unable to sleep. Then the sun rose and the kitchen was full of sun shine . . .

I hope you have some sun shine . . .

The little one seems to like the Corbiac air. He is very good. Really Corbiac looks a proper *mas*, apples scattered over the ground after the wind which has never stopped blowing. There are beans everywhere waiting to be shelled – in the kitchen, the bedroom, we're swimming in them. In the garden there are still some pears left to pick, I weeded some strawberry plants, the spinach is still not ready to eat.

'Ah, you wanted to come back to the land,' my grandmother always teases me. 'Now you see how it is!'

Even more than their concern for their loved ones, the women were worrying about next year. 'They are all asking: "How will we get the harvest in?" They are very nice to me, I chat to them all, and they talk about the baby.'

She writes about her problems with the neighbours. One wants to put her cows in the field, but Amélie says that Pierre doesn't like animals too close to his young trees. Another insists he still has a right to pick the apples. Then the neighbours accuse each other of stealing the apples. Someone else gets indigestion from eating too many snails. And a neighbouring farmer got caught under a fence wire while chasing a cow, and fell and hurt his arm. It all sounded very familiar. 'Time passes, a bit slowly,' writes Amélie, wryly.

By the end of October the weather had changed and they returned to Prades to escape the wind, the infamous Tramontane that scours the land and chills the bones. 'The wind drove us back to Prades – It was so cold we could not stay in the field, we really needed warm clothes. I must admit the wind at Corbiac gets on my nerves a bit. Which is grotesque for someone used to the mistral of Marseille!'

Already there was snow on the mountain heights, and as the weather closed in they went to salvage as much as they could from the garden at Corbiac, while Papa cut wood to store. 'Friday it snowed at Corbiac, but Finette managed to pick the last of the beans (me, I was by the fireside . . .). On Sunday morning Finette spotted the charcoal-burner's truck and he carried all the sacks. He wouldn't accept any payment, so we took a basket of apples to his mother.'

On 1 November, All Saints' Day, it is the tradition to take flowers to family graves, and Amélie fulfilled her obligations. 'I will go to the cemetery tomorrow. I picked a big armful of yellow chrysanthemums from Corbiac, it all looked like a Chardin painting, with your mother in her little bonnet, a big watermelon and some pears on the table . . .'

Amélie regularly sent parcels to Pierre, gifts of food, local honey and Banyuls wine for him to share with his comrades. She gave him regular updates on the progress of the socks Finette was knitting for him. 'Do you want them with or without feet, tell me soon before Finette gets to the heel!' (Perhaps Amélie didn't know that the Troyes region where Pierre was stationed was a major centre of hosiery manufacture.)

Since little was happening on the war front, Pierre and his comrades distracted themselves with football games and visits to the cinema. They went to Troyes to see the stained glass of the churches, to Reims to see the cathedral (difficult because the famous rose window had been covered up), and even made a trip to Paris.

'Have you been able to go to Paris again? I hope you can go and amuse yourself there and stop being a soldier for a few hours. I read in the Nouvelle Revue that Notre Dame without its stained glass is so bright that you can clearly see the bas reliefs around the choir.' Then Amélie joked: 'I hope you weren't tempted to use the addresses slipped into your coat pockets!'

Both of them read a great deal. Pierre begged Amélie to send him books, and she raided the attic of his parents' house for more. He sent her poems he had written, though she was a bit sceptical about some of his more sanctimonious sentiments:

Thank you for sending me your poems . . . Hope will come out of suffering? Do you really believe that? It seems to me that man has been suffering for centuries. But it is beautiful that there is in you a small glimmer of light, in the midst of all these shadows.

But Amélie begins to worry what he will think of his peasant wife when he comes back. 'You will come back very erudite, and what will you find, a fat peasant, with rough hands and tanned skin.

'Oh come back, come back . . .'

In October Edith Pye whizzed past Corbiac on a brief visit to La Coûme, driven by Howard and Gertrude Kershner, the American Quakers in charge of the International Commission for Child Refugees, in their large open-topped touring car, which was usually crammed with supplies. Edith made a report to the Quakers in Paris.

I paid a hurried visit to the farm and found Pitt Krüger had not yet been called up. (He said thanks to the efforts made from England on his behalf.) He has hopes of being mobilised in a factory near enough to enable him to spend weekends in Mosset. We found everything in beautiful order, the pear trees from which so much is hoped full of bud and the value of the property increased by a cement aqueduct which will enable the watering of the fields and garden to be done more easily. There was a large and healthy stock of rabbits and the sowing of seeds was well forward.

She asked the Krügers to take in more refugees, this time girls from Alsace-Lorraine. 'In the international atmosphere of the Auberge de Jeunesse these young creatures, speaking a German patois, and therefore looked on with suspicion in French households, will find a friendly welcome and the language will not be a problem.'

With the declaration of war the French government had evacuated half a million people from Alsace-Lorraine on the border with Germany, and sent them to safer regions of France. They had to leave their homes with only a few hours' notice, taking only what they could carry. They were accommodated in dire conditions in schools, churches and abandoned farms and could not understand why they were not allowed to return for more necessities, at least warm clothing for the winter, while there was no action at the front. Their villages were left empty, as the soldiers of the French army discovered. Herds of abandoned pigs and cows wandered the abandoned streets, and since their orders were to live on the produce of the country, the soldiers set to, slaughtering the animals, picking fruit and nuts and digging up potatoes and vegetables.

The news from Spain was equally disturbing, wrote Amélie. 'Today your father had a visit from a Spanish friend . . . In Spain, the misery is appalling, the prisons are full, and of course there are plenty of nouveaux riches!'

Both were concerned about their families, especially Clo, the husband of her sister Mimi, who was near the Belgian border. 'Clo is closer to the front day by day,' wrote Amélie anxiously. 'He is still waiting for leave. He is less optimistic than you about the duration of the war. I think perhaps you were trying to be encouraging . . .' Clo, who had been a teacher in civilian life, has reluctantly been obliged to ride a horse. 'They are now at rest after three days on horseback – poor Clo . . .' Despite the tanks in use, horses still formed a key part of the French army. Most of the German artillery was still drawn by horses.

Meanwhile Amélie had to take responsibility for Pierre's precious Peugeot. She wrote anxiously about insurance and repairs, the wayward battery, and most of all her own desire to drive. She noted enviously several times when other women had learned to drive, '*Hein*, these women!' It was all made more complicated because at that time women still did not have the vote and their husbands had to sign everything for them.

She had to chase patients who had not paid their bills, and recounted how much they liked to talk about the doctor.

How you wrapped them up, bandaged them and how bad they felt with their feet as black as the chimney? I met a Spanish woman in the street, who you treated in the summer, and she asked me if you could give her a certificate, because they want to send her to a camp. She begged me to ask you.

Yesterday one of your first clients came to pay you the price of a visit – 30 F and a bottle of vin rosé that she had promised, apparently. It is kind to pay without being asked – and rare too!

In mid-November she paid a visit to her grandmother in Arles-sur-Tech, slipping comfortably into the familiar round of daily activities – 'If we were all back together without any worries, how we would enjoy this peaceful life.' She describes a gentle walk along the river Tech:

The gardens look empty, just a few chrysanthemums left, dishevelled, red, yellow and gold. After the rain yesterday all the autumn has changed. Just tender shades – the mountain seems softer, the leaves have fallen, but are still at the tops of the trees. Even with bare branches the apple trees are still beautiful. And now we have chestnuts.

At the farm we chose straw for the cradle mattress. The pigs had been killed and we took Grandmère a *boudin blanc*. I joke it is she who has the cravings and not me.

Now we have a pretty wood-fire, and the mothers are knitting. Grandmère for Clo, Maman for our baby.

Most frustrating is the lack of information from Pierre.

How are you? Have you been able to take some walks, I hope the rain is not bothering you too much. I hope you are still in the same place . . .

What is it like where you are, are there rivers, forests, little hills and valleys? Tell me about the place you are staying, the house, the people. Are your patients sick – or wounded?

The weather in the north was appalling, with constant rain and plunging temperatures. 'Don't forget to put on your cape at night,' Amélie bids him anxiously.

It would be so stupid to get bronchitis. I'm sure your waterproof is not enough. The words of your last card were nearly washed out. I hope you have a second pair of boots, and the first get a chance to dry before you put them on again. That you get a chance for a bath, and clean linen . . .

are you still having bad weather? Does the country have pretty autumn colours, or is there lots of mud? Here it is beautiful . . . the fields all golden, so splendid, the river running full. On the hillsides the vines are red and yellow. It is the first time I have really seen an autumn.

It was worst of all when he seemed to be in danger. 'We have been so worried about the air raids. I hope the alerts are not too alarming . . . it must be terrible having to organise everything carefully at night, in case you have to leave in a hurry.'

Pierre described trying to find a warm bistro on a cold foggy night. 'What a difference between the life of the north and the Midi!' Amélie responded.

These big industrial regions must be horrible . . . Here at least be-tween each storm a ray of sun peeps through, the balcony is festooned with flowers, or a pot of basil. With sun and air it is not so bad. We can go outside, play boules, go fishing, visit our little cabins by the sea or in the country . . .

By mid-December they were anxiously awaiting Pierre, hoping he would make it in time for Christmas.

Do you know any more about your leave? We would like to send you a parcel for Christmas but if you come is it worth it? You know in the silence I hear the steps of rare passers-by, often in big boots, it seems always they will stop at our door, and it will be you.

Finally he did arrive and they spent his Christmas 1939 leave together. A photo shows them outside the old door at Corbiac, weathered oak planks held firmly together with medieval iron bands. The shadows are short in the bright winter sunlight. Amélie stands shyly, her coat buttons stretched tight over her stomach, hair cut short, leather boots snugly laced over socks and stockings, her hand on Pierre's arm. Pierre looks almost self-consciously manly, the soldier, farmer, prospective father, doctor, hands on hips, in open shirt and scarf knotted round his neck, army breeches and boots laced to the knee. Actually he looks so young. Behind them is the well, the pump, an axe and a heap of logs and kindling. Then he returned to the army, no doubt having left many instructions.

Food restrictions were beginning to be felt. 'Here we are missing a lot of basic commodities,' wrote Amélie. 'These restrictions! Three times a week the butcher will be closed. Is this how we begin to understand we are at war?' She has begun to appreciate their investment in the land. 'Everybody is talking about potatoes. People are really worried about the hard times to come – we did well to dream of cultivating the land.'

She missed her new husband. 'I spent a sleepless night, and when I turned to your side of the bed, there was a scent of burnt wood that puzzled me until I realised it was the smell of the wood tar you put on the apple trees. How you would have calmed me if you had been there . . .' And she sometimes found it difficult living with his parents. 'I've been chased from the kitchen by your mother – We will have a sauce Catalan, with an orange from the garden. Pity there is no partridge to go with the sauce . . .'

By January the weather had worsened, though it was much colder in the north.

Prades is shaken with wind, it is grey and snowing in the mountains. I hope the cold is not worse for you. Keep yourself covered up. Minus 11 degrees must be really cold but I hope there is no wind. Even here the rivers are frozen, if you could hear the joy of the children leaving school!

This is the weather to have a husband close by, at the corner of the fire, shelling corn. You know Papa now wants to have some chickens at the end of the garden. I promised him you would see to it!

And always the war loomed. 'Maman is very sad because she suspects the war risks being long . . . you seem to be thinking the same way.'

At last I find a brief, very faded postcard, complete with censor's stamp, from Pierre to Amélie, written in January 1940:

Ma chérie,

It is snowing and less cold. I am well.

If anything happens with the baby you can telegraph me at Villa Primavera, rue St Berry, Arcis-sur-Aube.

I'm sending you a photo of the snow here. It is very cold. Now it is sunny but it was minus 19 this morning. But the bronchitis has gone and there are no cases of congestion or pneumonia among 3 or 400 men. Morale is excellent. I have to go to Châlons now for a medical visit.

Arcis-sur-Aube, where Pierre was billeted, was a small village in north-east France halfway between Troyes and Châlons, east of Paris, about 70 kilometres to the south of Reims, behind the Maginot Line. The Aube is a gentle landscape of lakes, forest and vineyards; here and there stand riverside villages of half-timbered houses. The peaceful rurality of the region was captured by the Impressionist painter Auguste Renoir, but it was a peace that was frequently disturbed. Arcis was used to being close to the front line, and had suffered attacks from Attila the Hun and Napoleon, as well as the devastation of the First World War. It was in Châlons-sur-Marne that the Quaker Edith Pye had established a maternity hospital behind the lines.

For Amélie the imminent birth was beginning to occupy her thoughts more and more.

The cradle is ready, and it is really pretty. The mattress is made, and we've finished the curtains. I hope so much that our dear Pupot will sleep well.

Your mother advised me to put a handkerchief in my mouth to bite when the baby comes. I have an old pair of your leather gloves for the same purpose.

She received lots of advice from her husband. 'I've copied it all out for Maman in case I lose my voice.' In particular he recommended relaxing baths, not an easy proposition in those days, as Amélie described:

We install the antique seat bath, in front of the fire. I undress and wrap myself in an old coat, that maman calls 'Happy Days' because it is one I had to go to Paris. (It has a tartan lining and padded shoulders.) When I'm sitting down, my back resting against the back of the bath, Maman covers my knees with another sweater, and then she adds warm water bit by bit! And we think of the great aunts who took their baths in a bathing suit!

Maman had a lot to do looking after her elderly mother and her pregnant daughter, as she described in a letter to Pierre:

> I should have written sooner but there's so much to do, put wood on the fire, prepare the footwarmers and hot water bottles, make tisane and poultices, not to mention all the breakfasts and teas. We have got through this period of extreme cold, *grandmére* has not been too ill.

Amélie wrote, describing the first suggestion of spring in the Vallespir.

> I went for a walk in the sun, it is mild, with a trembling of colour, mauve, yellow or green, at the top of the trees. People are digging their gardens, and the earth is beautiful, really black, rich and shining. The river is flowing strongly, and now the trout fishing is open.

Then Pierre received another letter from Maman. After all their elaborate preparations for the baby to be born in a clinic in Perpignan with doctors on hand, and stay afterwards in Prades where the new cradle and anxious parents-in-law were waiting, he arrived early, born among the women at her grandmother's house in Arles.

> Feb. 10
> Your son was born in Arles after all. Despite not being expected till the 21st, it was peaceful, Amélie is not too tired. He is a beautiful boy with dark hair, round body, good colour. We have put Amélie in the back-room where there is a fire, and where she can be quiet. The little one is in a laundry basket because we have nothing else available here. Amélie is well cared for, the midwife is expert and devoted.
> I am sure you will arrive soon,
> Kisses from Maman

While Pierre went on leave to visit his new son, the *drôle de guerre*, the phoney war, rumbled on. Despite the declaration of war the Allies had not given any significant assistance to the Poles, and Hitler and the Russians had divided Poland between them. The Poles established a government in exile, and their armed forces and intelligence made a significant contribution to the Allied war effort. The Franco-German frontier remained quiet throughout the winter.

The Allies adopted a defensive strategy, and as they waited for Hitler to make his next move the lack of action weighed heavily on the soldiers. They sought distraction where they could, but boredom set in and morale was often low. Drunkenness became such a problem that special rooms had to be set aside in stations for soldiers to sober up before returning to the front. The intense cold didn't help –

temperatures fell to −24 in the east, the coldest winter since 1889. Even the Channel froze at Boulogne. They began to wonder what they were doing there.

Not least poor Folcher, dreaming of his southern home: 'It's horribly cold. The whole month of January it froze hard. The thermometer often going down to between −20 and −30, even going as far as −35. We have to saw the bread in slices that then have to be grilled to be unfrozen. The wine is in canteens from which nothing will flow. One morning at reveille our blankets are all white, the snow as much inside as outside.'

In *A French Officer's Diary*, an account of the war in northern France published in Britain in 1942, Major Barlone observed: 'Winter is on its way and we are convinced that Hitler will not attack before the spring . . . Shall we really have war? Or shall we remain facing each other, for years?' He admitted that the men had little enthusiasm for war: 'We know that our land is safe from invasion, thanks to the Maginot line; no one has the least desire to fight for Czechoslovakia or Poland, of which ninety-five Frenchmen out of every hundred are completely ignorant and unable to find on a map.'

In February Pierre wrote a note to Amélie on his way back to the front after his leave, from the station buffet in Dijon. 'After two excellent sandwiches and a *demi* of beer.' His journey had been easy: 'There have been no delays and I could even sit down and stretch out a bit. I am thinking of you and the baby.'

He wrote again the next day: 'The officers seem pleased to have me back. Here it is pleasant weather but the canals are still frozen along the Marne. It is since I have got back here that I can really think about being a father.'

Amélie wrote to him the same day:

It has been so hard to part this time, how cruel for you to leave me and your baby. Dearest, I can still see you, in your long nightshirt stoking the fire, scratching your head . . . you were so sleepy. To see the baby in your arms was such a joy. It was so sweet after the baptism the way you placed your child in my arms and embraced us both so tenderly . . .

She wrote about every detail of the baby's progress, his hands, his eyelashes, his ears like clover leaves: patiently she describes it all – 'the way he stretches out his arms, then puts two fingers stretched out on his face, or in his mouth, the other spread out on the pillow.'

Today I cut Henri's nails. He let me do it quietly, I can't wait to see you at the end of this month, you will find Henri so different. He seems to change from hour to hour. I love feeding him, every time he has different expressions and afterwards has such an air of contentment when he closes his eyes and his cheeks are all red and speckled with milk. I enclose a little lock of Henri's hair – isn't it soft! I got up for 2 hours, but still feel weak. I think about women in the past, getting up to look for wood only two hours after having a child – what were they made of?

Pierre wrote with instructions about the car, the battery, the water in the radiator, her attempts to learn to drive, and again, the seed potatoes. 'Sorry to load you with all this . . . Did you celebrate getting up – did you drink the bottle of champagne I brought?' But Amélie was still feeling tired, and told him the champagne must wait till he came back. 'And one of the neighbours has brought me two bottles of her wine that you can drink on your next leave. She waited for the old moon before she bottled the white wine!'

Amélie returned to Prades and her parents-in-law. 'The car was fine. I was delighted to see the trees in blossom, mimosas, cherry blossom, peaches, green fields, the snow on the mountains, and the sky so blue.' But she wishes they could all be together. 'I can't wait for you to come and move us to Corbiac. I want to be able to work beside you there. Your mother is doing all the cooking and I am forbidden to go into the kitchen.' She describes the baby's first bath. 'The event took place in the dining room, Papa lit the fire, warmed the water on the stove, and the bidet served as a bath.' She says she borrowed the rubber cloth Pierre had on his operating table. 'Your mother doesn't like marks on the floorboards, and it isn't always water that is spilt!'

In the north the bad weather continues, with more fog and rain. 'I am exhausted after so many vaccinations. We are seeing a lot of TB and I'm worried about the baby . . .' But at least, Pierre reassures her, he is comfortably billeted. 'We have found a new place where we can cook our meals with a woodfire in the chimney. Then we play bridge.' And, he adds: 'At least the war is still far away from us.'

Pierre came for his second leave towards the end of March. His first letter after his return arrived on headed notepaper from the café – Hôtel de l'Est – in Châlons. I imagine him in heavy boots and greatcoat, breathing steam, as he sits at a marble table, cold beneath his hand, and scribbles in his rapid doctor's writing:

I am sending you this note after arriving in Châlons. There was mist in Lyon but sunshine after Dijon.
    This time yesterday we were returning from our walk to Clara, I won't forget the clouds of white cherry blossom along the river bank. I

have thought so much about the baby, and this time I don't feel sad because I have such confidence in you now.

Meanwhile Amélie was planning to take her new baby and stay at Corbiac.

It has rained a lot today but I think the weather is going to be good so I can go to the country with little Henri. Your parents are making such a fuss about this little journey of 10 kilometres! Maman telling me about all the insects that will bite Henri in the fields . . .

Today was the foire in Prades. Maman is horrified at the price of food. Papa keeps talking about going up to Corbiac, and he has ordered turnip and bean seeds.

I can't wait to get there and stop being afraid of mice or the grunting of pigs, I am going to get a lamp so I don't have to light candles all the time, and then I can warm milk too. The baby is content today, feeding well. How sad it is so many children in the world are separated from their father.

Pierre spent another brief leave at home, enjoying the baby and planting potatoes, and then sends further instructions to his wife:

I am thinking of you this morning, of the bedroom, the cases, the unmade bed, the basin, the laundry, and you and the baby like two little ducks, big and small, the curtains on the cradle and the baby opening his eyes.

You asked me about vegetables. Remember I have not yet sown the leeks. Plant the lettuces in rows and water them well before and after planting. It would be good to get the potatoes in before 15 April, and dig over the earth ready to plant some beetroot.

But Amélie was struggling to cope at Corbiac:

Today has been terrible weather, with driving rain and a strong wind so we could not go out, the rivers are full of muddy water, this morning the floor was flooded and it was really difficult to make a fire and to cook.

Mme Riu came to clean – but there is still lots of manure and during recent nights the rats have been running about more and more. It is years since the place was cleaned properly. But I seem to be much stronger, and I can get the bucket up from the well more easily now. For the garden, Mme Riu has planted tomatoes, aubergines and peppers, I started to do the digging but she thought she would do it more quickly.

Around Mosset all is green and beautiful. All the poplars hold the light, and the fields are full of cuckoos.

For Pierre, her presence at Corbiac meant a great deal. 'The work on the land you are doing is such a consolation for me. We just have to accept these hard times. I hope we will always be able to produce our own staple food.' He reassured her about the progress of the war. 'Don't worry – it doesn't look as if we will be moving from here, despite all that is happening. I learned from the radio that Germany had attacked Denmark . . .' He was still optimistic. 'I have so much hope despite the scepticism of the veterans of the last war.'

Amélie had also heard the news:

> Yesterday Papa went out, and came back crying there is news . . . his face was so excited, I thought the war must be finished . . . and it was that Germany had invaded Denmark and Norway . . . I went to weep in our bedroom, not wishing to hear your father's explanations – he is convinced we will see a rapid victory for France . . .

While Amélie was feeding the baby and picking radishes, the Germans had attacked Denmark and Norway, and the French–British command sent an expedition to defend them. Many of the troops in the ensuing battles were Spanish, hundreds of whom were killed.

Pierre wrote, describing planting vegetables in the garden where he was billeted. 'I've just been digging my garden here, planting carrots and radishes, I know it is a bit late for garlic or shallots.' This was not unusual – Barlone records in March instructing his men to plant a garden with radishes, lettuces, spinach and carrots. They clearly expected to be there for a while. 'The Norwegian adventure seems to be turning out badly for the Germans. They can't get supplies through. The Boches have been cleaned out of Scandinavia, but Denmark has disappeared though, poor things.' He reassured Amélie: 'But you know that I am not really in any danger.'

The Allied campaign in Norway was at first successful, as Pierre recounted, but they were forced to withdraw in early May and turn their attention to the attack on Belgium and Holland. Denmark had surrendered to the Germans immediately.

Amélie had been looking for someone to help her with the baby.

> I went to to see the Spanish woman, but she asked for 10 francs a day! I don't like it when 'they take me for an *anglaise*' as we say in Marseille. Now I have found a young woman, Pierrette, age 15, from Mosset, the granddaughter of the roadmender. You took care of her sister once. We arranged that she would work here, sleep and eat here, for 100 francs a month. And she can help with watering and work in the fields, she is bigger than me, and very clean.

(Pierrette was the elder sister of Louisette, my informant on the village of Mosset.)

And she is finding contentment at Corbiac:

I am writing to you at the end of a sunny, windy Sunday at the window of the kitchen, while the mountain turns mauve. The baby is sleeping in a basket by the fire. I think I will be happy at Corbiac. Young Pierrette is helping me a lot. This morning we talked chickens and rabbits. Everybody has them, and we must do like everybody else.

Pierre was still awaiting action. 'I was invited to dine with the captains – a splendid meal in grand bourgeois style. This morning I went to communion, and prayed for everyone. My lettuces, onions, carrots are doing well and we also have 20 rabbits.' He begged for details of life at Corbiac. 'Have the peas flowered yet? How are the strawberries?' Amélie replied:

I can hear the wind, the toads as usual, the shaking of the tree. There are lots of birds now, and soon the strawberries will be ripe. You can be sure that the wood you chopped is keeping your wife and your baby warm. I always feed him in front of the fire. Yesterday there was rain and a bit of snow on Canigou, today the sky is blue but it won't last.

Then, at the beginning of May, a note of foreboding entered Pierre's letters:

Whatever happens we must stick to the land . . . but we will have to make sacrifices. I hope the hostilities will end in the autumn, so that I am not stuck here. I will do everything I can to return to you. I walked to Sens yesterday. But while I was enjoying some fine points of architecture, Paris was experiencing aerial bombardment.

I am off to look at the tomatoes in the garden, soon we will have the peas and we are already eating the lettuces. Have the haricots I planted been affected by the cold? Have you got any peas yet?

The family was anxious because they had no news of Clo, stationed near the Belgian border, and Pierre said he would try to pick up some information. He was clearly worried:

Sorry not to write, I have been so depressed the last few days, but happily I am surrounded by good comrades. You know from my letters how I feel about what is happening. We just have to await the storm with calm. The imbeciles who are fighting!

Even though I am with the army, I hate being behind the lines, unable to see what is happening, not being able to do anything. But this is certainly not the war of 1914–1918 . . .

And he added: 'Things could go one way or the other.'

# CHAPTER 6

# THE FALL OF FRANCE

Despite Pierre's reassurances, Arcis was actually in a very vulnerable position, only a few miles south of the border, and the western end of the Maginot Line, still at this point regarded as an infallible defence against the Germans. With the possible exception of the Great Wall of China, the Maginot Line, though it remained unfinished, was the longest and most complex system of fortifications ever built, an expensive 87-mile line of defensive steel and concrete forts along the Franco-German frontier. French confidence in its impregnability was so complete that the ladies of Paris had suggested planting roses along it to cheer up the soldiers.

On 10 May Pierre wrote to Amélie:

Pupot is three months old. He is strong, and laughing with you. I am happy. The storm we were waiting for has broken. The Germans are in Belgium tonight! I continue to look after my garden and my vegetables in Arcis. I will return whatever happens. Be patient, my dear.

At 5.35 a.m. on 10 May the Germans made their move. They invaded Luxembourg and attacked Holland and Belgium. The French had expected the main offensive through Belgium, and had stationed the best French troops on the Belgian frontier, including poor Clo. The Germans however had other ideas.

Amélie heard the news the next day, and wrote to Pierre:

Papa came up early this morning, and arrived in the kitchen with the bad news. It is as if we've been frozen, as if we knew nothing here. Corbiac is more calm than ever.

She was concerned about her family.

The serious tone of your last letters prepared me a bit, but I think of you all, of Clo at Maubeuge, of you, of my sister Louisette waiting for her baby, of Mimi in Toulon . . . all these unhappy people.

The Germans were advancing into Holland and bombing Allied troops across the border in France. Arcis-sur-Aube, about 70 kilometres from the border, was in their sights. On the 12th of May Pierre wrote:

No letters today, Which is not surprising since the Boches are bombing us right and left. Nothing to really be afraid of for now. Where is Clo? Have you any news?

I feel confidence in God, very little in men. But don't worry about me, here I am really not at risk.

Amélie, anxious that the big cities were threatened, wrote to her brother in Marseille to invite his wife and children to take refuge at Corbiac. But she knew little of what was really happening. 'All the papers are late. Oh what suffering, what sadness. Have you received my letters, are you well, are you safe? What anguish to know you are in danger. Poor people, poor world . . .' She continued the work at Corbiac. 'But when the harvest comes I don't know how we will be able to get it in with only old men and children to help.'

Corbiac remained calm and peaceful. 'The nightingales are singing in the ravine. It's so calm I can even hear the frogs. Henri loves being outside in his pram in the fresh air, sun, rain or wind. It astonishes me that the children of Mosset of his age don't go out – they are all surprised to see our baby out in the fresh air.' The water continued to be a problem. 'I have been hearing such stories about the water, it is not so bad now, but it seems you can't afford to miss your turn, even if you have to take it at 4 o'clock in the morning. It is exhausting, but this morning what a reward to see the grass so green.'

For Pierre her presence there remained his lifeline. 'At mass this morning in the middle of a new alert, I thought what happiness it was to know you are in the country, in a safe place. I love you more than ever. In the middle of all this carnage I think calmly of you. You seem to be becoming a real peasant . . .'

After drawing Allied fire to Belgium the main German attack finally came on the night of 12 May. They bypassed the Maginot Line completely and approached through the Ardennes, a sector of frontier the French believed was protected by the natural barrier of the Meuse River and the deep wooded valleys of the Ardennes forest. The inexperienced reservists defending the line were quite unprepared for the massive assault of German Panzer divisions. In only three days the French line was breached. The Germans crossed the Meuse at Sedan, north-east of Reims. Their most effective tactic was the dive-bombing, the heaviest air bombardment ever known, which totally demoralised the Allied troops. Groups of haggard and retreating soldiers were rapidly overtaken by the German army. The Germans then headed north-west towards the coast, in a rapid blitzkrieg operation of tanks and aerial bombing designed to encircle the Allied armies.

Surviving soldiers' diaries from that moment talk of 'total disorder and shameful despair'. Gustave Folcher wrote: 'It was terrifying to see those machines diving at us, spitting out their bombs.' After the German assault, the following morning there was chaos. Folcher wrote:

> Suddenly a lieutenant, I don't know which, and without any previous order, gives out a kind of 'every man for himself' directive. In five minutes, he announces, the withdrawal must have got over the hill. It's abrupt, and immediately there is a general panic, everyone thinking of his own skin.

The phrase '*Faut pas chercher à comprendre*' (No use trying to understand) was shortened to FPCAC by the soldiers, reminiscent of the American SNAFU (situation normal, all fucked up).

They were not exactly well-informed, as Folcher recorded, 'While with my own eyes I could see the tanks coming down to Sedan, the Paris radio was announcing that the enemy had been largely contained in Belgium, beyond our frontiers.'

Pierre, behind the lines, reassured his wife, but it was hard to believe he was immune from danger.

> I have so much work today . . . trainloads of refugees. I still hope that Clo has been in retreat with the army from Belgium, Mimi wrote today that until the 13th he had not been in combat.
>     My dear, if you are afraid go to my parents in Prades with the baby. So glad you are eating the cherries . . . how I would love to be eating some Corbiac cherries now!

The great exodus had begun. The flood of refugees from Belgium pouring into France was joined by the French themselves, fleeing the German advance. Major Barlone, whose unit was by then in Belgium, wrote:

> The number of refugees on foot, in farm carts, and cars, increases from hour to hour; they jam all roads and prevent the movement of military convoys. What are the army control doing? . . . The men want to know where I am leading them, but I conceal the fact that we are returning to France. They feel that things are not going too well, but do not suspect defeat.

On 15 May, Paul Reynaud, the French prime minister, telephoned Winston Churchill and said: 'We have been defeated. We are beaten.'
'Surely it can't have happened so soon?' asked Churchill.

But Reynaud replied: 'The front is broken near Sedan; they are pouring through in great numbers with tanks and armoured cars.'

When Churchill flew to Paris on the 16th the French government was already burning its archives. There was nothing between the German armies and Paris.

By the 16th civilians were fleeing Reims, about halfway between Sedan and Arcis-sur-Aube. Pierre may not have been on the front line but he certainly wasn't far away. The post was disrupted and Amélie waited anxiously for letters. She received a brief reassuring note on the 16th: 'Of course you are worrying about me but despite everything I am not in much danger. This morning I even managed to pick the peas and water the garden!'

But on the 17th she heard that the maternity hospital in Châlons had been bombed. She wrote: 'I just can't imagine the atrocities that are happening. The trains of refugees must be heart-breaking. To think that people like your father and mother must leave everything, and the children, and all the packets and parcels! We have had no news of Clo.'

On 19 May Pierre wrote again: 'No post today but I'm not surprised given the gravity of events. There were a lot of bombs yesterday and one death. Don't worry, I am not stupid – I take all necessary precautions.'

Both are waiting anxiously for news of each other. 'Today no news from you,' wrote Amélie on the 21st.

> I hope nothing bad has happened to you. I think of all the sick people you must be caring for, all the possible dangers, what suffering for you all! I feel so strange and ill at ease, I don't know how many times I have been into the garden, the field, looking for wood, huddled over the fire.
>
> Tomorrow there should be 22 strawberries in the garden, the peas are in flower, I'm sending you a photo of the garden so you can see it all. I hope soon you will be able to rest in the calm here. How you will need the mountains after all this. I would not dare talk about the simple things of Corbiac, so peaceful, so calm, and so eternal, if I did not know it would give you pleasure to rest yourself at home in your thoughts.

The first French refugees had already arrived in the Pyrenees, and Spanish refugees were moved from Molitg-les-Bains down the valley to make room for them. 'I must to go to your parents in Prades to arrange the house for refugees,' wrote Amélie. 'The first Belgians have arrived in Mosset. The poor things have been travelling for 16 days, and there are some children who have lost their parents. They had a quarter of an hour to prepare to flee, but you must know more about that than I can tell you.'

The French government had not anticipated such panic-stricken civilian evacuation, and often people started to leave while authorities were still telling them to stay. Sometimes the authorities were the first to flee. Roads were clogged by interminable columns of slow-moving cars, with mattresses on top to protect them from bombs. Every kind of vehicle was pressed into service – vans, lorries, bicycles, prams, even hearses. Some of the refugees were driving cars for the first time in their lives. It was an egalitarian rout, with high-powered Hispano Suizas jammed in between horse-drawn farm wagons. Wooden carts were crammed with furniture, tools, pets and birdcages. People on foot pushed wheelbarrows tottering with all their worldly goods. The roadsides were strewn with the corpses of horses. Cars were abandoned for lack of petrol. The horror and panic was made worse by German planes attacking the columns of refugees.

The official history of the 5th Royal Inniskilling Dragoon Guards paints a picture of: 'Townsfolk, clerics, professors, clerks, shopkeepers, country-folk with great panniers on their backs; here and there a sprinkling of bedraggled men in uniform . . . a pathetic mass of puzzled, distressed humanity bound together with a common bond of fear.' Barlone describes arriving back in France from Belgium at the town of St-Amand, already abandoned:

> Less than fifty civilians remain and the troops are allowed to take from the houses anything they need, for we know that the Germans will be here within a few days. I load up with fifty miscellaneous bottles; Burgundy, Bordeaux, Champagne.

There are more sombre sights:

> The convoys of refugees are much less numerous. Many of these poor folk have fallen victim to Hitler's bombs. Around a single crater I counted eighteen women and children killed.

On 19 May Pierre wrote, warning Amélie of the problems: 'Things are serious here, the German are pushing north. My dear, don't worry if you have no news from me for a while because there is huge disruption in this area. Yesterday Pétain was called to the government. May God go with him.' Like most of the French at that moment, the appointment of Pétain gave Pierre hope.

Marshal Philippe Pétain, then ambassador to Franco's government in Madrid, was called back by Prime Minister Reynaud, mainly to boost morale. People thought he would save the day as he had at Verdun. They still expected to fight on. 'Pétain is Verdun, and Verdun is resistance to the bitter end.' But the great hero Pétain was now eighty-four years old, and though his back was still ramrod straight, his eyes were rheumy and he was going deaf. He was in no mood for further battle.

They were all very worried about Clo. 'Have you any news of Clo?' wrote Pierre on the 20th.

> What was his last position? Poor chap, from what I can understand from here he must be in a tough situation.
>
> What a mess! Refugees, soldiers not going anywhere, German air raids, it is very demoralising. It is horrible hearing the German planes over our heads, calmly dropping bombs. You know now that our country has been defeated, and quickly too. To live we must work the land.

By the end of May the Allied troops had retreated to Dunkirk, completely surrounded. Barlone wrote:

> So we are encircled. It's flabbergasting . . . the whole of the North of France, Belgium, our lines of fortifications, our immense quantities of material, hundreds of thousands of men, thanks to this manoeuvre of unexampled audacity . . . what a disaster! We must reach Dunkirk at all costs.

Between 27 May and 2 June 320,000 men were evacuated from Dunkirk, two-thirds of them British, a fact that rankled with the French and was quickly exploited by the Germans, who put up posters showing British officers rejecting wounded French soldiers.

At Corbiac it was cherry time.

> The wind has blown down a lot of cherries – I know you said you wanted some but I don't think I dare send a parcel of cherries at the moment. You don't really want that do you? . . . You asked for news of the garden – I've just been weeding the beetroot – I used to wonder why the peasants always stood up with their tools in their hand when a train passed. Now I don't ask myself why – one stands up, that's all, it isn't out of curiosity.

Amazingly, on 7 June Pierre is still cultivating his garden in Arcis.

> We still don't know what is going to happen. Have you any news of Clo? Let us hope he is taken prisoner and not badly wounded. My favourite entertainment is still the garden. I watch the tomatoes growing . . . You must be eating the peas by now? My greatest comfort is thinking of you and the baby at Corbiac . . . here the sky is an implacable blue.

But then finally the next day he wrote: 'Since yesterday the great battle has begun. May God help France now. After the episode of Dunkirk we just have to hope . . . After two alerts our region is calm again . . . I ask myself what I am doing here.'

On 5 June the Germans had renewed their offensive. The French government fled first to Tours and then to Bordeaux. Paris was declared an open city and the Germans entered on 14 June. On 10 June Mussolini seized his opportunity and also declared war on France, keen to share in the spoils. The Germans continued their advance into France, and Reims and Châlons-sur-Marne were occupied by 12 June.

Finally Pierre's unit retreated:

> We have left Arcis. We are still on the road. I think we have done the right thing, in my opinion. We should get to the Côte d'Or tonight. I am not complaining, I don't have any feeling any more.
>
> Since the beginning of these tragic events I am sure you have been worrying too much about me. I think I may be able to get to Objat [a small village a few kilometres north of Brive in the Corrèze, where Amélie's sister Louisette had just had her baby].

Most of France by this point was in appalling chaos. Like Pierre and his unit, the French army had joined the civilian population in a headlong rush to escape the advancing German troops. There were reports of German soldiers stripped to the waist in the June heatwave, 'les torses nus', an image that carried terrifying force.

The French army had broken up into groups entirely separated from one another. There were some groups of soldiers with only a frying pan between them. Many thousands were taken prisoner. There was no longer a battle line but only isolated attempts at resistance, at a river crossing, in a village, at a crossroads, along the edge of a wood. It was hard to keep track of the German advance. Sometimes the only way was to phone the local Post Office and ask the switchboard operator if the Germans were there or not.

Abandoned villages were raided, wine cellars looted, the beds stripped of sheets and blankets. People camped out where they could, begging food and petrol, fighting over any groceries left in the shops. Everyone was trying to cross the Loire, to reach the rural *France profonde*, the fantasy land of peace and plenty for so many urban French. But when they got to the Loire River they found that many of the bridges had already been blown up to block the German advance. By 16 June the Germans were bombing the soldiers and refugees trying to cross the Loire. Many were killed. The roads were lined with bodies and nothing could be done for the wounded. Anguished relatives had to decide whether to stay or to leave their loved ones behind. Hundreds of thousands of civilians were trapped, and many children went missing. For months afterwards the local papers had advertisements for lost children:

> Mother seeks baby daughter, age two, lost on the road between Tours and Poitiers in the retreat.

> Generous reward for information leading to the recovery of my son Jacques, age 10, last seen in Bordeaux, June 17th.

Altogether around 8 million people fled their homes. The population of Reims fell from 250,000 to 500, of Lille from 200,000 to 20,000. In the village of Boselange in Côte d'Or all the inhabitants fled except for one family who committed suicide. The towns in the South were overwhelmed by refugees. The population of Brive grew almost overnight from 30,000 to 100,000, Pau expanded from 38,000 to 150,000, Bordeaux from 300,000 to 600,000. The Hungarian writer Arthur Koestler, who found himself caught up in this nightmare, found it 'a peculiar irony that the war had turned the most petit-bourgeois, fussy, stay-at-home people in the world into a nation of tramps'.

Prades too had its share of refugees, including five staying in the dining room at Pierre's parents' house. 'At Prades it's chaos, I am exhausted by it,' wrote Amélie. 'All Menton seems to be there! I told you the 625 Italians already in Prades must prove their loyalty, the same with those in Mosset. But they will still continue to make charcoal. Mme Krüger is still in Mosset because of her children, but can't even go into Prades . . .'

There is probably self-censorship at work here, since Amélie must have appreciated the delicate position of the Krügers, who had now become enemy aliens instead of refugees. A note from Hilda Clark to Edith Pye also mentions the Krügers, who had been temporarily interned as aliens in Thuès-les-Bains, a spa establishment about 20 kilometres above Prades, after the German invasion.

By 17 June Pierre has arrived near Vichy, which at that moment was still just a fashionable spa town tucked away in the Massif Central. The beleaguered French government would descend on it a week later, commandeering every hotel room and closet, and change its reputation for ever.

> They are talking about an armistice. I'm just writing to say I am safe. My unit retreated more or less in order, and I have no reason to

abandon it. Before the Loire I really thought we would all be separated. Between the Loire and the Allier the same. It was indescribable chaos, with French artillery still trying from time to time to attack the enemy.

We were only half a day distance in front of the Germans, making an irregular retreat because we had no desire to be taken prisoner. We have not lost many men – one motorcyclist was knocked down by a truck. He died immediately . . .

I think so often of my parents, of you and the baby.

Pétain has asked, with reason, to lay down our arms. At last it is done . . . it is useless to continue. I feel our retreat is like the Spanish Republicans.

The French government in Bordeaux was bitterly torn over the armistice. Those against it tried everything, even the idea of union with Britain. 'Why should France want to merge with a corpse?' asked Pétain, firmly in favour of surrender. Outmanoeuvred, Reynaud resigned, and on 16 June Pétain took over. He immediately asked the Germans for peace terms. In a broadcast made on 17 June, he said: 'I think of the unfortunate refugees who are clogging up our roads in utter misery. I express to them my compassion and my solicitude . . . It is with a broken heart that I say to you today that it is necessary to cease fighting.'

Next day in the newspapers this key phrase was changed to 'try to cease fighting', since they still needed to settle armistice terms, but it was too late. The soldiers had thrown down their arms in despair. There seems little doubt that French resistance collapsed after Pétain's speech. Though many felt they had been betrayed, there seemed little point in fighting on.

There seemed indeed to be general relief, as observed by one philosopher soldier, Georges Friedmann, who found himself in a small village south of the Loire when the armistice was announced: 'A whole country seems suddenly to have given itself up . . . I do not detect any sense of pain at the misfortunes of their country: during the days of this perfectly pure summer in these villages, towns and camp stations of Limousin, Périgord and Guyenne, I have only observed a sort of complacent relief.'

On 21 June Pierre made it to Brive, and wrote on headed notepaper from the Café des Sports. He had been to visit Amélie's sister and her new baby.

Louisette was overjoyed to see me. We have travelled without much danger in the middle of all the chaos. I am now trying to get back to Corbiac, if necessary on foot. It's very hard to find petrol now.

I hope you have received some of my notes on the road. I can't wait to lie down beside you – I don't want to think any more about all the terrible things I have seen in the last few days.

On 22 June the armistice with Germany was signed. In only six weeks the French had been defeated and totally humiliated. 'The armistice is concluded,' announced Pétain in a trembling voice, 'the struggle has ended . . . The conditions to which we had to submit are severe . . . but at least our honour is saved . . . the government remains free and France will be administered only by Frenchmen.' His voice grew more severe. 'It is towards the future we must, from now on, direct our efforts. A new order is starting. You have suffered. You have yet to suffer . . . Your life will be hard . . . but we must restore France. Our defeat was born of our laxity.'

As far as Pétain was concerned it was all their own fault, a defeat born of decadence. 'Too few weapons, too few allies, too few babies.'

The world was stunned. Czechoslovakia and Poland were one thing, France was quite another. 'One of the lights of world civilisation is extinguished,' wrote the *Sydney Morning Herald*.

But there were still a few more weeks of patience needed before Amélie and Pierre were reunited. Pierre awaited demobilisation in Salles-Corbatiès, a little village in the Aveyron, writing to his wife, whom he had not heard from since the retreat from Arcis. She meanwhile waited anxiously for news, along with her mother who was with her at Corbiac.

'I am in good health, I expect to be demobilised soon and can work and replace you in the potatoes and the beetroot. If you can buy a piglet, do it, and I will take care of it this winter.' Pierre has responded wholeheartedly to Pétain. 'Marshal Pétain has stopped the butchery his predecessors wanted to continue. His speeches have gone straight to my heart, above all when he talks about the land.'

Pétain's sentimental appeal chimed with Pierre's romantic notions about returning to the land. 'The land does not lie; it remains your recourse; it is the Homeland itself; when a field becomes a wasteland, it is a piece of France itself that dies; a land which has lain fallow sown again with cereals, it is France which is born again.' Thus Pétain reassured a nation of peasants. All they needed to do was cultivate their gardens and all would be well.

The British were so worried that the French fleet would fall into German hands that on 3 July 1940 they sent a naval force to Mers-el-Kébir on the Algerian coast where some of the French fleet was docked and delivered an ultimatum. The fleet must either scuttle itself, join the British, or sail to distant French colonial ports. The French admiral rejected their demands, and the British opened fire, killing almost 1,300 French sailors. This did not endear the British to the French. 'Now there have been French sailors murdered by British hands, how terrible!' Pierre exclaimed.

Poor Amélie was impatient and frustrated. 'I can't wait to see you, to hug you, and to show you your baby! Every day we hope for you and every car we rush to the window, or stand up in the field.' And she began to worry about how she would look to her husband.

> My dear, you must expect to see me looking older. In just a few months I seem to have got the rough skin and the colour of a peasant.
>
> What sad days we have spent, and still we hear horrifying news. In the city it must be dreadful. What is most upsetting is still to know nothing of Clo, and to think of Mimi alone in Toulon. She is so brave but how she must be suffering. The last bombing of Marseille caused many victims, but happily no relations or friends of ours among them. Many Italians have been attacked . . .

But she had been greatly relieved to receive Pierre's letter from Brive. 'When we got your letter we sat at the bottom of the stairs, Maman and I, and wept about everything that has happened.' She expected Pierre to arrive daily.

> I don't feel like writing much – I expect at any moment to see you appear along the road, I am waiting for you . . . Yesterday I got so upset – I had gone out on the road, with the baby, to wait for you and suddenly I heard a car horn and when it came around the corner it looked like yours . . .
>
> If it is going to be a while before you are demobilised, can't you ask for a few days' leave to . . . take care of the potatoes? Everybody is so busy cutting wheat and hay. I have nobody to spray the potatoes so we are picking off the doryphores by hand. It would be such a shame to lose such a promising crop which must feed all the family.

The crops they have planted are suddenly of great interest to their relations:

> They all keep talking to me about potatoes and beans and are relying on them to get through the winter. We can't find anything in the market any more but we eat very well – Maman is cooking all the garden vegetables in lots of different ways. But the pig – I have no money for that.
>
> I know it will be hard to feed ourselves in the winter – but your

country patients will pay you in food. Here we will have potatoes, beans, apples, tomato conserves. You will need to cut some wood because we don't have much left.

I understand you will need the peace of the country after these terrible weeks. We will stay here as much as you wish, but I think you will soon be needed as a doctor.

Pierre reassured her that he had no intention of abandoning medicine:

It's just that I want to put the property in better order. You know I am not fussy about food. If there's no wine I'll drink water. But I want to work with my hands until October. I won't get much from the town people in 3 months. I prefer to see my potatoes, my apricots, my rabbits. And I want to spend 3 months with you. Please buy a pig!

Amélie balked at the pig purchase:

And you – telling me to buy a pig – I am sure it would be useful but here it is impossible to find one to buy. They all have to be declared at the *mairie* and are immediately requisitioned. And how will we feed it? I hope you will soon be here, and you can sort it out yourself.

At long last there is news of Clo. 'Good news!' as Amélie put it. 'Clo is a prisoner. Mimi sent a telegram and said he was in good health. You can imagine our happiness.' Clo was one of 2 million young Frenchmen in POW camps on French territory waiting to be sent to forced labour in Germany.

Then Pierre's final letter: 'This war has ended much faster than expected but there is no reason for us to be unhappy. We have a lot of work to do at Corbiac but we will take a holiday this year. We will walk over the mountain to Arles . . .' Folded inside the letter I found a hand-drawn map indicating the roads to follow from Montauban to the Col de Jau and Mosset, with sketchy drawings of paths and instructions for short cuts.

I imagine him walking home up and over the Col de Jau. People did it often in those days, after all. Down through the pine forest, the oaks and chestnuts, sun glinting between the leaves, the cows in the summer pastures, their bells clanging, the fields of hay, past La Coûme, where he surely would have known there were German refugees. He would have walked through the village, past the church, past the forge and the café. He would have been known to many of the villagers. '*Le médecin est revenu.*' The word would have spread very quickly. Down the road to Corbiac he would have seen it below him, perhaps he spotted his newly peasant wife in the field, weeding beetroot, or hanging out the baby's washing. He would have left the road and turned into the path, past the cherry trees, a few still hanging on the tree, to see his potatoes, his pear and apple trees. To find his wife and baby son. There was a photo session, with the baby, the achingly proud Papa holding his son with such pride and tentative care.

CHAPTER 7

# DEFEAT

'Vichy was to be the last stand of men who believed a nation could be great without passing through the industrial revolution.'

Robert Paxton

There is a key moment in Marcel Pagnol's wartime film *La Fille du puisatier* (The Well-Digger's Daughter) when the local grocer, an upstanding bourgeois gentleman who fought in the 1914–1918 war, summons his family importantly to listen to the Maréchal. They all gather round the huge radio set. Then comes Pétain's fateful speech, 'You must lay down your arms . . .' They listen in silence, they all turn and walk away in silence. The grocer is left shaking his head. 'I don't understand, I don't understand.' It is appropriately ambiguous. (So much so that the film was actually shown in France at the end of 1940. Pagnol had begun filming before the fall of France, and finished it afterwards, so it was entirely contemporary with events.)

The whole of France was in shock after the collapse of their supposedly first-rate army and the blitzkrieg of the German invasion. To be defeated in six weeks was a shattering trauma. Many, like Pierre, simply felt relief that the fighting was done. Most like Pagnol's grocer did not understand, but were simply thankful that the war was over. The fatherly tones of Marshal Pétain were soothing and reassuring. He would look after them. Thus began *les années noires*, the black years, which even now are the subject of huge controversy, with layers of history peeling off like an onion as time goes by.

Under the terms of the armistice, France was divided, and its army reduced to 100,000. The fleet was disarmed and the ships docked in their home ports; the Germans promised not to touch them. French prisoners of war were to remain in captivity until the war was over. Alsace-Lorraine became German. In the north and north-east there were two forbidden zones of intense military occupation. The Occupied zone covered the north and the whole of the western Atlantic coast, the richest and most populated part of France. Here the Germans controlled transport and the economy, and the French were obliged to pay for the cost of German occupying troops. The Germans fixed the exchange rate so that France ended up paying a vast amount, enough for an army of 18 million men. The centre, south and south-east, separated by a heavily guarded demarcation line, became the so-called Unoccupied zone (soon nicknamed in inimitable French style the Nono, for *zone non occupée*). The Italians occupied a small section between Menton and the frontier.

The French government moved to Vichy, a spa town in the middle of the Massif Central. In former years July had been the Vichy bathing season. Elegant crowds still filled the streets, where all the luxury shops of the capital had branches. They listened to the best musicians in France at the Casino, and strolled on the banks of the Allier River. Now, though Vichy was already crammed with refugees, they had to yield to the government as ministries argued over the available premises. Pétain moved into the luxurious Hôtel du Parc, and various ministries took over other hotels. The Ambassador Hotel, appropriately, sheltered most of the foreign diplomats. Officials slept in the rooms where they worked and documents were mixed up with neckties and pyjamas. Hotel corridors buzzed with gossip and speculation. Tucked away in the tranquil hills of the Auvergne, Vichy was remote from the world.

Philippe Pétain became Chief of State, dissolving the Third Republic. On 10 July the National Assembly, elected four years earlier as the Popular Front parliament, met in Vichy. It voted overwhelmingly to give Pétain full powers to establish a new constitution. Only 80 voted against him. Pierre Laval became vice-premier. Laval was a lawyer from an Auvergne peasant background, a scruffy, stubborn chainsmoker, described by one French history of the war as 'the wily Auvergnat' throughout. Laval, born in 1883, began as a socialist politician but soon shifted to the right, the only French politician whose name was spelled the same whether one moved from Left to Right or Right to Left, as the joke went. He opposed the First World War, and the Versailles treaty, and always struggled to avoid conflict. But he believed that France had to reform like Germany or Italy, and he pursued a policy of active collaboration with Germany from the beginning, convinced that the only future for France was as part of Hitler's New Europe. His relationship with Pétain was always fraught and Pétain dismissed him in December 1940. He moved to Paris under German protection and was reinstated in the Vichy government at Germany's insistence in 1942. He is considered largely responsible for the increasing oppression and deportation of the Jews, though he had plenty of help. After the war

Laval was tried and found guilty of treason, and executed by firing squad in October 1945.

Pétain himself ended up with more power than any French ruler since Louis XIV. Indeed he and his supporters were keen to turn the clock back almost as far, aiming for a National Revolution to re-establish a traditional hierarchical order in society, with Church and family at its base instead of Revolution. Pétain blamed defeat on the moral collapse and decadence of society. One Vichy documentary described the problem of France as 'the English weekend, American bars, Russian choirs and Argentinian tangos', *Travail, Famille, Patrie* – Work, Family, Fatherland – would replace *Liberté, Fraternité, Egalité*. The battle axe of the ancient Franks was adopted as a symbol, the *Francisque*, designed by the famous French jewellery firm, Van Cleef & Arpels.

There had been no such cult figure since Napoleon. Pétain's image, the portrait with white moustache, straight back and all-seeing blue eyes, was seen everywhere, installed in homes, schools, churches, offices and shop windows (sometimes with a rebellious '*vendu*', sold-out, ticket attached). Marianne, the symbol of the French Republic, was moved out of the town halls in favour of Pétain. His image appeared on calendars, plates, cups, handkerchiefs, stamps, matchboxes, even pen-knives. A youth anthem was composed, 'Maréchal, nous-voilà', for children pledging to serve him, which was sung in school every morning. (A small boy offers it as an example of his singing ability much to everyone's embarrassment in Christophe Barralier's 2005 film, *Les Choristes*, set not long after the war.) Thus France was infantilised.

Pétain's strongest appeal to a nation of farmers was for a return to the land. 'The land does not lie' remained one of his most famous sayings. Such a dream resonated deeply for many, who, like Pierre, already longed for the simplicity and purity of a rural life. Amélie writes of reading Jean Giono, whose books romanticised the peasantry of France and rejected the decadent life of the city. (Giono said in August 1940 that the defeat of France was insignificant compared to the fact that a world of machines was coming to an end.)

France had remained a largely agricultural society later than much of Europe. Only in 1931 was France declared half urban, a stage Britain had passed in the early nineteenth century. The flight from the countryside after the First World War created a sense of loss, and encouraged the French romance with the land. To this day French families retain a deep attachment to their own *pays*, their own province. They love to have a corner of the country where they feel they have roots, an old family house with a long history, even if they only spend a few weeks of the summer there. Even before Pétain there was a growing tendency to romanticise rural values and the peasant past. People liked to believe that it was peasant tenacity that had triumphed at Verdun.

Agriculture was glorified, the French were encouraged to embrace the hard work and traditions of the peasantry. Basic agricultural skills were to be taught in school. Regional culture too was promoted, regional costumes appeared on stamps and architects were encouraged to build in regional styles. This land of happy peasants was to be purged of undesirable elements, foreigners, communists and especially Jews, considered the epitome of the decadent urban intellectual. Anyone considered politically dangerous would be interned in concentration camps, most of which were in the southern zone.

Pétain insisted that society needed a complete moral overhaul. Women should stay at home and bear more children. It became illegal for married women to be employed in the public sector. Divorce was abolished and the death penalty introduced for abortion. Mothers would be honoured with diplomas and medals, and Pétain would be godfather of all new-borns named Philippe.

French youth was to be regenerated by the Chantiers de la Jeunesse, youth workshops, where all twenty-two-year-olds were obliged to spend six months in training, partly a substitute for military service, and intended to instil moral values into the young. The Compagnons de France was another youth movement, which was voluntary, though participation was strongly encouraged. School books were revised, the French Revolution downplayed, and lessons in moral development introduced. The benefits of manual work, choral singing, sports, and work in the open air were exalted. Teachers who did not toe the line were soon dismissed. Socialist teachers were blamed for the moral decline of society.

In August 1940 the Légion Française des Combattants was created in the Vichy Zone, open to combatants from both wars, and uniting various veterans' organisations. Its purpose was to support Pétain, and his philosophy of national regeneration and moral improvement, 'to support France, the family and the fight against Bolshevism'.

On 29 August at 8.30 p.m. in the Café de la Bourse in Perpignan the departmental section of the Legion was formally launched, and by February 1941 the Legion had 590,000 members, 11,000 in the Pyrénées-Orientales. Colonel Jean-Jacques Ruffiandis, hero of the First World War, who also fought at the beginning of the Second

World War and escaped after being taken prisoner, was appointed chief for the department. The Legionnaires swore an oath of allegiance to Pétain, and formed uniformed guards of honour on his triumphal tour of the South. There is a grim photo of them all raising their right arms in the fascist salute for Pétain in Perpignan. Prominent among them is Ruffiandis, a stiff-backed figure in his Legion beret – Ruffiandis, whose family had owned Corbiac and whose book about Mosset had provided me with such a rich source of information. His celebration of country life and traditional values began to take on a much more ambiguous look.

Ruffiandis, I discovered, was still a sensitive subject in Mosset: one person said anxiously: 'You're not going to write about him are you?' In the village journal *Le Mossetan*, I read a laudatory article about him, decrying his treatment as a collaborator after the war, when he was condemned to prison for several months, describing him as a patriot and man of great culture. After he died in 1948 his articles continued to be published in a local history journal. Clearly in Mosset he was still respected, collaborator or not. I asked one of the old ladies in the village, Elvira, a peasant to her soul, what she thought of Ruffiandis. 'Oh yes,' she said, 'he was a gentleman, a fine man. He lived here after the war you know.' I don't think she even knew he was called a collaborator, or whether she would have cared. I found myself hoping I would find evidence that he had resigned from the Legion, or that perhaps, at least, he had secretly protected his beloved Mosset, that perhaps, like Mitterrand, he had switched sides. If it was so hard for me to square this man whose bucolic descriptions of the village and the landscape I had so much relished, with the idea of collaboration, how much harder must it have been for those who lived through that time?

I discussed this with Dr Goujon in Prades, in one of several conversations in his study lined with shelves of books on military history. At over eighty Dr Goujon is still trim and bright eyed after a lifetime of mountaineering, and his 'country gent look', the corduroy and tweeds, indicate a distinct anglophilia. Goujon had been a young Resistant in Mosset towards the end of the war, and had been Pablo Casals's physician for many years. I respected his opinion. He tried to explain the position of Ruffiandis. 'You have to understand that Pétain was the legitimate government . . . Somebody like Ruffiandis was just doing his duty.'

I was struck while reading Julian Jackson's illuminating book *The Dark Years* by the story of Jean Moulin, whom I knew of as the great leader and finally martyr of the Resistance. He was prefect of the Eureet-Loir region when the Germans arrived there on 17 June. The next day he was asked to sign a declaration condemning the massacre of French civilians by black French Senegalese troops. Moulin refused because he knew the deaths had been caused by German bombing. He was beaten up and put in prison. There Moulin, believing he might succumb to their demands under such treatment, slit his throat with broken glass. He survived however, and after hospitalisation returned to his post. There he stayed for the next five months, doing his duty as he perceived it, until he was dismissed by Vichy. He then went on to join de Gaulle and return to France to unite the nascent Resistance movements. I began to see that the ethical problems raised were very far from black and white.

In any case, most people at this point were more concerned with their families than with ideology. The threats to their men were a source of great anguish, and news of their fate anxiously awaited. Pétain's greatest support came from those whose sons, brothers and fathers were prisoners of war in Germany. If Pétain could bring them back, as he said he would, they were for him. One and a half million prisoners, about one-fifth of the male population of France from age twenty to fifty, had been transferred to German prison camps, and they became vital pawns in negotiations between Vichy and the Nazis. There were Prisoners of War Aid Committees in every department, and everyone became preoccupied with what they could provide to send in parcels.

In the handful of letters that remain from Amélie and her mother their concern for Clo, imprisoned in Germany, is a constant refrain. Amélie writes to her sister: 'We talk of you often, I understand your pain with Clo so far away, in a country so harsh, but I hope he receives your letters and parcels, and that soon he will return . . . if the promises to return the teachers are real.'

In the South people were still keen to believe in the protection of Pétain, and were grateful he had spared them the German presence. They were sure that there would be no help from the Allies – most were convinced that Britain would be the next to fall to the German war machine. Few considered there was the remotest possibility that Britain would fight on. And in any case, after the drowning of the French sailors at Mers-el-Kébir a great wave of anglophobia had swept the country. Perhaps collaboration with Germany was the only answer.

However the reality was that Germany was not really interested in collaboration. It wanted revenge and domination. The day after the

German invasion Strasbourg cathedral became a museum dedicated to the German soldier. 'We'll make of France a country half allotment and half brothel,' a German general said in the spring of 1940. The German propaganda ministry announced on 9 July 1940 that France's future would be as 'a greater Switzerland, a country of tourism . . . and fashion'. Hitler was not inclined to crush France straight away because he needed the French government in Vichy to control the country for him. He needed to exploit French economic resources for the benefit of the German war effort, so it was better that they appeared to be maintained by Frenchmen.

Still, the invaders set the rules, even imposing their own summer time in the North, so that it was one hour ahead of the South. The rules were different between the two zones. In the North there was a curfew between 10 p.m. and 5 a.m., but not in the South. American films were forbidden in the North, but could be seen in the South until 1942. In the South there were French flags, in the North swastikas. In the South they could still sing the Marseillaise, but not in the North.

Communication between the zones was tightly controlled, and crossing the demarcation line that ran through the middle of thirteen departments required a special pass, hard to get hold of, especially if you were politically suspect. People were only allowed to write to members of their family, and had to use a card of thirteen lines, where they ticked appropriate words – 'in good health', 'tired', 'ill', 'wounded', 'prisoner', 'dead', 'no news of'.

Food rationing was introduced and food shortages set in at once. Hunger and the quest for food began to dominate people's lives, and though quantities of produce and animals were requisitioned it was still easier in the country than in the cities. There the majority still lived entirely off the land, and hunting and foraging for food was something they took for granted. Happy were the citizens who could count on a brother or a cousin in the country, and many suddenly remembered distant relations with farms or smallholdings. A black market soon developed, and barter was common – a barrel of wine in return for some potatoes, butter swapped for espadrilles, tobacco for eggs.

The first ration cards appeared in September 1940, with priority accorded to pregnant women and mothers of large families, which soon caused resentment. Bread was strictly rationed. The export of potatoes outside the department of the Pyrénées-Orientales was banned. Meat soon became almost unobtainable. Coffee disappeared and people had to make do with ersatz coffee made from roasted acorns. Children were encouraged to forage for chestnuts and wild fruit, and pick off the Colorado beetles (*doryphores*) which threatened the precious potato crop. Nineteen forty was a particularly hard winter, and there were demonstrations against food shortages in several cities in the South. Rationed tobacco was replaced by dried leaves. Real soap became a precious commodity. Petrol was severely rationed, and soon was unobtainable, and charcoal became the ubiquitous substitute.

Wine consumption was also limited, linked to a campaign against alcoholism, which was cited as a factor in the defeat of France. France before the war had a bar for every 80 people compared with 270 in Germany, 430 in Britain and 3,000 in Sweden. Pastis, the universal aperitif of the South, was banned.

Political control was tightened. Left-wing mayors were evicted, including François Pujol, the butcher who was the communist mayor of Mosset. They were replaced by Special Delegations appointed by the Vichy government.

The media was censored. In August 1940 it was announced that no newspapers, even as wrapping paper for parcels, would be admitted from the Unoccupied zone into the Occupied zone. The radio was the main source of information, though only about 1 per cent of the population owned their own radio, in those days a notable item of furniture. People would gather at a neighbour's house or in the cafés to listen to the news.

Radio Londres was one of the main sources of uncensored information. The Free French had five minutes on the BBC at 9 p.m. every evening, which began with the warning to people to turn down their sets. Broadcasting in France by the BBC increased from two and a half hours daily in 1940 to five hours in 1942. The most popular programme was *Les français parlent aux français*, announced by a little ditty to the tune of La Cucaracha: '*Radio Paris ment, Radio Paris ment, Radio Paris est allemand.*' Radio Paris lies, Radio Paris lies, Radio Paris is German. By October 1940 people were forbidden to listen to the BBC in public places, and then forbidden to listen at home as well. Café proprietors were frequently denounced for playing Radio Londres for their customers. A young sandalmaker from Céret was sent to prison for two weeks for playing a fragment of the Internationale on his accordion when he passed the *sous-préfet* and several officers.

Cinema newsreels were strictly controlled. In the Vichy zone there was almost no foreign news, German soldiers were shown benignly looking after women and children, and France was portrayed as a peaceful rural country benefiting from visits from the fatherly Pétain.

Propaganda posters exhorted the French: 'Abandoned populations, have confidence in the German soldier.'

Opposition was fragmented at first. The socialists went home. The communists had been in disarray ever since the Nazi–Soviet pact the previous summer. There had even been suggestions that they should fraternise with working-class German soldiers. Still the communists were among the first to oppose the fascist invader.

Resistance grew only slowly. In the North the presence of the Germans made it difficult, though the daily evidence of their dominance encouraged people to rebel. Jean-Paul Sartre considered they were in a more acute state of awareness of the choices they had, and thus had more real freedom. In the South, free of overt German activity, the population reacted more slowly. The traditional ideas of Pétain appealed to many, and they also told themselves that he was actually playing a double game to help keep the Germans at bay. At this time most were convinced that Britain would be next to fall, and there was no focus for resistance. There were small prewar groups that tried to foster opposition, mainly by planning publication of newspapers and clandestine tracts. The British intelligence groups took their time.

There were symbolic gestures, organised via the BBC broadcasts, the first of which on 1 January 1941 called on the French population to leave the streets empty between 3 and 4 in the afternoon. Public holidays, the 14th of July, the 1st of May, became a focus for protests.

Not many heard the first historic call from Charles de Gaulle, broadcast on 18 June 1940:

> Come what may, the flame of French resistance must not die . . . I urge all Frenchmen who would remain free to hear me and follow me . . . Hope there must be. Somewhere there must shine and burn the flame of French resistance.
> France has lost a battle; she has not lost the war.

Probably a few more heard of him when he was sentenced to death for treason by Marshal Pétain. On 28 June Churchill had accepted de Gaulle as leader of 'France Libre', the Free French, and gave them financial and military backing.

As far as de Gaulle was concerned the Free French were not exiles but the embodiment of France. He distinguished between the legal government of France and what he called the legitimate government. Historians are still arguing over the legal status of the Vichy government. Right from the start de Gaulle did not make an easy ally – he was once reported as saying that Churchill always shouted when he was wrong, and he, de Gaulle, shouted when he was right, which meant they were always shouting at each other.

One of those who did hear de Gaulle's first broadcast was fifteen-year-old Pierre Solanes. He is eighty-three now, and spends much of his time in the quiet seaside town of Banyuls, where I went to visit him and his wife. I had been talking to Jean Larrieu, the historian who, with Ramon Gual, wrote the history of the war in the Pyrénées-Orientales, or northern Catalonia as they would have it, an exhaustive chronology in four volumes. He mentioned the first recorded act of resistance, a tract they had discovered in the archives. Typed on blue paper, the notice began: 'Français! France is not dead. She is waking up and will wake up more and more every day.' It gave news of the French colonies that were declaring for the Free French, and de Gaulle's determination to continue the war alongside the English allies. 'Keep your Resistance spirit! We are not beaten. Prepare for the struggle!'

We sat, Pierre, his wife and I, at a big round table in their sitting room, with amazing views through big glass windows, one side facing the sea, the other the vine-clad hills of the Albères, only a few miles from the border with Spain. As I asked about the war, Solanes seemed vague at first, as if he couldn't really understand what all the fuss was about. While he paused and tried to remember a detail, he was encouraged by his wife, a sprightly woman with smartly coiffed silver hair, who got out albums of photos and showed me Solanes's original Resistance armband, made in Algeria. As if she has to remind him of his heroism.

A smile lit up his face when I mentioned the tracts.

'It was about 1994 when I was approached by the historians Gual and Larrieu to talk about my Resistance experience. The subject of the tracts came up. It turned out that one of them had been put in the postbox of the director of the postal service, who was *not* for the Free French, and he had handed it over to the Prefecture and there it had been archived. Then I said to the historians, but it was me, it was me who wrote those letters!'

'What made you feel so strongly about supporting de Gaulle?' I asked.

Solanes clasped his hands together on the table.

'My father went right through the 1914 war. In 1940 he had very strong ideas, he was very patriotic. He was really shocked by the armistice, and was for de Gaulle right from the start. We listened to Radio Londres all the time, and we knew it was important to do something.'

'So what inspired you to write the tracts?'

'Radio Londres suggested writing letters, and gave out a text to copy – so that's what I did, my parents didn't know about it. They would have said it was too dangerous for me – but I made lots of copies of the letters and posted them in the letter boxes on the way to school. I was at the college in Perpignan then. Nobody ever said anything, nobody ever mentioned it. Nobody kept the letters, the neighbours would come round to listen to the radio but nobody would keep letters like that . . .'

With more encouragement from his wife, Solanes went on to talk further about his Resistance activities a few years later, and how in 1942, when he was still only seventeen, he had helped a Dutch soldier to escape across the mountains from Banyuls. 'We are all great friends now,' added his wife. 'We met up with him after the war. In fact he is coming to stay in a few weeks' time.' Then they invited me to return and meet Willem Brederode, who had recently retired as Governor of the Royal Netherland Academy, 'the equivalent of Sandhurst', Madame Solanes proudly explained.

It is a cliché now that all the French claim to have been in the Resistance, and indeed there were plenty of turncoats who donned Resistance armbands at the last minute. But there were those who resisted actively right from the beginning, those known proudly as *Résistants de la première heure*.

When I reviewed the material for this chapter, I thought that the interviews I had done were perhaps unrepresentative – two women and one boy of fifteen. And then I realised that perhaps they were indeed representative.

Two stories had moved me greatly, the stories of the Sabaté family and Rose Blanc. Odette Sabaté-Loiseau, I discovered, was still alive, and living just outside Prades in the village of Ria-Sirach. She gladly agreed to see me, and was waiting at the door when I arrived at her small modern house with a garden on the outskirts of the village.

She came out to guide my car into a parking place, a tiny upright woman, leaning on a stick. I would have recognised her from the photos I had seen of her as a child. The same straight hair cut in a simple bob, now silver, the same round clear eyes, now framed by spectacles. And the same open clear expression, in a face now lined with age, but with smile lines above all. She grumbled gently about her knees and her hip, but it was only later I discovered she had always suffered, like her sister Francine, from a hip dislocated at birth.

There were doors onto the garden, and a fine view of Canigou through the window. On the wall were many pictures and photos, a framed embroidery from South America, and biggest of all a poster of La Pasionaria, the communist heroine of the Spanish Civil War. Clearly Odette Sabaté had never lost faith with the cause she espoused as a teenager.

It began with the International Brigade, she explained.

'After France signed the non-intervention treaty in 1938, the International Brigade were forced to leave Spain, and about twenty of us went to welcome them at Cerbère. The trains coming into the station were covered in flowers and Republican flags, full of thousands of men, broken-hearted, sure that Franco would win the war. I will never forget it, it was an experience that affected me deeply. I swore then to fight against fascism, for freedom, for a better life.'

She was then fourteen and was already involved with her mother and sister in supporting the Republican cause, collecting funds, and sending supplies to Spain. Her family came from this village, Ria. Her mother, Josephine, and elder sister, Francine, were born here, but then they moved to Thuir, where Odette was born, and thence to Perpignan, where her father kept a small grocery. After he died of wounds suffered in the First World War, her mother had been politicised, Odette explained, by her experience trying to get support as a widow for herself and her children. She became a socialist and committed to the Spanish Republican struggle against fascism. Her young daughters went further, joining the Union des Jeunes Filles de France, affiliated to the Young Communists.

The organiser of the Jeunes Filles was Rose Blanc, aged nineteen, also active in the Republican cause. Another young girl from a Roussillon farming family, she had been sent to work as a maid in Paris when she was fourteen. She met Danièle Casanova, 'the French Pasionaria', the legendary Corsican Resistant, and they had travelled to the Madrid front together with a convoy of supplies. By 1939 Rose was running the Young Communists of the region, passionately committed to the anti-fascist cause, spending many nights typing furiously. Both Rose and Casanova would eventually share the same fate. Odette told me that Rose's sister was still alive, and I resolved to find out more.

Odette produced a sheaf of papers, an account of her experiences in the Resistance which she consulted from time to time as we talked. Unlike some who never speak about their wartime experiences she often gives school talks and shares her memories.

When the Republican refugees poured across the frontier at the end of the war, the Sabaté family did everything they could to help, supplying food and clothing and smuggling false documentation into the camps.

'It was easy for me to go there by bike – at that age no one suspected me,' said Odette with satisfaction. Soon their home was full of Spanish and became a centre of clandestine activity. 'But it was forbidden to take the Spanish into our homes, and my mother was eventually arrested for helping them, and sentenced to a month in prison.'

Once war broke out in France they continued their activities, helping escaping Allied airmen and soldiers as well as the Spanish. Francine worked as a typist for the Prefecture and could smuggle out identity cards, official stamps and a precious supply of paper. She taught Odette, then still at school, to type. 'We were well organised,' Odette recalls. 'We had a hiding place in the attic where we kept our supplies and the typewriter.' There they created false identity papers, and typed tracts of Resistance propaganda. But as conditions became tougher, and once the Germans invaded the southern zone, they soon came under suspicion.

The position of the Spanish refugees helped by the Sabatés and Rose Blanc became more delicate than ever at the outbreak of war. Some returned to Spain, having no desire to fight for the French. But many joined the French army, determined to continue the fight against fascism. Their contribution to the war has been historically sidelined, but they fought with great courage (they were after all experienced). Six thousand Spaniards died in battle before the armistice. But to have fought against fascism twice made them doubly suspect. After the collapse of France Spanish soldiers were segregated by the Germans and deported to the concentration camp of Mauthausen. Of 12,000 Spaniards sent there during the war, only 2,000 emerged alive.

The Vichy government did not return the Spanish wholesale to Franco, having decided that they were more useful as forced labour. (By the end of 1940 over 200,000 Spanish were working for French or German enterprises in France.) But the Spanish were always considered to be dangerous elements, and every department was instructed to compile lists of suspected Spanish communists. Some were forcibly sent back. This was the experience of José Sangenis, as he described it to me, still angry at the treatment they received, the day I talked to him in the Perpignan café.

In December 1940, still in the Auvergne, the women were given a choice: 'You can go back to your husbands in Argelès or return to Franco.' All chose to return to the camps, rather than Spain. Women, children and war-wounded were all put on a train.

'We travelled through the night,' said Sangenis, 'so we couldn't see the names of the stations.' It was only when they arrived in Bayonne in the first light of morning, close to the Atlantic coast, the other end of the Pyrenees, and a few miles from the Spanish border, that they realised what was happening.

'They're sending us back to Spain, to Irun.' Panic-stricken, they poured off the train as soon as it stopped. 'But the police arrived, and made us all get back on. My mother showed them her CNT union card [the Spanish Confederación Nacional del Trabajo], and told them, "If I go back to Spain I will be killed immediately." But they pushed us back on the train, brutally. One man, who was wounded, refused to get back on, despite blows, and the women screamed at the police for hitting him. The children were crying in fear. But the police kept hitting him, and finally killed him with their bayonets.'

The train left, leaving his corpse on the platform.

José shook his head sadly. 'The horror of that night has stayed with me for the rest of my life. We arrived in Hendaye, then Irun, in tragic silence. We were put in a stable full of fleas and vermin, for five days, without eating or washing. Then we were packed off in closed cattle wagons, so we could not escape, and sent to Zaragoza [midway across Spain]. There they gave us a piece of bread and half a sardine each. That was so good!'

They were sent on to Barcelona and imprisoned in Montjuich, the hilltop fortress infamous for the number of prisoners killed there by Franco. Women and children were put in one prison, and men, including José, and the wounded in another.

'I was there for three months. We were close to the sea and I could hear the waves crashing against the rocks of our prison. I wept night and day knowing my mother and sisters were nearby and I could do nothing to help them. I was the only child amongst all the men, and one day they got hold of some girl's clothing, and disguised me as a girl.' During the morning reveille, the guards sent him to the women's quarters, where he stayed for another two months. 'But of the 150–200 men I was imprisoned with I have heard of no one. They must all have been killed.'

Eventually José and his family were released and returned to their village, where they found the ruins of their house and where their mother, despised as a 'Red', struggled to find work to feed her children. They did not hear from José's father again until 1945.

As resistance grew in France, the groups of Spanish workers scattered all over the country. The workers in northern industrial regions,

Massif Central quarries and the dams of the Dordogne, the forest workers and charcoal-makers of the Pyrenees, perhaps most of all those who were already hiding out in the hills, were to prove invaluable. Resistance was their natural state, and they were motivated above all by continuing the fight against fascism in their own country. As one Spanish Resistant said to de Gaulle, when asked how long he had been in the Resistance, 'With all respect, General, before you.'

The Spanish were among the first to establish escape routes across the Pyrenees, at first in the opposite direction, smuggling guerrillas into Spain, and then helping others escape to France. After the armistice the flood of escapees ran both ways. They ran tremendous risks on both sides of the frontier, and many were executed in Spain.

Nineteen forty was a terrible year for France, but for most people in the Mediterranean Pyrenees that date is still remembered for an even greater disaster. If you mention the catastrophe of 1940, people won't think you are talking about the defeat of France. They will only remember the Flood.

### 17 October 1940

Everybody had their eyes fixed on the mountain that day. At noon the sky was so black it blotted out the plain, the village, the farms, the heart of man. The darkness was almost complete. It rained as it had never rained before. The Têt was unchained, the Tech wailed. All the rivers roared together. In each valley all the rivers in flood swept everything along with them.

A millennial fear took people by the throat. In a few hours the face of the mountains was unrecognisable, the valleys ravaged, the plain submerged. Of the houses built beside the river banks there was no trace, countless animals and people were carried off to the sea.

Michel Maurette 1992

Ever after it was called *la semaine terrible*, the terrible week. Never in living memory, not in the last two centuries, had the region endured such a flood, such a natural catastrophe. More than three hundred were drowned. People already frantic at the events of the year, the moral shock of defeat, the absence of so many men killed or taken prisoner, the economic problems of daily life, searched for an explanation. Had Canigou, the god of the land, exploded under the onslaught of the storm? Or would it appear again tomorrow more beautiful, more grand than ever? Many people thought it was an earthquake, that the mountain had riven itself in two.

Later a rational explanation emerged. Two masses of air had collided:

warm unstable air from the Mediterranean had met polar cold air from the mountains. After five days of rain the river basins of the plain were already saturated with water, when on 17 October there was a further deluge. At least 800 millimetres of water fell on the southern flank of Canigou, the record in Europe for twenty-four hours. During the same day the Haut Vallespir received as much water as it normally did in a year. By the evening of the 17th, all rivers had exceeded their maximum levels. In forty-eight hours the Roussillon was transformed into one vast swimming pool, awash with trees, walls torn from houses, dead livestock and human bodies.

There was a terrifying growling sound of bricks and stones dragged along by the water, and there had indeed been a split in one side of Canigou, where part of the left bank of the Têt River slipped away, creating a small lake. Dozens of bridges collapsed, communication routes were cut and railway lines destroyed. In Perpignan the main bridge was under water and the riverside population had to be evacuated. The entire spa at Vernet-les-Bains, once so popular with the English, was completely annihilated, all the grand hotels and the thermal baths were swept away and hundreds left homeless. There were forty-eight deaths in the Tech valley. In Arles-sur-Tech the chocolate factory was destroyed and sixty houses with it. In Amélie-les-Bains the casino disappeared. Thousands of hectares of farming land were flooded and covered in sand and gravel, hundreds and hundreds of houses were flooded. Many of the villages in the Vallespir could only be supplied by mule.

The refugees suffered appallingly. Those Spanish refugees still living on river banks drowned. The camps, especially Argelès, were flooded, but the authorities were slow to evacuate them. When the water level reached the roof of some of the barracks there was collective panic. Finally the women's camp, under 2 metres of water, was partially evacuated, but several women died when two of the trucks that took them floated away. The hospital which had been constructed at Argelès for the Spanish refugees had been built on marshy land near the mouth of the Tech River, but the necessary retaining wall had never been built. The flood inundated the hospital, destroying all the equipment.

Amélie and her mother both wrote about the catastrophe. Maman was with Grandmère when the flood happened. On 20 October she wrote to Mimi, her account of the disaster eclipsing her concern for her imprisoned son-in-law:

You must have heard of the unprecedented disaster which has befallen us. All the Tech valley in ruins with so many victims. At Arles many houses have been swept away, from the terrace I can see the furious river Tech which has drowned the fields and carried away the new bridge. We thought it was going to take the entire village. The water came within 10 centimetres of the barriers built in the street. We are exhausted after nights without sleep.

Don't worry about us – but I can't send any parcels to Clo until things get back to normal.

So many people have been left with nothing that one dares not complain. The worst is the lack of water and light these short days. If you could see us with our one candle at night. The night comes so early and the weather is grey, and it rained again last night. Amélie has written to us, but they can't get supplies to us, because communication between the two valleys is impossible, though there are lots of teams at work repairing the roads and the irrigation canals.

The people of Arles believe they have their saints to thank that the town has not perished. When the water had stopped rising and the rain had nearly stopped, there was a huge procession, carrying the saints' remains, with bells ringing, followed by the pious, those who think they are, and those who don't know what they believe!

I'm getting used to the ruins now. Sometimes I try to remember what it was like before but it is hard.

In Mosset there was damage too, with land flooded and bridges carried away. All the lower fields at Corbiac were flooded and the garden wall slid down the hill. The precious crops of apples and potatoes were lost. Amélie and Pierre returned to Prades to live.

In December Amélie wrote to her sister Mimi:

What we saw at Amélie-les-Bains was beyond anything you could imagine. It left me stupid and mute, the little Tech running in an enormous bed full of huge rocks, the debris of houses and bridges. And the road, no, you have to see it to understand.

Pétain sent a telegram: 'Profoundly moved by the disaster which has attacked your department, my affectionate thoughts to the sorely tested population.' The minister of agriculture came to inspect the three devastated valleys, and millions of francs were given to pay for the disaster. The memory of the flood surpassed all others in the collective memory of the department, but coming only four months after the defeat and armistice, outside it passed almost unnoticed. On 24 October 1940 Laval arranged for Pétain to meet Hitler at Montoire, and France entered formally on the path of collaboration with the enemy.

# CHAPTER 8

# SURRENDER ON DEMAND

In July 1940, while Pierre trudged thankfully home to the calm of the Castellane valley, returning to the land as instructed by Père Pétain, thousands of refugees headed south. All were desperate to escape the Germans, hoping to find a way out by sea or across the Pyrenees into Spain. As well as French refugees, who could theoretically take their chances and return home, there were many people who had no desire to be caught. There were all the Allied soldiers, British, Belgians, Polish and Dutch, who had avoided or escaped capture and wanted to return to the fight. There were the anti-Nazi refugees, especially Germans, who, like the Krügers at La Coûme, had found a haven in France, but were now considered enemy aliens, even though they too had been opposing Hitler. And there were the Jews, who were already being singled out for special treatment.

The Pyrenees has a 435 kilometre frontier with Spain, which was one of the few countries of Europe not controlled by the Axis powers. Franco was reluctant to align himself with Hitler; he had no desire to plunge Spain into further war, and preferred to keep his options open with the Allies. (Hitler was not too keen on Franco, either.) The British therefore still had a diplomatic presence in Spain, with an ambassador in Madrid and a British consulate in the big cities, including Barcelona. Thus, despite its own misery, Spain became the country of hope for the escapees and undesirables of Fortress Europe.

Normally most passengers and freight would cross the Pyrenees via road and rail routes at both extremes of the chain, but with the Germans in occupation of the Atlantic coast, the eastern end of the Pyrenees became the only way out. In the early years as many as 70 per cent of escapes from France were made via the hills and beaches of the Pyrénées-Orientales.

Some came by train from Toulouse through the Ariège to Puigcerda and Latour-de-Carol, a tiny station with an international connection to Barcelona. Others arrived at Latour-de-Carol via the Petit Train Jaune from Perpignan, a narrow-gauge railway winding up through the steep valley of the Tet, via Prades. There was the also the frontier crossing of the coastal railway at the station of Cerbère on the coast, and there were heavily patrolled road crossings at Cerbère and Le Perthus, which so recently had seen the Spanish refugees fleeing in the other direction. But otherwise the roads and paths wound discreetly and tortuously through the mountains, few of them passable by car, and often, as the Spanish had found, subject to hazardous weather conditions.

The cols or portes were always the lowest convenient points to cross the mountain ridge, ancient paths marked by centuries of men and animals. One of those was the Col de Mantet, the most direct route to Spain from Prades, just east of the massif of Canigou. Here Pierre came to visit his patients in the tiny village of Mantet, cradled in a bowl of sheltering peaks, and still remarkably remote. Even driving up there today it is easy to understand his new wife's anxiety, and it is hard to believe it was possible on a motorbike. We stopped for lunch in the village, now restored by a devoted colony of hippies, and bought goat's cheese made from the flock reared there. Then we walked part of the way up the worn old path which led towards the frontier, over soft tussocky grass and rocks, past grazing cows. It was a warm October day with just a little cloud of a sea breeze dancing over the hills below us, but above there was already snow.

A guide would be essential for anyone trying to escape from here. Lower down the mountains were patrolled, higher up there was less surveillance, but it was Nature who stood guard. In winter, snow and avalanches made the higher reaches inaccessible for up to six months of the year. There are many sad stories of escapees dying in the snow between November and May, deceived by the palm trees of Perpignan or the mimosa of Amélie-les-Bains. In summertime there could be sudden mists which obscured the paths, and there are also plenty of stories of people spending days going round in circles, without meeting anyone at all.

Those who knew the mountains were highly sought after; both the legitimate denizens, the shepherds, who spent many months in their primitive shelters at high altitudes, and the smugglers for whom frontiers were a challenge rather than a restriction. There had always been a certain natural anarchy in these mountains. Sheep paid scant attention to frontier posts, and the shepherds were more likely to negotiate with each other over grazing rights than with some distant authority far below. There were also foresters, woodcutters and charcoal burners, all of whom knew their own patch of land and might be asked to help a refugee.

Some were simply lucky like the Dutch soldier, Major-General Willem Brederode, who met Pierre Solanes one day on the beach near

Banyuls, the little fishing village not far from Cerbère. I had revisited the Solanes family in order to meet him and heard his tale of escape. We sat on the terrace, drinking Banyuls *naturellement*, as the sun faded over the sea, while the old men studied the map spread on the table and worked out the route that Brederode must have followed. He had escaped from Holland in 1942, and wandered across France, a tall blond blue-eyed northerner pretending to be French, increasingly desperate, until he met young Pierre on the beach near Banyuls.

'I asked myself if it could all be true,' said Pierre, 'but he insisted, he said he was finished, exhausted, he had no money, could I help him escape to Spain?' Pierre took him to his family. 'Opposite us lived a *vigneron* with vineyards outside the town, and he agreed to help. We hid Willem in the *vigneron*'s cart under a pile of sacks, and then early the next morning, they set off.' They had to pass a German guard post – although at that time this was still in the *Zone Libre* there were Germans posted at all strategic points along the frontier. 'But they knew the *vigneron* and waved him through as usual.' He indicated the hills behind the house, the vine terraces where Willem began his journey to the Spanish frontier.

But for most of those escaping it was simply the Pyrenees they had to cross and few had much idea of where they had been. Most accounts simply say they crossed the Pyrenees, but rarely do they mention whereabouts as if they have no idea just how long a chain of mountains it is, and certainly little idea of where they were. Often of course this was deliberate as the escape networks tried to keep their routes secret.

A tangled international web of escape networks soon emerged: Polish, Greek, British, French, most of all Spanish. They seem to have had little idea of each other's existence, a reflection of their clandestine nature and a tribute to their discretion. Many claim to have been the first. Even now in books written about specific escape lines, French, American or English, the activities of other networks are barely registered.

Immediately after the Fall of France in June 1940, the Pyrénées-Orientales began to see some exotic fugitives, including the Duke of Windsor who got stuck there on his way to Spain. He had been in Antibes on 10 June, having lunch with his neighbour Maurice Chevalier, when Italy declared war on France and the Riviera expats decided it was time to leave. The Duke telephoned the British embassy, which by then had decamped to Bordeaux, to ask them if they could send a warship round to pick him up. He was told the ships were needed for British troops, and advised to head for the Spanish frontier. Visas however could not be guaranteed.

So on 19 June the Windsors, along with the British consul of Nice, set out for Spain. Eventually they arrived in Perpignan hoping to obtain visas to cross the border from the Mediterranean port of Cerbère to Port Bou. They found a hotel and the men set off for the Spanish consulate, where at first they were obliged to join the queue, treated like anyone else without papers. Meanwhile the Duchess of Windsor and the other women in the party were evicted from the hotel because it had been requisitioned by the French government, who at that point apparently planned to move there from Bordeaux if the armistice talks broke down. Finally the visas were issued and the royal refugees crossed the frontier that evening, heading for Barcelona.

Jean Cocteau also turned up in Perpignan, well supplied with opium, to stay with a wealthy doctor friend, Dr Nicolo, in his house on rue de la Poste in the old town. Cocteau was soon joined by several young men, including Jean Marais, his boyfriend, who had been a rather nervous aircraft lookout in the army. He had ended up in Gascony camping out with gypsies, and arrived in Perpignan in the only civilian clothes he could find, turquoise trousers he had worn to act in Cocteau's play *Les Parents terribles,* a white shirt and an opossum waistcoat that Coco Chanel had sent to him at the front. In Perpignan Cocteau entertained himself with costume parties fuelled by opium and cocaine, but he returned to Paris in the autumn, apparently unable to resist the spectacle of Paris full of German uniforms.

In Prades there had been panic. Pablo Casals was one person who certainly could not cross the Pyrenees into Spain. His supporters in the USA and Britain had been begging him to leave, and he had been offered a quarter of a million dollars to play in America, but he felt he must stay in France, out of duty to his compatriots. But once France fell, and they heard that the Germans were approaching Paris, it was rumoured that Franco would declare war on France and occupy French Catalonia. The head of the Prefecture in Prades told Casals he must leave. If the Nationalist forces of Franco crossed the frontier he would face execution. Casals, his then companion, Señora Capdevila, and the Alavedras decided to leave. There was the chance of places on a boat, the *Champlain,* due to sail from Bordeaux for South America. It was hard to get there with all public transport at a standstill, but Joan Alavedra found two taxi-drivers willing to make the trip. They burned all correspondence in their files, so as not to compromise the anti-fascist refugees left behind. After two days on the road, via Perpignan, Narbonne and Toulouse, they found Bordeaux in utter chaos, over-flowing with refugees, trucks, carts and cars loaded with furniture.

Eventually Alavedra managed to arrange passage on the *Champlain*, but just as they were about to go to the dock they heard the boat had struck a mine dropped by German planes, and had sunk.

Famished and exhausted, with no hope of finding hotel rooms, or even food in the cafés, they had to return to Prades. They started back in the taxis, along roads clogged with troops and refugees, and arrived in Prades at midnight, but when they came to the Grand Hotel they found the doors padlocked. Alavedra pounded on the doors, and the proprietor who had been so honoured by their presence appeared at an upstairs window. He told them there was no room, they were full up. Alavedra begged for beds for the night and said Casals was ill.

Casals recalled the moment in his autobiography. The hotel owner said: 'The Germans may arrive at any time. What if they find I have given shelter to Casals? Everyone knows he is an enemy of the Nazis. I have my family to think of.' With that he closed the window.

Opposite the hotel was the Grand Café. The proprietor's wife, Pierrette Hostelrich, woken by the noise, offered them a room. After a few days they found temporary accommodation and she provided them with furniture. Casals would stay in Prades for almost two decades.

Many of those trying to escape were artists, writers and intellectuals, 'the flower of European culture', who had already fled the Nazis in Germany and other occupied countries. The refugees descended on Marseille, where they hoped to be able to take a boat, or find a way across the Pyrenees into Spain, and either British-controlled Gibraltar, or neutral Portugal.

For a few weeks at the beginning it was possible to escape through the coastal frontier points. The international station at Cerbère on the coast was the most obvious point of departure for many. Here on Friday 13 September 1940 – the inauspicious date was sourly noted – a bizarre party scrambled their way up the steep cliffs that divide Cerbère from Port Bou, the first village on the other side of the frontier. Alma Mahler was clad in a billowing white dress, and clutched a bag containing her jewels and the precious Bruckner manuscript which in happier times had hung in the marble hall of her Vienna home. This was the latest scene in a dramatic life. After the death of her husband Gustav Mahler, for whom she had given up her own musical ambition, Alma had had an affair with Oskar Kokoschka, who painted her as the Bride of the Wind. Then she had married Walter Gropius, founder of the Bauhaus movement. Three of her four children had died. Now at sixty she was accompanied by the last great passion of her life, the Czech writer, Franz Werfel, ten years her junior. He was under sentence of death for his anti-Nazi writings, in particular *The Forty Days of Musa Dagh*, published in 1933, a novel about the Armenian genocide which anticipated the siege of the Warsaw ghetto and was believed to be an allegory about Nazism.

Both were more used to taking taxis than climbing mountains, and Werfel had a heart condition. Their companions were Heinrich Mann and his wife Nelly. Heinrich, brother of Thomas Mann, had been a very popular novelist in Germany, but his anti-militarism was not appreciated by the Nazis and he had gone into exile in France in 1933. He had been living in Nice, smuggling his anti-Nazi writings back into Germany, where he was now banned. He was author of the novel that would become *The Blue Angel*, starring Marlene Dietrich. With them was Golo, the son of Thomas Mann, who had been a history professor at Renne University before he was interned. All were being actively sought by the Gestapo. They were accompanied as a guide by Dick Ball, an American ambulance corps driver who had landed up in France in the 1930s, and as a travelling salesman for his lard factory outside Paris had got to know France well. He spoke the language with a foul-mouthed fluency all his own.

Alma Mahler recalled the climb in her autobiography. 'It was sheer, slippery terrain that we crawled up, bounded by precipices. Mountain goats could scarcely have kept their footing on the glassy, shimmering slate. If you skidded there was nothing but thistles to hold onto.' Finally they all scrambled up, and were stopped at once by French *gardes-mobiles*, the motorised police force. Their prospects looked grim.

The refugees had all brought with them a giant stack of luggage, despite being told only to bring essentials. Alma had insisted on her twelve suitcases, which contained original scores of Mahler's music, not to mention her clothes. The luggage was travelling by train, through the tunnel to Port Bou and to Spain with their American saviour, Varian Fry. He had been obliged to lie on the floor of the toilet to burn the forged documents they no longer required and he did not want to be found with.

Varian Fry, sometimes called 'the American Schindler', a preppy young American in suit, bow tie and horn-rimmed glasses, had arrived in Marseille in August on behalf of the American Emergency Rescue Committee. He brought with him $3,000, a list of artists and intellectuals stranded in France, and a fierce commitment to rescue them from the Nazis. Fry had been a reporter in Berlin in 1935 when he had seen the growing Nazi threat, and witnessed the violence and brutal attacks on Jews at first hand. 'I saw with my own eyes young Nazi toughs gather and smash up Jewish-owned cafés, watched with horror as they dragged Jewish patrons from their seats, drove hysterical, crying women down the street, knocked over an elderly man and kicked him in the face.' His reports made the front pages of the *New York Times*.

So in 1940 when the Germans invaded France he knew what was coming. One of the most sinister terms of the armistice signed in July stipulated that people were obliged to 'surrender on demand' anyone the Gestapo wished to interrogate, imprison, intern in concentration camps or return to Germany for trial.

Fry realised that many refugee artists, writers and politicians were at great risk, and must be rescued before the noose tightened further. His list included Germans like Konrad Heiden, Hitler's biographer (who claimed to have coined the term Nazi which Hitler was forced to adopt, despite the fact that it meant 'bumpkin' in Bavarian slang), the philosopher and critic Walter Benjamin, the Jewish novelist Lion Feuchtwanger, who had been deprived of his German citizenship, and the poet Walter Mehring, whose books had been burnt by the Nazis in 1933. All were high on the Nazis' execution list. Among others on Fry's list were André Gide, Marcel Duchamp, André Breton, Max Ernst (who had refused to return to Germany on Nazi orders, and had married a Jew), Marc Chagall and Henri Matisse.

As soon as Fry reached Marseille, he was besieged by people desperate to escape. Marseille was a tough, edgy city with a thriving underworld. Its Vieux Port contained a network of hidden streets, and was honeycombed with secret underground passages. Now it was crammed with refugees, who filled all the hotels and even the brothels (these were considered safer because there was no register for the police to inspect). The French police were on edge, and would sometimes subject them all to a *rafle*, a mass round-up. You could be picked up anywhere any time, and end up in jail, or back in a concentration camp. The Kundt commission of German army officers and Gestapo agents were visiting French concentration camps and selecting those to be sent back to Germany. Even in the Unoccupied zone the Germans made their authority known: a large car running on precious petrol would purr to a halt, and out of it stepped German army officers, very correct in their long grey overcoats, shiny black leather boots and peaked caps adorned with eagles and swastikas.

Arriving at the American consulate visa section, Fry saw the signs that would dismay so many:

APPLICATIONS FROM CENTRAL EUROPE CLOSED.

PASSAGE FROM LISBON SOLD OUT FOR MONTHS.

It seemed as if there was no way out, especially as it soon became clear that the Americans were not at all keen on refugees. They presumed that if they were anti-fascists they were probably Reds, and communists would not be admitted to the United States. Only Vice-Consul Hiram Bingham was doing anything to help, trying to speed up visas, even hiding refugees in his own home. He told Fry that US policy was, 'Issue all the visas you want, but not to those people who apply for them.' But Fry was determined, and immediately addressed himself to the problem of obtaining visas, tickets and boat passages and distributing funds. A committed team soon emerged around him, of refugees with connections, sympathetic French citizens and other Americans who donated money and time to the cause. Under cover of relief work, handing out meal tickets and emergency funds, they arranged escapes from French internment camps, forged passports and other vital travel documents, arranged boat passages and discreetly investigated illegal border crossings.

Fry made contact with others in Marseille who were officially working with refugees – Richard Allen of the Red Cross, Howard Kershner of the Quakers and Donald Lowrie of the YMCA, with whom he cooperated in printing false passports. Before long his name was on everyone's lips – he heard that in Toulouse a man was selling it for 50 francs to refugees bound for Marseille. A constant stream of people arrived at his room in the Hôtel Splendide. At first he had expected to stay only a few weeks, rescue his list and return to America, but it became clear that there was much more to be done. Soon his operation extended way beyond his initial list, some of whom in any case were already dead. He heard for example that the German art critic Karl Einstein had hanged himself at the Spanish frontier when he found he could not cross.

Fry struggled to help as many refugees as he could, though he found it invidious and unfair to have to choose those who could go. 'See you in New York,' he would say to them, inspiring confidence with his immaculate dress, the handkerchief in his breast pocket and a carnation in his lapel.

He found office space and set up the Centre Américain de Secours, with a polyglot medley of staff; as well as Dick Ball, they included a German political refugee who had volunteered for the French army; an

Austrian Catholic; Lena, a multilingual Russian travelling on a Polish passport; an Austrian cartoonist whose cartoons depicting Hitler had not gone down well, and whose talents were turned to forging documents. Plus a crew of underworld characters who helped Fry launder the funds being raised in the US, and included the owner of a café who was also head of one of Marseille's Corsican gangs.

After the first few months Fry was exhausted by the pressures in Marseille and had rented a villa outside the city, the Villa Air-Bel, where he could work in peace; it was a magnificent decaying mansion, and soon attracted a motley company of guests, in particular André Breton, the dean of the Surrealists, who held reunions on Sunday afternoons of his Surrealist disciples, most of whom were waiting for visas. 'The whole Deux Magots crowd,' Fry wrote, 'as mad as ever.' Food was scarce (rarely bread or meat, just boiled squash or artichokes, pasta without sauce or oil; they even ate the goldfish from the pond) but they had lots of wine, and conversation was entertaining. Visitors included Max Ernst, Kay Boyle, Consuelo de Saint-Exupéry and Peggy Guggenheim.

When Fry began his rescue work there had been a brief window of hope. At first the Germans were focused on tightening up the demarcation line, and at that point were actually rounding up Jews from Germany and Poland and dumping them in the Unoccupied zone of France. When the Vichy government tried to deliver Jews to them in the Occupied zone some were even sent back.

Refugees who were actively wanted by the Germans were caught in a Catch-22. In order to leave France by plane or ship they needed to apply for an exit visa, but to do so meant betraying their presence. Thus only one way out remained: the Pyrenees. To begin with the Spanish police were not concerned about exit visas, only that people had transit visas, so all they wanted to see was a Portuguese visa.

Fry's team had checked out the route over the Pyrenees, via the cliffs between Cerbère and Port Bou. To avoid the French frontier post at Cerbère, the escapees had to leave the railway station, walk down to the cemetery, climb the wall and then up the slope. It was no great distance, but it was very steep and difficult terrain, exposed to the elements and easily visible from the town. Then they were to go to the Spanish border post at Port Bou for an entrada stamp.

Alma Mahler and Franz Werfel were among the first refugees Fry tried to help. Fry found them in their hotel room in Marseille. Franz, whom Alma once described as 'a stocky man with sensuous lips and large, beautiful blue eyes under a Goethean forehead', looked according to the prosaic American 'large, dumpy and pallid like a half sack of flour' attired in a silk dressing gown. Alma, once a great hostess in Vienna, proffered chocolates and Benedictine, her favourite tipple.

The Werfels had escaped from Austria after the Anschluss in 1938. They had been living in Sanary-sur-Mer on the Côte d'Azur, then something of a writers' colony which had also included Aldous Huxley and Arthur Koestler. Once war was declared the local police soon became suspicious, so they went to Paris to avoid arrest and internment. Then when France collapsed in June they joined the rush of terrified people heading south in the June heatwave.

After expensive taxi rides around the south-west the Werfels landed up in Lourdes, on the 'free' side of the demarcation line. There they bumped into Walter Mehring, the voice of radical Berlin till Hitler threw him out. He was lurking in a souvenir shop, in the same predicament as the Werfels. They managed to make their way to Marseille, and had got hold of American visas but had no exit permits. After frustrated attempts to leave by sea, they resigned themselves to crossing the Pyrenees. Since none were very accustomed to hiking, they all hoped this would be by train, until they heard the news that Spain had closed its border to those without nationalities or passports, that is, those who had been stripped of citizenship by Hitler. They decided to chance the train all the same.

The party had gathered on 12 September at Gare St Charles in Marseille at 5 a.m., travelling first class, so as to be less suspicious, through the dark outskirts of Marseille, past the wild flatland of the Camargue along the coast to Sète, and its huge port and a first glimpse of sea. It was a very hot day. They arrived at Perpignan, where they had to change trains, and had a three-hour wait. Fry insisted they stayed in the station. (Walter Mehring, the little poet who was to prove one of Fry's most tiresome charges, later disobeyed this instruction. He had blithely strolled out to a café for a glass of wine and was arrested at once and put in the concentration camp of St-Cyprien. Only by the efforts of Fry and the Quakers was he winkled out, to turn up like a bad penny in Marseille. Mehring's misadventures were the plague of Fry's life, till Mehring finally got away.)

The train to Cerbère was smaller and slower, but they could see the Pyrenees ahead. Here they were in concentration-camp country, as Fry well knew, since his team was in the process of collecting reports on the camps, and were especially concerned about the numbers of children still interned there. Beyond the sandy beaches of the Golfe du Lion they tunnelled into the Albères, the arid hills that form the final easternmost reach of the Pyrenees before they plunge into the sea. Through shadowy canyons carved from the rocks, past terraced vineyards and glimpses of cool blue sea, they passed the stations of Collioure and Port-Vendres, through another tunnel to the little white-washed fishing village of Banyuls, and finally arrived at the viaduct of Cerbère, from which the station looked down on the town below.

The journey had taken twelve hours, and by the time they arrived the sun was already sinking behind the hill. Ahead they could see the rails that should take them to Spain. But they had to leave the train – Spanish railways have a different gauge of track, so all were obliged to change trains – there were police on the platform and all the passengers were lined up for inspection. Nobody without an exit visa would be allowed to travel on to Port Bou. Since the only thing they could be sure of was the inconsistency of both the rules and the border officials, they decided to stay in Cerbère and try again the next day.

But the next morning prospects looked no better, and they gloomily accepted the necessity of going over the cliff on foot. Fry was highly dubious about the Werfels and the infirm Heinrich Mann, but they would have to manage. He bought them lots of packs of Gauloises and Gitanes for the Spanish guards, and they set off, with Ball to lead them across the hillside until the customs post at Port Bou came in sight. Fry, who was 'en règle' with an exit visa, would go through on the train with the luggage.

It took only twenty minutes before he was in Port Bou, and then he began to fret about his charges, and walked up the hill to try and find them.

Guards had stopped the party of escapees and asked them if they were looking for Spain. When they admitted that they were, the guards miraculously pointed out the footpath. At the border the Spanish officials looked hard at Golo's affidavit in lieu of passport. 'Are you the son of Thomas Mann?' asked one of them. Golo would not deny it.

'I am honoured to make your acquaintance.' The Spaniard bowed. 'The son of so great a man.'

They made it to Barcelona, then to Madrid, and finally took ship from Lisbon to the USA. They ended up in Hollywood, where Werfel finished the novel he had begun in Lourdes, which was made into a highly successful movie, *The Song of Bernadette*, before his death in 1945.

Organising the border crossing was always nerve-racking for Fry and his team. They never knew what would happen. Some refugees were stopped and searched, some had luggage sent through and collected it successfully. But then they heard that someone who went over the day after the Werfels had seen uniformed German officers on the road near the cemetery of Cerbère. What was much worse, some of the successful escapees had sent indiscreet postcards back with details of their escape, thus compromising the escape route. They needed to change the route.

At this point Fry met the Fittkos, who were then living in Banyuls, close to the frontier, planning their own escape. Hans and Lisa Fittko had been on the run for a long time. Both were Germans who had been committed to the struggle against fascism since Hitler's rise to power. And Lisa was Jewish. She had gone into hiding in Berlin after 1933 when the arrests and torture began, but soon had to escape. In Prague she met Hans, another fugitive. They continued to smuggle anti-Nazi literature into Germany, until the Gestapo tracked them down and they escaped again to Switzerland, where they lived on false passports. Through the 1930s they kept moving, still printing counter-propaganda, escaped again to Holland and finally to Paris.

In a photograph from that time Lisa looks so pretty, slim, with curly dark hair and dark eyes, a full mouth with a distinctly defiant expression. While she was impulsive and impatient, Hans was always calm and analytical, restrained with a discipline born of years of clandestine activism.

When war broke out they were interned as enemy aliens. Lisa was taken to the Paris indoor sports stadium the Vél d'Hiv, along with thousands of other women, with a light suitcase and a blanket. She wrote a list of personal essentials:

Toothbrush
A pot with a handle, a spoon
Lipstick
Razor blades [in case there was no other way out]

The German women were packed onto trains and sent south, jeered at and stoned by the French along the way. They were sent to Gurs, a camp in the western Pyrenees near Pau, originally erected for Spanish Republicans. Now 10,000 women arrived. (The camp commandant had apparently collapsed in a faint when he learned that so many were coming.) On the first day all those who were pregnant spontaneously aborted. Conditions were disgusting: barracks with rows of straw pallets, open latrines, washing at an open trough in front of the guards. Lisa recalled the satisfaction of stealing a few nails to hang things on. On a meagre diet of chickpea soup, soon most had dysentery.

The clay soil became a sea of mud when it rained. A survivor recalled: 'Gurs was a camp full of mud. It was clay. When it rained, you sank into the clay up to your knees. One woman choked to death in the mud. I would not say Gurs was Auschwitz, but it was what they called the little Hell before the big one, meaning Auschwitz.'

Today the camp at Gurs has become a memorial. You can walk down the paths through the woods where the barracks used to be, and visit the cemetery with its rows of graves. A simple but affecting sculpture of rails disappears into the distance, the prospect for many of the inmates.

Lisa knew she had to get out before the Germans came for her, and needed to find Hans, who had also been interned. In the chaos after the military collapse in June she managed to escape. It was second nature to her to maintain a network of contacts and details of other refugees, and soon the refugee telegraph put her in touch with Hans, last seen heading for Montauban on a 'liberated' bicycle. There they met up again. Both had managed to find adequate papers; Hans a military release pass, Lisa a forged camp release certificate and a travel permit issued by a sympathetic French commandant in Lourdes. Learning of Article 19, the clause to 'surrender on demand', they realised their lives were at stake. They had to get out of France. They went to Toulouse where they stayed in a cinema cleared for refugees, several hundred sleeping on the bare floor. Like so many others they headed for Marseille. There they managed to find acommodation in a school auditorium, along with Lisa's brother and family.

Where would they go? They had no connections, money or legal papers. Boats to the United States or South America sounded like fantasy. Perhaps they could get a transit visa to Portugal without a final destination visa. Or perhaps they should simply go underground in France – after all they were used to that. They managed to get passports from the Czech embassy and a Chinese visa for a hundred francs. (These were readily available, though it turned out later that the Chinese characters apparently read: 'It is strictly forbidden for the bearer of this document under any circumstances to set foot on Chinese soil.') They queued for Portuguese transit visas, then for Spanish visas. Only the French exit visa was impossible, because to apply for it would reveal their presence to the Germans. They would still have to cross the border illegally.

In mid-September, Lisa set off for Port-Vendres to scout out the territory. The Cerbère route had become too well known, but she made contact with the sympathetic socialist mayor of Banyuls, Vincent Azéma, who told her about a secret smugglers' route over the mountains. But he wisely insisted they must organise the crossing themselves. 'Perhaps one day I will no longer be here,' he said.

He offered to help with housing and food, and handed her cans of milk and vegetables. It was a heavy load for Lisa to carry back along the path between the cliff walls from Banyuls back to Port-Vendres, but what did that matter, she wrote in her memoir, *Escape through the Pyrenees*:

> Milk and vegetables and above all a new, safe border route. I remember returning on that path back then and seeing the region with open eyes for the very first time – the incredibly blue sea and the mountain chain, on its slopes green vineyards with a hint of gold between them, and a sky as blue as the sea.

While Lisa was in Port-Vendres, staying in an attic room with a group of other émigrés, she received a visitor. It was Walter Benjamin, the German-Jewish critic and philosopher who had escaped Berlin and been living in Paris. He was forty-eight, rather stout, unfit and awkward, his grey hair close-cropped but his gaze, Lisa recalled, still searching behind the thick lenses of his round glasses.

'Gnädige Frau.' He bowed politely. 'Please forgive the intrusion – I hope this is not an inopportune moment.' Hans had told him that Lisa could help him across the border. 'That was just like him,' wrote Lisa, 'always taking it for granted that I'd manage.'

Lisa explained to Benjamin that the route was strenuous, but he insisted, explaining that he would have to walk slowly because he had heart trouble. And he wanted to bring with him two more refugees he had met in Marseille, Henny Gurland and her son. By this time Benjamin was truly desperate. He had already tried, along with another grey-haired German professor, to disguise himself as a French sailor, in order to board a freighter from Marseille. It didn't work.

Lisa and Benjamin went to see Azéma again in Banyuls to make sure of the route, and they decided to explore it partway. After a couple of hours when Lisa was ready to return, Benjamin insisted he would stay the night in the open and wait for them there, in order to conserve his strength. Early next morning Lisa and the others rejoined him, and they set off on a gruelling journey, first through the steep amphitheatre of terraced vineyards heavy with ripe grapes, then over rough mountain tracks, sometimes on all fours. The climb finally brought them to a point from which the coastlines of France and Spain were clearly visible.

After the steep ascent to the plateau between Banyuls and the slopes east of Cerbères, the route headed south, then looped around the ridgeline that is also the international border. It was a secure route because the path ran parallel to the road that led along the mountain ridge, an ancient smugglers' path concealed by the mountain over-hang, so they could not be seen by French border sentries who pa-trolled above. At some places the road and path ran close and they had to be very quiet.

Benjamin stopped every ten minutes to rest for one minute. He had worked it all out precisely, as an intellectual exercise. While he was interned in a concentration camp near Nevers, the previous winter, where he had met Hans Fittko, he had decided to give up smoking on the principle, 'I can bear the conditions in this camp only if I'm compelled to concentrate my mental strength on one single effort. Giving up smoking costs me this effort, and thus will be my deliverance.'

He refused to be parted from his black leather briefcase, heavy with his last precious manuscript (a subject of speculation to this day). Though critically respected, Benjamin was still a struggling, poverty-stricken writer. He is now considered one of the foremost original thinkers of the twentieth century; he was the first to consider the city as a place of memory, to appreciate the topography of the metropolis as a world of life and experience, once trying to draw a map of his life in Berlin. He is best known today for the Arcades Project, a labyrinthine exploration of Paris. His writing can be lyrically beautiful but also obscure. (About an essay on language, even his biographer Momme Brodersen says: 'This text seems to reach the outermost limits of what is still linguistically and logically comprehensible to mere mortals.')

There is a sad irony in the image of this urban philosopher strug-gling for his life on the rugged mule paths of the Pyrenees. Finally, after walking for nine hours, they saw the sea and Spain before them, and Lisa left them to make their way down to the border post at Port Bou. But when they arrived they were told by the Spanish customs that though they had US visas and Spanish visas they must now produce a French exit visa; they were not allowed into Spain, and would be escorted back to France the next day. Benjamin was trapped on the frontier unable to go forward or back, in total despair. He committed suicide that night, 26 September, with a heavy dose of morphine. The manuscript has never been found.

Now there is a remarkable memorial sculpture to Walter Benjamin by the Israeli artist Dani Karavan outside the cemetery where he is buried in Port Bou. A rusted metal chute descends from the cliff down to the sea, pink against the blue of the water. In the glass frame at the bottom of the chute you can see white waves pounding threateningly, and as you walk down the steps within the chute it is as if you are plunging to certain death. Climbing back up again to the small square of sky above invokes an unlikely but palpable sense of hope. On the glass is engraved this quotation from Walter Benjamin: 'It is more arduous to honour the memory of the nameless than that of the renowned. Historical construction is devoted to the memory of the nameless.' Benjamin's younger brother, Georg, who had continued to publish communist underground newspapers under the Nazis, died two years later, in August 1942, in Mauthausen concentration camp.

Hans summoned Lisa back to Marseille by telegram; transit visas had to be renewed at once. Then they met up with Varian Fry, who wanted to know about the new escape route Lisa had discovered. He proposed that they should stay in France to escort other refugees. Even though helping men of military age over the border carried the death penalty, they could not refuse. After the years they had devoted to the cause of freedom, and the risks they had taken, it would all have been meaningless if now they decided to save their own skins. Just this last time, said Lisa. They would only accept money for essentials, they didn't want to be paid. There were plenty of others with their hands out, people-smugglers who sometimes charged extortionate fees for the passage, and even occasionally abandoned their charges.

The mayor of Banyuls found them a house, identity cards and ration cards. They were identified as French refugees, and the locals soon got used to them; even the local gendarmes turned a blind eye. For the next few months, two or three times a week they smuggled groups of refugees over the mountain route to Spain. They would set out early in the morning, leaving the village with the vineyard workers, dressed in dungarees and espadrilles, carrying only a canvas lunch bag. When Hans and Lisa returned they always brought firewood with them, needed anyway for cooking and heating as the weather grew colder. Often the refugees were difficult. They were old or sick, they grumbled about the distance, one refused to abandon his fur coat. The British were always a problem, so tall and fair in contrast to the short dark Catalans, and they always spoke dreadful schoolboy French. But they were strong, self-disciplined, and never complained.

At the end of November, Mayor Azéma was removed from office and replaced by someone loyal to the Vichy government. Food, much of which was requisitioned by the Germans, was becoming more and more difficult to find, and soon Lisa fell seriously ill, with jaundice, and had to spend a month in hospital in Perpignan. Finally on 25 May 1941, a month before Hitler invaded the Soviet Union, a decree of the Vichy government proclaimed that all border areas had to be cleared of foreigners within ten days. They had to leave.

I had been told there was a memorial to the Fittkos in Banyuls, and since Banyuls has always been one of my favourite places on the coast, less crowded, more down-to-earth than Collioure, it was pleasant to spend a day there. There are a few more restaurants along the harbour now, some dubious modern pavement tiling and rather too many estate agents, but it is still recognisably the old fishing port, marina to one side, to the other the old village of steep cobbled streets winding up from the harbour, the whitewashed walls festooned with splashes of purple bougainvillea.

My enquiries yielded nothing. No one seemed to know about the Fittkos any more. Finally I asked at the *mairie*. (I was pleased to note that the list of mayors engraved in marble included Mayor Azéma, the friend of Fittko, who though dismissed in 1941 and replaced by a Vichy appointed delegation, had returned in 1945 and remained there until 1953.) The deputy mayor was called. He shook me by the hand and, typically, instead of giving me directions he insisted on taking me there himself, so we drove a kilometre or two inland, across a bridge and up to the old village of Banyuls, Puig-del-Mas, the original inland village, which was on the route the Fittkos took with their charges. In the middle of a housing estate of curious children and barking dogs, there it was, a simple slab of rusting iron on the ground, representing the path, pointing out to the hills beyond. The inscription, in English and German, pays tribute to the Fittkos: 'Despite being in danger them-selves they guided others, persecuted by the Nazi regime, to the other side of the Pyrenees.'

The deputy mayor's name was Escalida. I asked if he was Spanish. He explained that his mother was from Tarragona and his father from Barcelona and they had both come to France in the Retirada, crossing the Pyrenees in the other direction. His mother, aged about five, was put in the Rivesaltes concentration camp near Perpignan. 'They came to take some of them to work in these vineyards,' explained Escalida, 'but then delayed paying them . . .' he added bitterly.

I spent the night in the Hôtel Canal, where many of the fugitives stayed before crossing the mountains. With the collusion of the *patron*, it was often crammed with refugees and escaped soldiers. It doesn't seem to have changed much. It is a couple of streets back from the harbour, a classic old-fashioned *pension* hotel, where you get a ring to keep your napkin for the next meal. The dining room has Spanish patterned tiles on the floor, wooden wainscoting, and bevelled glass

French windows stretching the length of the façade. At the door an old man and a little boy were sitting together on the step, surveying the street. Behind them blared a dubbed Clint Eastwood film on TV.

I enquired about the refugees, and was given a key for the attic rooms upstairs. Under the sloping ceiling were simple single beds, wooden furniture, bare floorboards. From the window you could see over the terracotta roof tiles and chimney pots of the village, to the sea in one direction, the hills in the other. You could also look down several storeys to the street, and any passing gendarmes or military. What hope and fear these humble little rooms must have seen.

The Fittkos left Banyuls for Cassis, a small fishing port between Toulon and Marseille, where Lisa's brother was living, evading checkpoints at the stations they passed through on the way. There they spent the summer, bathing in the clear blue sea, grilling sardines and eluding the police. There is a photo of the group of refugees, with rocky white cliffs and sea behind them, Hans in dark glasses, shorts and espadrilles, Lisa in a bikini top she has made from her Provençal headscarf. They look almost relaxed. But by the autumn of 1941 they were still struggling to renew expired documents to satisfy the Kafka-esque bureaucracy, and find another way out of France.

They were assisted by the American Emergency Rescue Committee, though Varian Fry himself had been expelled. He had long been under suspicion, but his cover was comprehensively blown by the novelist Lion Feuchtwanger, who when he reached the USA in safety gave interviews to the *New York Times* describing his daring escape and the Americans who had helped him. Then German radio reported they had uncovered a refugee smuggling ring, and the Spanish border was officially closed.

Fry had been more and more closely watched. It was very hard to send telegrams, or any messages, so they came up with a scheme to use toothpaste tubes. Messages were written on onionskin paper snipped into single lengths, glued end to end and tightly rolled, wrapped in a condom and inserted through the crimped end of the tube.

Fry was frequently questioned, and on one occasion imprisoned in Marseille during a round-up to tidy up the streets for a visit from Pétain. Neither the French authorities, the Germans nor the Americans approved of what Fry was doing. Eventually he was arrested and thrown out at the end of August 1941. In all his operation had helped about 4,000 refugees, and enabled about 2,000 to escape. All this was done without the approval, indeed with the distinct disapproval, of the United States consulate in Marseille.

On his return Fry became an editor for *The New Republic*, writing about France. His most vehement article entitled 'The Massacre of the Jews', published in December 1942, about the deportations from France, was prophetic. In 1996 he was posthumously honoured by Yad Vashem as the only American to be named Righteous among the Nations, to have saved Jews from the Holocaust.

The Fittkos were finally issued with visas for Cuba. They could sail from Lisbon. They took the train for Cerbère and crossed into Spain, their documentation legal, but with a few too many tubes of toothpaste and shaving cream in their luggage.

# CHAPTER 9

# ESCAPE NETWORKS

Helping Allied servicemen to return to the fight was a priority for the escape lines crossing the Pyrenees. After the fall of France there were thousands of British and Allied soldiers and downed airmen, Belgian, Dutch and Polish, who headed south, hoping to cross the Pyrenees to Spain and Gibraltar. Most lacked documents, money for food, or any means to exchange their uniforms for civilian clothes. Few spoke more than schoolboy French. Often they had untreated wounds.

Private Gordon Laming was one of them. He was recommended to me by the Royal Escaping Society, and I went to meet him at the charming red-brick villa in a small Buckinghamshire village outside Aylesbury, where he has retired with his wife, after a career as a senior civil servant. Laming, silver-haired but still spry and acute at the age of eighty-eight, sat comfortably surrounded by piles of books, his scholarly manner enlivened by an ironic sense of humour. I was most struck by the sheer modesty with which he described his extraordinary adventures as he tried to escape from the chaos of defeated France in 1940.

When he was called up, aged twenty, in October 1939 he was working as a civil servant in London. He had a Methodist background and little inclination for soldiering, but was nevertheless assigned to the Royal Army Ordnance Corps and sent for basic training in Portsmouth. 'We were only trained to salute officers and march properly. No weapon training at all!' he said. The raw recruits embarked for Cherbourg in March 1940 and ended up in the suburbs of Metz, billeted in a derelict château. 'We were not too worried, as a few miles in front of us was what we believed to be the impregnable Maginot Line,' he told me drily.

On the night of 9 May Laming heard his first bomb drop, and heavy artillery fire, but the German invasion bypassed them completely. 'It seems amazing in view of the mayhem going on in other parts of north-east France. Not that we were told anything about all that! No one ever said keep a lookout for twenty German tanks and a battalion of infantry . . .'

The troops were kept busy with training – Laming fired his rifle for the first time on 10 June, a bit late in view of what was happening elsewhere. They finally had orders to leave on 13 June by train and truck. (The Germans arrived in Metz the next day, they heard later.) The train dragged along, occasionally bombed by Italian planes, and no one had a clue what was happening. Finally they came to a complete halt. The major set off to get information in a nearby village, and heard that the French had asked for an armistice. 'He just told us, "Switzerland is over there. It's every man for himself!" and we jumped off the train and ran into the woods.'

A small group including Laming wandered about rather aimlessly for two days in the Doubs forest, given food by apprehensive villagers, and bivouacking in the woods. 'We were complete innocents. Our training was to obey orders, so we had no idea how to cope with the order, "Every man for himself." '

It seems that the French were no different. 'Some French troops even surrendered to us, not being familiar with the British uniform – they thought we were Germans!'

They were taken in by a French couple in a small village, but on 23 June they heard that the armistice had been agreed. 'There were Germans in the village so we realised we had to get out fast. We were told we were supposed to give ourselves up in Besançon so that's what we pretended to do.' They stopped in a café where Laming drank cognac for his raging toothache, but they were picked up by a German officer and shipped off to the fort in Besançon.

Several thousand prisoners were being held there. Rations were meagre. 'There were army horses tied up in the barracks – they were the ingredients for the midday soup. I had some mints left, about the size of a sixpence, and we broke those up between us.' They were transferred to another barracks where they found most of the rest of their division, and put to work.

Eventually a number of the prisoners devised an escape route, in inimitable British style, via drainage sewers, and at the end of October Laming and several others got out and made their way to a safe house. They were rowed across the Doubs and finally escorted across the demarcation line, where they hid out in the Arbois forest and then found shelter in a magnificent château owned by an English family, where they were served fine food and wine by a very English butler, and telegrams were sent home for them.

They set out for Lyon, but were picked up by gendarmes, and sent to the Fort St Jean internment camp in the Vieux Port of Marseille. 'It was pretty civilised, with passes out for the evening and weekends. It wasn't

difficult getting information about crossing over to Spain. All you had
to do was go and have a cup of tea with Donald Caskie at the Seamen's
Mission.'

Donald Caskie was a devout Scottish Presbyterian who had been
minister of the Scottish church in Paris. Having denounced Hitler in
ringing Scots from the pulpit he felt it best to flee with all the rest in
June 1940. He headed south with his kilt and his Bible. When he
reached Marseille he found the streets and waterfront in a turmoil,
packed with soldiers in a lamentable state, many of them wounded, all
of them hungry, without documents or ration cards. He felt God's call
to stay on, and arranged to reopen the abandoned Seamen's Mission in
the Vieux Port as a place of refuge. There he provided meals, beds and
blankets, washing facilities, playing cards, billiard tables and English
books. He was not supposed to admit soldiers, only civilians and
sailors, but soon he was hiding men in secret boltholes and supplying
them with civilian clothes. Discarded uniforms had to be clandestinely
chucked in the sea.

For a while the authorities were aware of his activities, but they saw
the Mission as a source of information and for a while allowed it to
remain open. Soon anxious soldiers were arriving in droves. 'Knock
three times on the door and ask for Donald Duck,' they were told. In
January 1942 Caskie was forced to close the mission, and in April he was
arrested. He ended up as a chaplain in Grenoble, where he continued
helping with escape and Resistance, until he was arrested again. He was
imprisoned in seven prisons in all, including San Remo in Italy, where
his torments included a stretch in a bottle cell – twenty-four hours in a
hole shaped like a man but not big enough to stand upright. By 1943
he was in the Paris slaughterhouse prison of Fresnes, under a death
sentence, which was lifted after the intervention of a German padre.
Caskie, mercifully, was one who lived to tell his own tale.

Duly equipped by Caskie, and provided with funds for clothing and
train fare by the American consulate (I asked if this was Varian Fry, but
Laming had never heard of him), Gordon Laming set out for Banyuls
by overnight train with four others, seeing the mountains ahead of
them as they approached in the early morning, already with snow on
the hill tops. It was 9 a.m. next day when they arrived. 'We got by the
control at the station, but it was bitterly cold, and we were tempted by
the chance of coffee, and went into a café.' They were immediately
picked up by the local gendarmes, locked up and sent back to Marseille.

About a month later they tried again, this time hiding out in the
Mission for the night, to catch an early train the next day, taking with

them bread, biscuits, tins of salmon paste and figs, provided by the padre. 'This time we arrived in Banyuls at 8.30 in the evening, jumped out of the train *not* on the platform side, ran up the line and hid until the train left. Then we set off in the dark to climb up into the hills.'

Laming considers his escape largely a matter of luck. 'A measure of resolve and determination was graced by good fortune, basically. In our case there were no established escape lines, we simply strode into the Pyrenees hillside at night, ill-clad, with no guide – and no knowledge that such a breed existed, hoping to cope with whatever weather hazards we might encounter in late December.'

Laming is still not sure of the route they followed. 'We just stumbled through the vineyards, and across open fields, keeping the sea to our left,' he recalled. 'We were lucky, there was a full moon, and it was a cloudless night.' At daybreak they headed down into Port Bou. There however they were spotted by the border guards, taken into custody and packed off to jail in Figueres. They ended up like so many British escapees interned in the concentration camp of Miranda del Ebro, west of Zaragoza, where they stayed a month.

'It was a pretty dreary experience,' said Laming, something of an understatement, 'and I still had terrible toothache among all the other problems.' Twice a day the prisoners were obliged to salute the Spanish flag, and chant: 'Viva España, España Grande, España Libre, Viva Franco.' 'Otherwise you got thumped,' said Laming, adding with a little smile: 'But with no capacity for foreign languages, the British just responded with anything that came into their heads, and when it came to Franco there was a certain alliterative unanimity . . . and we reckoned it made it evens for having to give the fascist salute. It didn't seem to do Franco any harm.'

They were finally released and sent to Gibraltar. 'It was good to see British bobbies again. And we were given eggs and sausages for supper, three blankets, a mug and even a knife and fork!'

Perhaps he was lucky. By the autumn of 1940 escape was already becoming a much more dangerous business. Security in the internment camps was tightened up, the Spanish guides were chary and were often obliged to charge more. This was when the escape lines began to develop, in particular the so-called Pat Line, which was originally started by Ian Garrow in 1940, and was known to the Germans as the Acropolis Line because of the number of Greeks involved.

Ian Garrow was a captain in the Seaforth Highlanders, a very tall man with a strong Scottish accent, who had decided to stay on in France rather than escape himself, in order to help other soldiers. He established contacts all along the south coast and with the Spanish network of guides run from Toulouse. Garrow also worked closely with Donald Darling, who in 1940 had been sent to help run an escape line from Marseille into Spain, working under the cover of British vice-consul in charge of refugees, based in Lisbon.

The network soon became very efficient at moving escaped Allied POWs and downed airmen who had evaded capture out of France into Spain and so to Britain. They were provided with false identities and disguised in shabby French clothes, then passed through several agents down the line to the South. They were often fed, hidden in safe houses, or concealed by loyal French people. Everyone involved did so at great risk. Everywhere the Germans had put up posters threatening the death penalty for aiding a foreign soldier. Many suffered that punishment.

All over France were safe houses, and especially in Marseille there were people willing to take grave risks. One was George Rodocanichi, a distinguished grey-haired doctor, then aged sixty-five. He was born in Liverpool of Greek parents, and after medical training in France and service in the First World War had become a naturalised French subject. With the help of his wife and-sister-in-law and nephew, he worked with Caskie to treat wounded soldiers, and help them escape. He ran a safe house in his huge twelve-roomed apartment in the Vieux Port, a flat full of heavy mahogany furniture, with a trusted elderly maid who helped hide and care for hundreds of Allied soldiers on the run. Because of his doctor's practice, people could arrive at his flat at all hours without suspicion. Right from the start of the war Rodocanichi had helped hundreds of Jews in particular, giving them the necessary medical certificates to board immigration ships for the USA.

Another key person in the Marseille network was Louis Nouveau, a French stockbroker with strong ties to Britain. He was an anglophile, always dressed in perfectly cut Savile Row suits and bow tie. His elegant apartment on the Quai Rive Neuve in the Vieux Port was full of art and antiques and had an amazing view of the port. He carefully noted details of each of the escapees who stayed with him, in the margins of volume 44 of his 70-volume complete works of Voltaire, an invaluable record which is now in the Imperial War Museum in London.

Louis Nouveau helped finance the line and also acted as a courier himself, crossing the demarcation line with the 'packages' as they were called, and bringing them to Marseille. Even though Nouveau and

Rodocanichi were family friends neither knew the other was providing a safe house.

Nancy Wake was another larger than life character in Marseille, who became known to the Germans as the White Mouse for her unfailing ability to slip through their hands. After an astonishing career as a secret agent with the Resistance she became the Allies' most decorated servicewoman of the Second World War. As of this writing she is still alive. She was born in New Zealand in 1912, of English and French stock but with Maori blood from her great-grandmother. The family moved to Australia when she was two, but as soon as she was old enough she moved to Britain to work as a journalist. In 1930s Europe she witnessed the rise of Nazism and in Vienna she saw horrific scenes of Jews brutally whipped by Nazi stormtroopers. The sight fed an early determination to work against the Nazis.

In 1939 in Marseille she married Henri Fiocca, a wealthy French industrialist fourteen years her senior. (She was apparently seduced by his ability to tango. 'He was the love of my life,' she said later.) They led a life of luxury in a splendid apartment on a hill overlooking Marseille and its harbour. But once Hitler invaded France both were drawn into the Resistance. By September Nancy was helping soldiers and airmen to return to Britain, feeding them and acting as a courier. Her charges included Air Chief Marshal Sir Lewis Hodges. After his bomber was shot down over France, she helped him to cross the Pyrenees into Spain. Nancy herself made seven attempts to escape across the Pyrenees. She finally succeeded, smuggled out in a coal truck, followed by a forty-seven-hour march over the peaks. She was retrained as a secret agent and parachuted back to support the Maquis in the Auvergne.

The sea provided the other significant means of escape. It was at the little port of Collioure that Pat O'Leary came ashore on his first mission as a secret agent. O'Leary would give his name to the Pat Line (officially known as the PAO Line) which became one of the most famous escape lines of the Second World War. He was aboard the HMS *Fidelity*, a U-boat hunter disguised as a cargo vessel, with a captain and crew who could have walked straight out of a novel by Graham Greene.

Claude Peri and Madeleine Bayard had met in Vietnam in the 1930s, working as French spies. Claude had been born in colonial Hanoi in 1908, where his father was a wireless pioneer. His parents were often absent and he was brought up by Vietnamese maids, in a poverty-stricken colony of brutally oppressed workers. Peri left when he was seventeen in 1925 for naval training in Toulon, but was thrown out after three years, and returned to Indochina. He worked as an insurance agent but his greatest passion was hunting elephant. Madeleine was a Parisian, the illegitimate daughter of a seamstress. Madeleine had married a rubber plantation owner and went to Vietnam in 1932, to live a life of luxury as an elegant colonial wife, while the menace from disaffected workers grew around them. She and Claude apparently met when he rescued her after she had been raped in a rebellion of workers on her husband's plantation.

By 1937 they were both working as spies, for a French government increasingly worried by communist influence and Japanese aggression in Indochina. They were experts in the use of plastic explosive, and with the prospect of war they returned to France. Claude had a brilliant scheme to travel undercover through Nazi Germany, Turkey, Syria, India and Thailand, driving himself in a black Ford. He was a plausible character and his many adventures in an increasingly tense Europe included a very convivial dinner with Göring, who made him a member of the German Hunting Association. He finally met up with Madeleine and her beloved terrier, Totoche, in Calcutta, a final hiatus of hedonistic freedom.

They returned to Paris, from where they were sent to Marseille with suitcases full of explosives. There they boarded the SS *Le Rhin*, an ancient merchant vessel with a single funnel and vertical bow, and sailed for Casablanca. Claude seems to have persuaded the captain to give him charge of the ship, while Madeleine played with Totoche and practised her marksmanship with a pair of pearl-handled pistols. In Casablanca they occupied themselves blowing up German U-boats. After the fall of France they switched from the French to become British agents. They returned to Marseille, headed for Paris for instructions, and found themselves in the chaotic exodus south, in a truck they had loaded with machine guns.

In Marseille they found *Le Rhin* miraculously unbombed and filled it up with anything they could find on the docks: paper, scrubbing brushes, jute sacking, pig iron, cement, medical supplies, 6,000 pairs of leather boots and 10,000 bottles of claret. They recruited a crew of mixed nationalities, but mainly French, and sailed for Gibraltar.

It was here they met Albert Guérisse, alias Pat O'Leary. Guérisse had been with a Belgian cavalry regiment in May 1940. He managed to escape to England through Dunkirk, and offered his services to the British. He persuaded the British Navy to take him, and was commissioned as Lieutenant Commander Patrick Albert O'Leary RN, taking the name of a Canadian friend. In Gibraltar Claude and O'Leary made a start on the claret, and soon these two mavericks became firm friends.

Claude was determined the ship should be used to support the British, though most of the crew wanted to take orders from the French. A dramatic fight ensued for control of the vessel, but Claude eventually prevailed and most of the crew left the ship. Claude persuaded the British to take him on, along with his ship. 'It was as if he planned to win the war all by himself,' they observed drily, accepting that this eccentric, belligerent character could indeed be of use to them.

Claude changed his name to Jack Langlais, Lieutenant Commander RN, and adopted a British naval uniform. After major refitting in Britain, *Le Rhin* was equipped with disguised cannons and machine guns, and rechristened HMS *Fidelity*. The ship set sail again, to carry out secret missions in the Mediterranean, packed to the gills with explosives, but disguised as a cargo vessel. This ruse solved the problem of Madeleine too, since in wartime women were not allowed to serve on fighting ships. Now Madeleine's presence could improve the disguise. She thus became the only woman to serve on a British fighting ship during the war. HMS *Fidelity*'s first mission under SOE was to land two groups of agents on the south coast of France and pick up escapers.

Pat O'Leary was on board on his first mission. The *Fidelity* set course for the southern French coast, where O'Leary's instructions were to drop off two agents with a radio – they were to establish a two-way escape and infiltration route across the Pyrenees. Then his mission was to rescue twelve officers from the Polish air force, hidden in Collioure by the Resistance, presumably Spanish contacts of Garrow, since there was little organised French resistance at this point.

On a cold night with the Tramontane blowing, HMS *Fidelity* lay two miles offshore, all lights doused, the engines silent. It was O'Leary's first mission, and the parting with Claude was emotional. At midnight the old lifeboat with its 5 hp engine was swung over the side and six men climbed in along with bicycles, luggage and a radio set. The radio operator, Egbert Rizzo, an elderly Maltese civil engineer, was codenamed Aromatic, due to his exotic smell.

It took nearly an hour, while tension rose, to get the outboard motor going. One of the crew members, Fergusson, whose real name was Fourcade, came from Le Barcarès and reckoned he knew the coastline intimately. He confidently took the tiller. As they approached the coast, they cut the motor, and began rowing, hands poised on their revolvers, until they reached sand. They could see nothing, there was just the sound of the wind whipping the waves into crests. Two men steadied the boat while the agents climbed out, Aromatic with the radio high on his shoulders. The lifeboat was pushing off again when they heard a frantic cry.

'You've put us on an island!'

They had landed on a sandbank and had to be taken off again.

Finally they really struck shore and the agents successfully disembarked and disappeared into the night. Unfortunately the boat was now firmly embedded in the sand. They were obliged to unload all the ballast, until they could free the vessel and set course for Collioure.

The pick-up of the escapers was due to take place at dawn on 23 April on the stone breakwater of Collioure harbour, but delays meant they were an hour late in arriving and dawn was already lightening the sky as they approached the harbour. They could dimly perceive a line of fishing boats, a few nets on the sea wall, and then at the end of the jetty they spotted their connection, the leader of the group of fugitives, wearing a Basque beret and a red scarf around his neck as planned.

'How far is this from Perpignan?' they hissed.

'I'm sorry, but I'm a stranger here myself,' was the reply.

Password and answer. But the Polish airmen had expected the boat the night before and were now asleep at their hotel. O'Leary cursed. 'How long will they be?'

'Not long, don't worry. Come into the harbour.' O'Leary was dubious, surveying the houses along the shore, roof tiles glinting red in the rising sun, but in they went and waited, pretending they were fishing from the boat. But then a man in uniform appeared and challenged them, demanding to see their papers. When they did not respond, he disappeared, and quickly O'Leary and his team started the motor and put out to sea again. It was rough, the wind got up, and suddenly the engine stopped. The petrol pipe had broken and petrol was flooding the boat. At this moment a French cutter appeared, full steam from Port-Vendres, alerted by the Collioure customs official, and they were lost. They managed to slip the grenades and machine guns overboard as they were towed into Port-Vendres.

Under questioning they claimed to be Frenchmen trying to reach de Gaulle, hoping for sympathetic support. But it was not to be. As they were marched off they attempted to escape, but O'Leary was captured and taken to prison in Toulon.

HMS *Fidelity* waited in vain for the appointed rendezvous at 6 a.m. that morning. Nobody returned. They had no idea what had happened to them. Claude and Madeleine continued operations, dropping off agents at Canet and Leucate and picking up escaped prisoners of war. They did not see O'Leary again until December 1942, when he appeared in Liverpool before Claude and Madeleine set course for Burma. He adored them both, but felt the greatest affinity with Claude, 'the finest warrior I have ever known', according to O'Leary. The *Fidelity* was torpedoed by German U-boats in the Atlantic on New Year's Eve 1942. The bodies of Claude and Madeleine were never found.

O'Leary meanwhile ended up in St-Hippolyte-du-Fort, near Nîmes, where British officers were held under light security. He managed to escape with the help of Ian Garrow, and went to hide out with Dr Rodocanichi in Marseille. Garrow realised how useful O'Leary could be and arranged for a coded message to be broadcast by the BBC if checks in London confirmed he was genuine.

They listened anxiously to the BBC every night at 9 p.m. 'Ici Londres. Turn down your sets!' After the news came the code words, and a fortnight later O'Leary heard the agreed message, '*Adolphe doit rester*' – London's message saying he was *all right*.

He was more than *all right*. A small, graceful, apparently almost delicate man, he had nerves of steel. People described him as talkative and charming, a man who liked a drink, with a great sense of humour. He spoke almost perfect English. But he had been brought up by Jesuits who had perhaps helped inculcate a profound inner strength and determination. He would need it all and more in the next few years.

He joined Garrow's network, which soon spread its tentacles from one end of France to the other, with agents and safe houses to pass escapers rapidly down the line, give them forged papers and identities and shepherd them over to Spain. As the network grew there were more and more people involved. Among them was Gaston Nègre from Nîmes, like a character from a Pagnol film with an easy laugh, a thick Marseille accent and a cigarette always in the corner of his mouth. Nègre ran a black market operation from his huge rambling wholesale grocery store in Nîmes. He entertained lavishly in his fourteen-room apartment, sometimes with Germans and local collaborators eating dinner at one end and concealed Allied pilots and French Resistance workers knocking back champagne and caviar at the other.

Another agent was Paul Cole, a red-haired Englishman who seemed to have an astonishing range of contacts, and a remarkable capacity for bringing escapers across the demarcation line without being apprehended. One of them was Peter Scott Janes, who had been called up in December 1939, a cheeky twenty-one-year-old grocer's assistant from Esher, Surrey, until then cheerfully delivering turkeys to his round of customers and kissing girls under the mistletoe. One day, searching the Internet for escapers, I had come across the website Conscript Heroes and discovered the story of Janes, which had been painstakingly reconstructed by his son Keith. After his father's death Keith had discovered his war diaries, some of which had been left behind in Marseille, and posted back to him by Louis Nouveau after the war. They were still in the original envelope.

Janes, passionately interested in guns and keen to get into the fight, was shipped out to Le Havre with his Surrey regiment as part of the British Expeditionary Force in April 1940. They spent a month there, technically in training, in reality getting spectacularly drunk, especially after they moved into an abandoned château near Dieppe with a fine wine cellar. Janes's irreverent, cynical diary describes the bombing of Le Havre and the news that Germany had invaded Holland and Belgium. He spent the same day sunning himself on the château roof, and records that his captain was bathing at the beach and sent a message by Signals, semaphore and Morse code, for someone to bring him a towel. On 14 May they received orders to move north to Abbeville at the mouth of the Somme. Janes was thankful. 'We should be in action very soon. Hope so anyway, the only thing I have used my rifle for is to knock in nails and toast bread on the bayonet.'

But the Germans had already got to Abbeville. Their battalion was shot to pieces, and Janes escaped by the skin of his teeth, joining the retreat of the Belgian and French armies, and the massive exodus of civilians. On 12 June they were taken prisoner and marched for several days, many of the thousands of men dropping by the wayside in total exhaustion. They were gathered in camps with a rainbow tribe of the Allied armies, French, English, Scots, Belgians and Poles. Janes seems to have been a canny lad, who wisely hung on to his water bottle and the cigarettes he did not smoke in order to barter them. He comments that they were not badly treated by the Germans at first, and is admiring of their efficiency and fine equipment. 'And to cap it all, every man seems to be well trained and well fed. The food they gave us last night was the two things they were supposed to be short of, lard and herrings. Makes one believe very little of what our papers and radio have said.'

Then the armistice was announced and the French went mad with joy, 'rushing about and kissing each other'. Janes was gutted. Suddenly the French peasants who had given them food and water as they passed their villages now refused to have anything to do with them. They were obliged to drink water from duck ponds. Then just outside the village of Divion Janes was grabbed by a young girl, who pulled him behind a wall and gave him civilian clothes to put on. He had been rescued, still unaware of the cataclysm of the defeat, the retreat, or the evacuation of Dunkirk.

He spent the next fourteen months hiding out with French families in the Pas de Calais, a poor mining area, just north of the Somme. The women at least welcomed them, quite literally with open arms. The French, he says, seemed resigned. 'The war is finished – fine.' News seeped through of the continuing conflict, mainly from the clandestine BBC broadcasts. Janes notes what became known as the Battle of Britain, with satisfaction; on 15 August, Germany lost 75 aircraft and the RAF lost 34. This was the air battle that inspired Churchill's oft-recited speech: 'Never in the field of human conflict was so much owed by so many to so few.' Still, as far as Janes was aware most of Britain was already in ruins. He met up with other escaped prisoners and they began to plan escape to unoccupied France. There were many complications, including arrests, but finally they were approached by an agent offering to escort them to Spain. In the end their departure was none too soon, since of the family sheltering one of his chums, both mother and daughter were unexpectedly pregnant.

Janes finally left towards the end of August, with Arthur Fraser and Fred Wilkinson. In Béthune they met up with Paul Cole, the mysterious English officer who had first approached them. According to Arthur: 'Cole was in charge but in my mind did not inspire much confidence. He was tall and thin with reddish hair and small moustache. His whole appearance was the continentals' idea of a typical Englishman.' Arthur's suspicion was not misplaced, as it turned out. Cole took them to Abbeville and the house of Abbé Carpentier, a quiet, self-effacing priest who had installed a printing press in his kitchen, and kept the line supplied with false documentation. He gave them false identity cards which would enable them to get to Paris. Janes found his ID made him out to be a clergyman.

The group included a Czech pilot, two Poles and an English officer, the po-faced Crowley-Milling, who, remarks Janes, 'never during the whole trip forgot that he was an officer and we were not'. The whole of the north of France was packed with thousands of Germans, and Janes noticed in particular one woman lieutenant: 'she weighed perhaps twelve stone, of which not much was fat,' he comments admiringly. They eventually crossed the demarcation line into the *Zone Libre*, and after numerous narrow shaves made it to Toulouse, and finally Marseille. Here they were met by Louis Nouveau, who took Janes and Arthur and the Poles to his house. Peter Scott Janes's name was duly noted in the Voltaire list. The rest stayed with the Rodocanichi family. Then they set off for Perpignan by train, and met a guide in a garage who drove them into the mountains.

Keith Janes has worked out that they must have left from Laroque-des-Albères, well inland, which his father describes as 'a sort of hiding place for doubtful characters', as indeed it was. They set off the next evening, squabbling with the guide, who said he was only paid to take them to the frontier, and paying him more money to get them down the other side. They made their way in the dark through a cork oak forest, and after climbing the steep slopes were soon panting for breath. Janes got sick from the altitude, and collapsed at one point. Then it began to rain, but they struggled on. They crossed a high plateau, where they heard the sonorous tinkling of cowbells. The guide finally left them about 4 a.m. and they set off in the direction of distant lights, but it was still another two-hour slog through the rain, enduring rocks and thorns that tore their skin to ribbons.

Finally they came upon a vineyard and knew there must be habitation somewhere near. After dawn they found an old deserted mill, where they took shelter, made a fire (they burnt the door for fuel) and dried their clothes. Janes describes going outside 'as naked as the day I was born', finding a huge millpond and a garden full of tomatoes and ripe peaches, which cheered him up a lot. He appreciated the view almost as much. 'The beauty of the mountains with the sun on them was striking, enhanced by the clear blue sky and pure white clouds.'

When a Spanish fisherman came by, they confessed who they were, and though he warned them the Guardia Civil was on the way, they waited, having been instructed to give themselves up as escapers once they were in Spain. They were given an excellent meal – Janes records it in detail as usual: he especially appreciated the melons – and then locked in a filthy prison for the night. Then they were taken by a ludicrously overloaded bus to Barcelona, riding on the roof. 'It stopped several times and still more people got on, no one ever seemed to get off. At one place a man climbed on and then proceeded to haul up basket after basket of fruit.' Janes noticed the villages on the way, 'picturesque but pathetically poor'. They were imprisoned in Barcelona, where in the gallery above them were five young men condemned to death for offences committed during the Civil War. Then they were all shaved, fingerprinted and sent off to Miranda del Ebro. There Janes made the best of it as usual, despite the horrible conditions, yet again acquiring an impressive amount of booze. They were bailed out by the British consul and taken to Madrid, where says Janes he 'practically ate himself to death'. Then down to Gibraltar, where after several days of brawling and drinking he decided to sober up before going back to Blighty, just after Christmas.

The suave Englishman Paul Cole later turned out to be a traitor, and it eventually transpired that it was through his betrayal that the gentle Abbé Carpentier and many others were arrested. He had been under suspicion already and there had been a dramatic scene in Marseille when Cole was accused of fraudulence with money. Although there were those who thought he should be killed there and then, Pat had demurred, and Cole had managed to escape.

In October 1941 the French at last caught up with Ian Garrow, and he was arrested and sentenced to ten years' detention in a concentration camp at Mauzac, 25 kilometres south of Toulouse. O'Leary took command of the line, which became officially known as the PAO Line (his initials) but more famously as the 'Pat' or 'O'Leary' Line. Part of his job was fund-raising, since money was a constant problem. Each 'parcel' cost over £200 to get home, with Spanish guides needing payment and money to buy food along the way.

O'Leary travelled frequently between the Dutch frontier and the south of France, often escorting the 'parcels' through numerous German controls, disguised sometimes as a priest in a black soutane, or as a businessman. In a photograph of him snapped in the street in Marseille (an indiscretion that annoyed him) he looks the part, striding along, smartly attired in blazer and tie, leather briefcase in his hand. In particular he made it his business to repay Garrow for getting him out of St-Hippolyte-du-Fort. He had a guard's uniform made and by means of bribery had it smuggled in to Garrow, who walked out of Mauzac at dawn, joining the night shift of guards coming off duty. London summoned him back to England, and he too followed the escape line across the Pyrenees.

Garrow was sheltered in Toulouse by a fiercely determined Frenchwoman, Marie Dissard, code-named Françoise, who lived quietly with her little black cat in the middle of town, and harboured a hatred for the Nazis which made her a key refuge for escapees. She was about sixty years old, with her grey hair wound in two plaits over her head and a cigarette in a bamboo holder always clenched between broken teeth.

Marie Dissard was the spinster aunt of a young man in a POW camp in Germany, and she spent hours each week preserving food and then actually canning it for her nephew. Later she became leader of the network, and travelled all over France escorting escapers. In Toulouse the Lycée Marie Louise Dissard Françoise is named in her honour.

The network was looking more and more threatened. How much longer could they continue? Airey Neave also wondered how long they could go on once he returned to London and joined the British Intelligence operation, after passing down the line himself. Neave, later a British Conservative politician who was killed by an IRA bomb in 1979, escaped across the Pyrenees with a Spanish guide in April 1942. In 1941 he had made a spectacular escape from Colditz castle in Germany, through Switzerland to Marseille. There he was hidden in Louis Nouveau's apartment, obliged to creep about in slippers to muffle his footsteps. 'The chaps downstairs . . .' Nouveau had indicated, with palms uplifted and a moue of distaste.

According to Neave's own account he crossed the mountains with a group including Captain Hugh Woollatt, who had also escaped from prison camp in Germany, a M. Coubert, an elderly Belgian tourist agent, Coubert's nineteen-year-old son, who was keen to join the Free French in London, two Poles and a Canadian priest. Their first stop was the Hôtel de Paris in Toulouse, a dilapidated hotel with a glass-roofed courtyard, where they found the formidable Madame Angeline Mongelard, in her high-buttoned black dress and white headscarf. From behind her glassed-in reception desk she too fulfilled a key role in the network. They were provided with forged Czech identities (especially suitable for those who spoke no French) and then they travelled to Port-Vendres. There they met José, a small, wiry Spanish guide, and paid him his fee. There was an argument with M. Coubert over his luggage and he was finally persuaded to abandon a suitcase of precious travel books, though he hung on to a case of clothes. (Neave says he himself took only dry socks and chocolate.)

At midnight the party was shepherded out into the night, led by José, wearing white boots so that they could see to follow him up the dark mountain paths. They started off well, but as scrub gave way to stone and the black mass of the mountains towered above them, Coubert soon became exhausted and everyone else grew heartily sick of helping carry his suitcase, even more so when they had to carry him too. As they approached the higher peaks there was an icy wind and it began to rain, with freezing torrents rushing down the mountainside. They were all soaked through but they staggered on. The suitcase was finally flung into the depths. The white boots kept moving ahead of them, like a ghostly mirage, but finally the gradient levelled and they began to head downwards. By now the rain had stopped and they were surrounded by fog. They tramped for hours across soaking tracks and fields, eventually arriving at the border. They were then transported by train, with the discreet connivance of Spanish contacts on board.

One of the key figures in the network was the legendary Vidal. It has been suggested that it was he, not O'Leary, who was the real mastermind of the Pat Line. It is certainly true that the Spanish contribution to the Resistance in France and the escapes over the Pyrenees is still woefully underestimated. In 1940 there were still an estimated 236,000 Spanish Republican refugees in France, and of these it is reckoned that 40,000 Spanish anarchists, communists and Republicans joined the Maquis, their experience proving invaluable to the nascent Resistance movement.

Vidal was born Francisco Ponzan in 1911 into a large family in Aragon. Though he hated school he had a passion for reading, and became a teacher. He was a militant anarchist, and played a notable role during the Civil War, involved in counter-espionage in Nationalist territory. It was probably during this period that he began relations with British Intelligence. After the collapse of the Republican army he crossed the Pyrenees into France, and ended up in the concentration camp at Le Vernet in February 1939. There with the help of Spanish families lodged nearby he created an escape network for those fleeing Franco's Spain. In August 1939 a local communist garage owner recruited Vidal as a mechanic to get him out of the camp.

Then his activities expanded. After the fall of France he was recruited to help escapees in the opposite direction, and from September 1940 he lived in Toulouse with his sister Pilar, and organised a spreading escape network.

Vidal's Spanish network helped O'Leary himself to make a clandestine crossing into Spain. Early in 1942 Pat was summoned urgently to see Donald Darling, the MI9 agent in Gibraltar. The message had been brought by Spanish agents working for Vidal, and Pat went to see him in Toulouse. According to O'Leary, Vidal didn't much like the English, the French or the Germans. All he cared about was undermining Franco. He was always seeking more arms, which Pat quietly supplied. They met in Vidal's dark shuttered house in Toulouse, sitting in the kitchen where a log fire continually burnt. The table was laden with food and good wine, as befitted one underground chief entertaining another.

Vidal arranged Pat's crossing himself, employing the services of the mysterious Melis, who was working for the Germans, Franco and Vidal simultaneously. Melis made a lot of money. Pat's true identity was concealed and he travelled to Perpignan, then Banyuls, where he joined another party crossing the Pyrenees, Melis met him there, escorted him to the train, and then to the British consulate in Barcelona. Pat was smuggled down to Gibraltar to meet Darling, where he demanded more money, a wireless transmitter, and most of all a skilled radio operator. He returned by trawler with wireless and operator, to be dropped at the little seaside resort of Canet-Plage, not far from Perpignan, where Madame Suzanne Lebreton took care of them at the Hôtel du Tennis.

Pat had another grim encounter in the mountains with the Spanish. He had been approached by a French double agent offering details of German activities. Pat consulted Vidal, who said the same agent had already tried to penetrate his organisation. 'We have proof that he is a German agent,' said Vidal. It was arranged for Pat to meet the young man in Port-Vendres. Vidal's men would be waiting. They went up into the mountains to talk, and the Spaniards began to question him. At last the agent broke down and confessed. He was terrified and volunteered to give them all the information he had. But it was too late.

'We have to kill you,' the Spaniards told him.

The double agent begged for mercy, but Pat had to harden his heart, remembering the mistake he had made with Paul Cole. The Frenchman screamed and began to run, but the Spaniards caught him, strangled him, shot him through the head for good measure, then removed all his papers and sent his body crashing into a ravine.

As the conflict intensified the Pat Line became more ambitious and plans were made to take off larger groups of escapers from the coast. In August 1942 a shipment of forty was planned from the beach at Canet, a long wild stretch of coast south of Canet-Plage. It is now a protected zone without any buildings: the saltwater lagoons behind are dotted with ancient reed huts, and provide a peaceful sanctuary for birds.

Every detail was meticulously planned, including springing several of the English from prison and bringing pilots down from the north. Among them was Postel Vinet, who had been working with the Pat Line in Paris for months. He had been arrested, and while he awaited his fate in the notorious prison of Fresnes in Paris, decided that he was not sure he could withstand the inevitable torture, and concluded that suicide was better than betrayal. So he tried to kill himself by throwing himself from the high window. He hit the stone courtyard 30 feet below, fracturing his spine, pelvis and thigh, but found himself still alive. He was dragged back to his cell and left untreated for two days. After six months in hospital he was helped to escape by a French doctor, and managed to stagger into the street, where he begged money from two small boys and managed to contact his sister. Six weeks later, still painfully weak, he was on his way south.

Also in the party was Paula, Pat's secretary, whose anti-fascist German family had fled Germany in 1933. They had been interned in the camp at Gurs, and then her father had escaped to Algeria with the help of Varian Fry, though he had ended up imprisoned there. Paula was fluent in French, German and English and she was responsible for writing and coding Pat's reports for London.

The escapers assembled in Marseille, where tension rose as all were obliged to stay indoors in hiding, especially since the prison breakout had caused a commotion and the countryside was swarming with guards, gendarmes and tracker dogs. Finally the fugitives set off by train for Perpignan, with their French disguises and false papers. One of them recalled his amusement at seeing twenty other 'French' passengers getting off the train, all of them very familiar faces. They all made their way discreetly to Canet-Plage, a few miles away. Soon thirty men were crowded into a small villa in Canet, a safe house lent them by Andrée Bourrel, a Frenchwoman who was early active in the Resistance and later returned to France as an SOE agent. They included English, Poles, Belgians, French and the pale crippled Postel Vinet.

They waited for darkness. Before they left, Pat instructed them to observe absolute silence. They would move singly at intervals along the silent edge of the sea, below the sand dunes. It was a calm night, with bright stars, and a dark glittering sea. Pat's flashing light signal was answered and a rowing boat pulled in to shore. Two trips and they were all aboard. Two days later they were in Gibraltar.

Several further large pickups followed along this coast, but the sixth, again from Canet, did not go so well. Thirty-two fugitives were waiting, including six in Nouveau's apartment in Marseille, five in Dr Rodoca-nichi's, and seven in the Hôtel de Paris in Toulouse. Gradually, accompanied by Nouveau and Pat, they all assembled at the villa, thirty-two men crammed into one small house with a dining room, kitchen and three bedrooms. All the shutters had to be kept closed, and it was stifling. Food supplies were brought, no small feat for so many, and they ate sprawled everywhere, in rooms thick with cigarette smoke. At 1.15 it was time. They slipped out from the back door into the garden and along the beach. The night was warm and still, with a moon reflected in the dark sea. Their black shapes merged into the dunes, their footsteps muffled by the sand.

One of the French civilians was struggling to carry two heavy suitcases, which were taken over by two cursing English airmen. The call of a seabird unnerved them all.

At 1.25 they reached the mouth of the river Têt, where they had to cross 150 yards of shallow water with quicksands a danger. They waded through, some taking off shoes and rolling up trouser legs, and hunkered down in the sand to wait in silence. No smoking. At 2 a.m., the rendezvous time, Pat flashed his light, but the darkness remained. The wind got up and the men huddled deep into the sand, like the Spanish refugees before them. Sand got into their clothes, eyes and nostrils. Two hours dragged by, till at 4 a.m. Pat gave up, and the column of depressed men wound its way back to the villa.

The next morning Canet-Plage woke up in the sunshine, the fishermen reeling in their catch, the cafés full of gendarmes. The escapers stayed cramped in the villa. By 10 p.m. that evening the citizens of Canet went back to their cottages, and streets emptied. From the dedicated Madame Lebreton at the Hôtel du Tennis five men brought a suitcase full of sandwiches. They ate and set out for the dunes again. A fishing boat appeared and Nouveau tried the password, to be rapidly disillusioned as the fisherman cursed and demanded to know what they were talking about. Again they crossed the river, again Pat sent the signal. But there was no reply. Finally again they had to return to the villa.

Some of the men began to doubt Pat, and the entire operation. Next morning he and Nouveau took the first train to Marseille, where they drafted a coded telegram to London, demanding to know what had happened to the ship. Nouveau decided it was not worded strongly enough, and added: '*Pas plus de bâteau que de beurre au cul.*' An army expression: 'No more sign of a boat than of butter on your arse.'

London got the message. Pat and Nouveau had to wait till the next afternoon for a reply, painfully aware of the conditions in the Canet villa. They laboured to decode the reply they received, which said the ship had been there both nights, but would try to return. They then had to wait again for confirmation of its arrival time. They sent telephone messages to Canet, where the food supply problem was critical, their presence was being noticed, and worst of all the lavatories had seized up. The reply said the ship would return on two further days. Pat and Nouveau returned to Canet. They went through the night-time charade again on the beach. As they waited in tense silence for a reply to the light, they saw another man slip by. They exchanged *bonsoirs* and he disappeared. An insomniac night owl, enjoying the beach perhaps, or another agent, another network? They would never know.

Another no-show. The tenth day came and they were still stuck inside the stifling, by now stinking, villa. The next night they tried again. Pat spread the men right along the beach to cover all eventualities. Suddenly a black mass materialised in the sea. It's a boat!

They heard the splash of muffled oars, the password.

'*Où sont les fraises?*'

'*Dans le jus!*'

It was way out off course but it was there. As a seaman held the rowing boat steady they climbed aboard. One of the men was weeping from relief, but most of the others simply demanded: Where the hell have you been?

After four trips they were gone. All they could see beyond the beach was the silhouette of the mountains in the moonlight. Nouveau and Pat returned to Marseille. Four more airmen were waiting for rescue.

The organisation continued to grow, with about 250 men and women involved. Pat no longer knew everyone, and the dangers escalated. They spanned the borders of Belgium, Italy and Spain. Many ordinary people took the risk of sheltering the escapers, and Vidal and his guides crossed the Pyrenees many times. They could acquire false papers, ration cards, black-market food, and a Jewish tailor in Marseille could turn out perfect copies of uniforms in twenty-four hours.

But the war had escalated. The Germans had conquered most of Europe and had turned their attention to the east, and by October 1941 were besieging Leningrad and approaching Moscow. However, they were halted by the ferocious Russian winter and finally defeated at Stalingrad. After the Japanese attack on Pearl Harbor in Hawaii in December 1941, the Americans had entered the war making the conflict global. When the Allies landed in North Africa the Germans entered the *Zone Libre* in November 1942 in order to defend the Mediterranean coast. Sea evacuations for escapers were no longer possible.

The escape lines continued, but both Pat O'Leary and Vidal paid heavily for their resistance. In February 1943 Pat was betrayed by a double agent, persistently and horribly tortured and sent to Dachau concentration camp. He survived. Vidal was arrested and executed – they say burnt alive – by the Germans on 17 August 1944, the day before the liberation of Toulouse. The gentle Greek Dr Rodocanichi was also arrested a few days before O'Leary. He died in Buchenwald concentration camp in February 1944. Louis Nouveau also ended up in Buchenwald but survived.

The daring escapes across the Pyrenees continued, but it became necessary to find more and more obscure routes. They must head higher into the mountains. Meanwhile the concentration camps were filling up.

# CHAPTER 10

# RIVESALTES

Every person I knew who was saved during the war was saved solely by the grace of someone who, at a time of great danger, extended a hand to him. It was not God that we saw in the camps, but good people. The old Jewish saying that the world continues to exist only by virtue of a few righteous people is as true today as it was back then.

Aaron Appelfeld, *The Story of a Life*

If any place is infused with emotion in this region, it is the camp of Rivesaltes near Perpignan. We tried to find it one day in late summer when all the vineyards around were in the middle of the vendange, so our progress was slowed by tractors pulling trailers overflowing with ripe grapes. The smell of new wine filled the air as we passed through the villages, unusually animated with their *cave* doors open to receive the harvest. Beyond the vineyards to the north the limestone outcrop of the Corbières provided a romantic backdrop. To the south was Canigou, clad in autumnal russet and green.

Sign-posting was reticent but we found the site at last. It occupies 600 hectares, some still in use by the army. It is appalling in its magnitude, visible from the air as you land at the nearby airport, though its outlines are slowly fading in contrast to the red roofs and blue swimming pools today.

Before us lay a bleak vista of ruined cement barracks and roofless latrines, the ground strewn with coils of rusting barbed wire, broken tiles and rusty sardine cans, all overgrown with prickly scrub and thistles. It was desolate and grim even under a hot sun. In 1852 it had been considered as a base for an artillery regiment but dismissed as not fit for the horses. Though to our eyes now the landscape has a certain wild beauty, for those interned there between 1940 and 1942 it was ugly, cold and very inhospitable.

We found the memorial steles, rugged boulders of granite with engraved marble plaques, erected in memory of the Spanish refugees, the gypsies, the Algerians and the Jews who spent months and years in this place.

For the Spanish there is a quotation from the poet Antonio Machado:

> Live, for life goes on;
> the dead die and shadows pass;
> the man who leaves all takes something with him, and it
> is he who has lived that lives on.

The stele for the Jews was the second to be erected here, after the first was vandalised in 2003. It was dedicated to the thousands of non-French Jews who had been interned in Rivesaltes:

> delivered to the Nazis in the Occupied zone, by authority of the French government, deported to the extermination camp of Auschwitz, and murdered because they were Jews. We will never forget these victims of racial and xenophobic hatred.

Until 1997 when we came to live here, Rivesaltes meant two things: a delicious sweet muscat wine that we drank as an aperitif, and the name of the airport at Perpignan. That was pretty much what Rivesaltes meant to most of the French here too, until 1997. Then we read on the front page of *L'Indépendant*, the local newspaper, that archives about the Jews interned at Rivesaltes had been found by a municipal employee, thrown into a public dustbin.

The article, by the journalist Joel Mettay (whose subsequent book on Rivesaltes explored the story further), became a sensation, and finally drew attention to the existence of the camp. Plans were made to establish a memorial and museum here. In 1999 local schoolchildren visiting the site discovered murals, fortuitously preserved under a coat of whitewash, of animals, rainbows and mountains, painted by refugee children. Restored, the frescoes would make a fine centrepiece for the new museum.

Every year in September France has a museum open day, and in 2006 I went to see how the Rivesaltes project was progressing. The project is being led by the regional government with the support of the US Holocaust Memorial Museum in Washington, the Red Cross, the *Fondation pour la Mémoire de la Shoah* in Paris, and others, including Germans, Spanish and Israeli. An architectural design has been proposed; it would combine exhibition spaces with a long concrete corridor 'to inspire silence', and would leave some of the crumbling barracks in silent testimony. The estimated cost is around 18 million euros and there is some local controversy about whether the museum is really necessary; and whether they really want it to become an important tourist attraction.

Temporary marquees had been erected for exhibitions and presentations. Most were full of visitors, only the bravest venturing out into the driving rain, huddled under umbrellas and picking their way through craters of yellow mud. It somehow seemed appropriate that it was cold and wet, with a bitter wind sweeping through the empty barracks. They call this area the Catalan Sahara – too hot in summer, too cold in winter, and exposed to the full force of the Tramontane wind.

One of the buildings had collapsed completely and the cement walls lay fallen like a pack of cards. A young man with a ponytail was writing poems on the walls in French and Spanish, in chalk, the rain blurring his words almost as soon as he wrote them. He told me he was the son of Spanish immigrants, working in collaboration with a photographer, who has hung photos of the Ebro valley, the village there, a burnt husk, left in memorial to that terrible battle of the Spanish Civil War, the skulls and bones that can still be seen. As I watch the poet I realise there is a pool of mud around my feet, and I roll up the bottoms of my trousers, thinking of the mothers and children trying to survive here.

Rivesaltes was only one of numerous concentration camps in southern France. They were originally set up for the Spanish refugees in February 1939, like those at Argelès and St-Cyprien, on the Roussillon coast. They came in useful at the declaration of war in September 1939 when suspect foreigners and 'undesirables' were interned. There were plenty of these, including gypsies, anarchists, communists, and most of all suspect foreigners, some of those many thousands of foreign émigrés who had sought refuge in France throughout the 1930s: foreign workers, anti-fascist Germans like Lisa Fittko and Walter Benjamin, the Spanish, fleeing the fascist forces of Franco, and the International Brigaders who had tried to support them. They were soon followed by the Austrians, Czechs and Poles as the Germans invaded their neighbours.

But then France too was invaded, and in June 1940, after the cataclysmic defeat, the south was flooded with people – who now included the French as well – fleeing from the Germans. Many of these were Jews, already aware that they were the most in peril from the Nazis. At that point perhaps they did not fully realise that they were also at risk from the French themselves.

The treatment of Jews by the French remains the most controversial aspect of the Occupation. Right up until 1983, French school textbooks continued to declare that the Jewish deportations had been an entirely German affair. Not so.

Before the war nobody even knew exactly how many Jews there were in France, nor was it agreed exactly what defined being a Jew. Not everybody even knew who Jews were – according to the historian Rod Kedward, in his book, *In Search of the Maquis*, throughout the war in a small village in Provence they referred to all foreigners as 'Jews', including two Irish Protestants. It is estimated that there were probably around 300,000 Jews in France in 1940, of whom 200,000 were in Paris, the third-biggest Jewish community after Warsaw and New York. Almost half of these were recent immigrants, Jews who had fled Germany in the 1930s, and those who had escaped the German invasion of Holland and Belgium in 1940.

At first the Germans took no action against the Jews in France, but simply tried to exclude them from the Occupied zone and send them to the South. But the Vichy government began to introduce anti-Jewish legislation almost as soon as it came to power. There had always been a strong thread of anti-Semitism in France, with the right-wing press grumbling about the Jewish problem, blaming the depraved urban Jewish intellectual for the weakening of French morals. They insisted that Jews were incapable of national solidarity, and were anyway inclined to be communists as well.

Anti-Semitic laws were passed by the Vichy government, defining what it meant to be Jewish; anyone with three Jewish grandparents or two Jewish grandparents and married to a Jew was defined as Jewish. Physical examinations began to be used, to check for circumcision or 'Jewish' features. In July 1940 the first statute (in the name of free speech) removed penalties for anti-Semitic defamation which unleashed virulent denunciations of the Jews, caricaturing them as hook-nosed and avaricious, and blaming them for the defeat of France.

The second statute of 3 October 1940, the *Statut des Juifs*, effectively rescinded the equal rights for the Jews which had been gained at the Revolution. It excluded Jews from many professions, including teaching, journalism and the civil service, film and television, and permitted the internment of foreign Jews. Later laws further restricted their participation in professional and commercial life, and permitted the confiscation and sale of Jewish businesses. They ultimately created a framework of laws that were later used to justify the actions of French administrators on trial after the war for their role in the deportations.

Further restrictions were imposed by the Germans in the Occupied zone; Jews were not allowed radios or bicycles, were banned from hotels, cinemas, theatres and museums; children's parks were closed to Jewish children. Gradually life became impossible for the Jewish population. By the summer of 1941 more than half the Jews in Paris had virtually no means of support. Many tried to emigrate. Despite the risk of crossing the demarcation line illegally, many fled to the South, where at least initially they felt less threatened and it was easier to hide, especially in the big cities. A very significant number joined the Resistance. One historian estimated that about 25 per cent of the Jewish community was involved in resistance, far more than any other group.

Nevertheless many thousands were interned in camps in the South, such as Gurs, Noé and Récébédou near Toulouse, Les Milles near Marseille, Le Vernet and Rivesaltes, a number of these in the Pyrenees. It is estimated that by the end of 1941 there were 40,000 Jews in the camps in southern France. The administration of the camps posed enormous problems for the authorities, who were overwhelmed with the necessity to provide accommodation, medical care and food supplies for so many desperate people.

The relief organisations tried to respond to the challenge, wearily continuing the work they had already been doing for decades, most recently in Spain. They included the Quakers, who began to distribute food, clothing and medical supplies. They set up a refugee centre in the Archbishop's Palace in Toulouse where trainloads of refugees were arriving every day, and sought out accommodation in dilapidated old châteaux and hotels to try and shelter the refugees.

Edith Pye was there, as concerned as ever about accommodation and supplies. In one of her reports to the International Commission for Child Refugees, she wrote:

> One of the most interesting projects we were considering was for the rapid housing of refugees drawn up by M. le Corbusier, the famous French architect who devised a plan for huts with log roofs, constructed of cement blocks that could be made in wooden moulds by the refugees themselves.

This particular scheme seems not to have been pursued.

Edith's budget for the following week in Toulouse gives some idea of the pressure they were under:

Already spent on urgent supplies: food      40,000 francs
Feeding 10,000 youths      80,000
Mattress material      90,000 (many people are sleeping on earth floors)

Canteen     6,500
Potatoes (Belgians eat these inordinately, it appears)     1,000
Tinned goods     20,000
Clothing, underwear, stockings and shoes for those worn out on
    the journey, linen towelling etc     40,000
Kitchen stoves, wood for burning . . .     10,000

But Edith as a British citizen had to leave France and embarked from Bordeaux with the rest of the British Quakers in June 1940. Fortunately there were aid workers of other nationalities, including Americans, able and willing to continue. Alice Resch Synnestvedt, a Norwegian nurse, spent the entire war working with the Quakers and refugees in Toulouse and various camps; in her memoir she records meeting Edith in Bordeaux: 'I met Edith Pye, who was famous for her wonderful work with the British Friends Service Council at Châlons-sur-Marne during the First World War. Now, she was tired and depressed.' Having done all she could, Edith went back to Britain and to Hilda Clark. There she became the driving force behind the famine relief committee, which eventually became Oxfam. She returned to more aid work in France at the end of the war.

Alice Resch almost immediately found herself travelling over the Pyrenees to Mosset and La Coûme, and she offers a brief glimpse of how the Krügers and the community there were faring. One of the other Britons leaving from Bordeaux had given Alice her car, a blue Simca, and she set off at once for Toulouse. As soon as she arrived at the centre there, she had met a French woman whose husband, a Russian communist, was a prisoner in the concentration camp at Le Vernet in the Ariège. Their two children, Pitchou and Nadine, were at La Coûme. Before the armistice was signed the Germans were still expected to arrive in the South at any moment, and the woman was worried she would never see her children again. Could Alice drive across the mountains to Mosset and collect her children?

'The next morning we drove south,' wrote Alice in her memoir,

The sun was shining, and I enjoyed the countryside and the mountains. Near Ax-les-Thermes, we saw a narrow yellow road on the map. It wound around, but was a much shorter route to the little Quaker farm in the tiny, picturesque, walled-in Middle Age village of Mosset. But that 'yellow' road turned out to be a steep curvy path through the woods. We went as quickly as we could in first gear. I was worried the car wouldn't be able to navigate the steep hills on the awful wartime gasoline. Finally we were rewarded with an amazing view of the snow-clad Pyrenees, dominated by Mount Canigou.

La Coûme, she writes, had become renowned as a welcoming international meeting place. 'The beautiful area was perfect for walks, there was a small centre for children and plenty of spiritual nourishment.' Still she acknowledged how hard it had been,

> La Coûme was no guarantee for an easy life; they worked extremely hard to make ends meet. Something was always happening to thwart their attempts to eke a living out of the land. There wasn't much arable earth in the small valley, but floods washed the soil away and droughts ruined the crops. The ground was strewn with debris from the erosion of the surrounding mountains.

With the outbreak of war, La Coûme had become established as a centre for refugee children, including the Russians Alice had come to collect. Their return trip through the mountains was dramatic.

> We loaded the children and started home, driving as fast as we could. Dark clouds appeared on the horizon, and the wind started to blow. When we reached the 'red' main road, the heavens opened and rain poured down! The river Aude flooded, and the road became a waterfall between the steep mountain wall on the one side and the river on the other. Finally we could make out the grey walls surrounding Carcassonne. We reached the main road to Toulouse, and got home without further incident.

Resch's book describes many of these dedicated women, Quakers and others, working tirelessly to help the refugees, and rescue the children, especially the Jews, caught up in the war. Photos show them immaculately dressed, loading supplies on to trains, nursing children, delivering food to the camps – the journalist Margaret Frawley, for example, who took over running the American Quaker operation. She was famously elegant in all circumstances, and always wore a smart pillbox hat with little white wings on the side – she was once asked if it was the Quaker uniform. A few like Alice wrote their memoirs, but most of their stories remain unknown. They were just doing their duty and would not have wanted a fuss. Most remain in the obscurity they chose, the work they did, and the real dangers they risked, unacknowledged.

One of the Quakers who stayed was Mary Elmes, born in Cork in 1908, and as an Irish national considered to be neutral. The work of the British Quakers was taken over by the American Friends Service

Committee, and under their auspices Mary Elmes went back to Perpignan and the camps there. Tantalising scraps of information about her emerged from the local histories and personal memoirs I read, including an ID card that read: 'Mary Elmes is a member of the American Friends Service Committee. The travel on which he [sic] is engaged is a necessary part of his duties as a representative of the Committee.' In her photo – issued on 24 April 1941 – she looks modest and kind, with neat short hair, and a pussy-bow-tied blouse. But a hint of determination shows in her raised chin. She needed it.

Mary Elmes, a trained nurse, had already spent several years in southern Spain during the Civil War looking after the wounded, and children in particular. In 1939 she came with the refugees to Perpignan and continued her work. She organised the distribution of aid, food and clothing to refugees, and found refuges for the children. She took a group of Jewish children to the Château Hille near Toulouse, from where they were eventually smuggled to safety. She escorted several groups of children from Rivesaltes, established a colony for them in Canet, and later another in Vernet-les-Bains, in the Hôtel Portugal, which had in palmier days been a favourite with Rudyard Kipling.

Her papers were apparently deposited in the Perpignan Municipal Archives, and although at first the archivist said they had no record of her, I finally found a reference to the Quakers, and inside a handful of letters relating to Mary Elmes. The first letter, dated January 1943, two months after the Germans entered and took over the Unoccupied zone, is from Mary asking permission from the Vichy government to distribute food to foreign prisoners in Perpignan. This was refused, very elaborately, apparently because some of the Quakers were suspected of helping clandestine escapes. A month later Mary herself was arrested, accused of organising escapes and spying, and imprisoned for six months, first in Toulouse and then in Fresnes in Paris. At about the same time – America having entered the war at the end of 1941 – the American Friends Service Committee was closed down and some of the American Quakers were interned. At that point they changed the name to Secours Quaker and said they were now French, and they struggled on with the work of aid and rescue. Mary too, after her release in July 1943, went straight back to work. Alice Resch mentions seeing her in Toulouse just after she got out of prison. 'Mary managed to talk her way out after only a few months. She arrived in our office, as attractive and well-groomed as always, as if she had just made a journey like any other.' Mary clearly did not give up on the prisoners either, since the last letter in the Archives folder was from the *préfet* of the Pyrénées-Orientales responding to her 'verbal enquiry' and again refusing her permission to take food to the prisons. In a memoir entitled *Picking Up the Pieces from Portugal to Palestine*, by a Quaker official, Howard Wriggins, who saw her in Perpignan at the end of the war, she is described as 'a tall, thin upright woman . . . reserved but determined, with a certain presence'. When he enquired about her time in prison she simply said: 'Well, we all experienced inconveniences in those days, didn't we?' She would say no more.

During the Rivesaltes open day one of the historians engaged in research about Rivesaltes, whose book *Le Camp de Rivesaltes, 1941–42* is an exhaustive account, Anne Boitel, a clear-voiced young woman with a mass of dark curly hair, was giving a tour of the camp. Among those listening was a tall woman leaning on a stick, who asked her about the Quakers. As we walked on I spoke to her.

'Why are you interested in the Quakers here?'

'My mother was here,' she said.

'Who was your mother?'

'Her name was Mary Elmes.'

Her mother had married a Frenchman, Roger Danjou, after the war, and stayed in Perpignan, giving birth to a daughter – this woman, Caroline Danjou. I mentioned my interest and what I had gleaned, but her daughter could add little more.

'My mother never wanted to talk about that time,' she said sadly, leaning on her stick, and looking round the camp. 'She was discreet, didn't want any fuss or awards . . . but I don't want what she did to be forgotten.'

The existence of the camps is still a thorny subject in France, the darkest point of those shadowy years. Nobody likes the term 'concentration camp' for a start, which is now associated with the extermination camps in Germany and Poland. But the term '*camp de concentration*' was used at the time by the French government. And although the French camps were never intended for such an appalling purpose, many people did die there as a result of the atrocious living conditions and starvation rations, and some of the camps, notably Rivesaltes, were the first step towards extermination, as internees were deported to the East.

When I began talking about the subject I was warned how difficult it would be. Claude Laharie, who has written extensively about the camp at Gurs, *Le Camp de Gurs*, near Pau and was instrumental in the memorial project there, said to me: 'Knowledge of the camps is only slowly emerging, with Americans who want to bring everything out into the open. The French are not like that. People still wonder why we want to talk about it. You are English, they will think you can never understand, they don't think what happened in the camps is really very important.'

It was certainly hard to find out. As I began to read different historical accounts I found frequent contradictions. The numbers of those deported never seemed to agree. No one seemed to know the real number of children that were deported. The best report I read, because it was made at the time, came from Hiram Bingham, the American vice-consul in Marseille at the outbreak of war, who had collaborated discreetly with Varian Fry to help people escape. During November 1940 Bingham visited several of the camps himself, at his own expense and to the great disapproval of his superiors, who soon recalled him and packed him off to Argentina. He resigned in 1945 and his brave work only became known after he died, through the diligent research of his children after they discovered letters from refugees thanking him for his help.

Bingham counted a total of twenty-seven internment camps, some sited in old army camps, others in old factories or hotels, and he visited those at Gurs, Vernet, Argelès-sur-Mer, Agde and Les Milles near Marseille. He was accompanied by Dr Donald Lowrie, a veteran aid worker who had been working in Russia. Lowrie was chairman of the Committee of Nîmes, formed in September 1940 to coordinate the work of over twenty different relief organisations in the camps. They included the Quakers, various branches of the Red Cross, Jewish relief organisations, the YMCA, the Unitarian Service Committee and the *Secours Suisse aux Enfants*, Red Cross Aid to Children.

Bingham estimated that there were over 50,000 people in the camps in November 1940, including over 8,000 women and 2,000 children. He was very critical of conditions, and horrified by the mortality rate. Here is his report of the camp at Argelès, where conditions seem not to have improved since the Spanish arrived there, and where there were now also 600 Jews desperate to emigrate to America:

> Many if not most of the barracks were without floors and the Com-
> mandant told us that a number of women and children had to sleep on
> the damp sand . . . at least 60 persons were understood to share each
> of the long wooden buildings or barracks . . . Some barracks, notably
> the barracks for women at Argelès-sur-Mer were reported to be infested
> with rats and mice and lice which disturbed sleep and were not

pleasant to have around particularly where there were many small children.

Further recent research suggests that St-Cyprien, which had been virtually emptied of its Spanish detainees by January 1940, was used again for the new wave of refugees, especially Jews, in June 1940. According to one report there were 7,500 German and Austrian Jews in St-Cyprien in August 1940, suffering from a terrible typhus epidemic. In October over 3,000 of them were sent to Gurs.

Rivesaltes at that moment was still under construction, though Spanish refugees from the coastal camps of Roussillon had been sent there anyway after the terrible flood in October 1940. In November 1940 the Vichy government made part of the camp a *centre de héberge-ment*, accommodation centre, to shelter refugees, and about 2,000 people were transferred there in January 1941, soon followed by entire families from other camps such as Gurs and Argelès. Rivesaltes was theoretically intended to be a camp for families, but in practice the men and women were separated and children under sixteen stayed with their mothers. The internees were not criminals and, again theoretically, had the right to apply for permits to leave the camp for a limited period. In practice this was extremely restricted.

Almost 20,000 people, including thousands of children, passed through the camp between January 1941 and November 1942, among them 4,540 Jews. To begin with over 50 per cent of the camp population were Spanish, but soon there were also Czechs, Romanians, Germans, Hungarians, Belgians and Poles. Most of them were Jews, either transferred from other camps or picked up while trying to cross the demarcation line.

'The camp was never finished,' explained Anne Boitel, as we toured the barrracks in the rain. 'Sewers were not finished nor the roads, wells were still not dug.' Apart from being a perpetual building site, the location was totally unsuitable; violent storms in January 1941 destroyed several new buildings and buried some of the workers. Boitel went on, 'It was hard to heat, exposed to wind on all sides. There were not enough stoves, no hot water, the sanitation was disastrous and the latrines infested with mosquitoes.' It reeked of mud, manure, urine.

Letters begging for help never got further than the censor's office. There was little furniture or bedding provided, and the lack of wood or charcoal those freezing winter months forced the inmates to burn the wooden beds they had for fuel. Most of the refugees had only the clothes they arrived in, and once shoes wore out they had to tear up blankets to wrap around their feet. Mattress covers were used for clothes, and, as became increasingly necessary, as shrouds.

There were many deaths, especially among the children and babies who succumbed to gastro-enteritis. People died from malnutrition even though in principle the internees were entitled to the same rations as the French population. But rations were cut, food parcels rifled, provisions sold on the black market by the guards. Even though Roussillon is an abundant source of fresh fruit and vegetables the diet rarely varied, mostly a watery soup of cabbage leaves and turnip. The sugar ration was put directly into the coffee, which made it easy to skimp. When the internees tried to cook food for themselves the guards would often kick out the forbidden fires.

Ironically, according to Anne Boitel, in good French tradition they were still offered a menu, which for Monday 19 October 1942 included:

*Potage aux haricots*
*céleri au four*
*boeuf en daube*
*confiture*
*pain*
*un quart de vin*

The reality was:

soup with 4–7 beans
5–10 grammes of beef
a teaspoon of jam
100 grammes of bread
a *quart de vin*

Sometimes they would try to get exit permits to buy extra food, but without ration tickets this too was very difficult, and the locals resented their presence. The mayor of Rivesaltes complained about the invasion of 'undesirables' in his town. Local merchants sometimes came to the camp to sell food, setting up their stalls against the barbed wire, offering their produce – potatoes, peaches, apricots, according to season. The internees paid with what they could. According to Claude Belmas in the introduction to Joel Mettay's book, 'After the war a friend discovered in a drawer of an old cupboard a huge quantity of jewellery, wedding rings and gold watches inscribed with the name of the town from where they came, Prague, Madrid, Amsterdam, Warsaw.'

In April 1941 the Jews in the camp had been separated from the other inmates on the cynical pretext that they could thus celebrate

Passover together. They were moved into their own barracks, in a driving rainstorm, and the building chosen was the most decrepit of all, though surrounded by an extra cordon of barbed wire. It was the beginning of the Final Solution. Restrictions were tightened, authorisation to leave the camp became even harder to get, and they were no longer allowed to receive visits, or go to the other compounds. They had been put in the building with the worst conditions, with rats and vermin, no windows, sometimes only straw on the floor to sleep on. Rations were further reduced. The children had to walk about a kilometre for the distribution of their daily ration of milk, and were often too weak to struggle out in the cold or rain. Out of 1,800 people in the Jewish compound, 30 died between March and July of 1941.

In November 1940 the Vichy government had been persuaded by the Nîmes Committee to authorise the relief organisations to enter the camps to carry on their humanitarian work among the refugees. Some of the volunteers lived in the camps, sharing the harsh conditions of the internees. They were grudgingly accepted by the camp administrators because they could take responsibility for some of the overwhelming problems, in particular the care of the sick.

It was a morally difficult decision for the relief workers, and there were those who criticised the aid organisations for getting involved, arguing that by taking care of the internees they were helping perpetuate the camps. Further, the aid workers themselves were supposed to remain neutral and not get politically involved, and certainly not to try to help people escape.

Aid organisations involved with Rivesaltes included the American Quakers, the YMCA and the OSE (*Oeuvre de Secours aux Enfants*, a Jewish organisation for children's relief). They gradually helped to organise the life of the camp, distributing food and clothing, taking care of the sick, setting up schools for the children, sewing groups, and libraries for the adults. Their commitment to the care of the refugees, and increasingly to helping them escape, despite the risk to their own safety, is the sole gleam of light in this whole grim episode. Hannah Schramm, an inmate at Gurs, later described in her book about Gurs how important the aid had been:

> The representatives of these agencies obviously did not realise the kindness they performed for us and how much comfort they gave us. For us, they were the emissaries whose absence we had felt so acutely most of the time: emissaries of the outside world. Now, we were no longer on an abandoned and forsaken island. We recovered our courage because we felt that now someone was concerned about us,

someone was trying to help us. Our complaints no longer vanished into a void and our fate was known to the outside world.

Their greatest concern was the child detainees, and huge efforts were made to find refuges for them, sometimes with sympathetic French families or in dozens of children's colonies – they called them 'homes' – such as Château Hille near Toulouse, and Chambon-sur-Lignon, hidden high in the Cévennes hills, which was one of the most important refuges for Jews. The aid workers did all they could, by means both legal and illegal, to rescue the children.

Mountains of bureacracy were scaled to fix emigration papers, especially for America. Doctors were begged to issue exit permits to those who were ill. Others were given false identity cards, and there were priests who specialised in faking baptismal certificates for Jewish children. Others were simply smuggled out – the redoubtable Mary Elmes is reported to have taken some of the children out under the seat of her car. These efforts were remarkably successful; thousands of children were rescued from the camps, found accommodation or helped to emigrate.

In his 1962 book, *The Hunted Children*, Donald Lowrie, chairman of the Nîmes Committee, estimated that in all they rescued over 6,000 children. They were hidden all over French territory. 'On 6 September 1944,' he recorded, 'we received a letter from a Jewish chaplain with the American forces advancing up the Loire valley. "This territory," he wrote, "has just been liberated. I have been here five days and every day some more Jewish children come out of hiding. One day five, the next eleven, and so on. There must be hundreds of kids scattered all over this territory, and they owe their lives to the courage of hundreds of Christian families." '

Some of their stories have emerged over the years, as have a few memoirs like Alice Resch's. But it is an area that remains little-known. No doubt justly, more research has been done about those who died in the death camps than those who lived, or those who saved them. For those children who survived it was simply too painful to remember the mother they would never see again. And those who helped them were either too modest, or themselves had no desire to remember, or in many instances simply got on with the next task.

Henri Parens did try to remember. He escaped as a twelve-year-old from Rivesaltes and was sent by the OSE to America, where as a psychoanalyst he was to spend many years working with aggressive children. He did not bring himself to write about his own experience of

Rivesaltes until he was seventy-five. In his book, *Renewal of Life*, he recounts how he lost most of his family in the Holocaust and does not know to this day what happened to the father and brother he left behind in Poland. He ended up fleeing Belgium to France with only his mother, Rosa. A photo shows her with her little son, both looking at the camera with serious expressions. Henri is standing on a chair, and his mother's hand dents his plump thigh, she is holding him so firmly.

After three months in a small village in south-west France, the October *Statut des Juifs* was passed, and they were rounded up and sent to the camp of Récébédou, near Toulouse. In November they were transported again, this time to Rivesaltes. They were allowed just one piece of luggage, and Henri never forgot the bananas his mother had miraculously acquired and insisted on saving, packed in their bag. But their luggage arrived only weeks later, pillaged and trashed, and the bananas were rotten.

They arrived on a bleak and windy winter's day. The camp was desolate and depressing, 'round and round we had been brought down to this next circle of hell'; Henri describes the huge unpartitioned barracks with rows of beds on each side, which had to do as chairs and tables, coarse blankets, straw mattresses and no stoves. He recalls gathering bits of wood outdoors to make fires, the toilets in another barracks, just a hole in the cement floor and no paper, the food brought in drums, one piece of bread with a spoonful of brown syrup at midday, the evening soup of turnips or rutabagas.

He remembers the Jews being moved together, 'further separating out the Jews from the rest of this abominable universe', the lack of food and the terrible cold. 'Our blankets served as coats, and my mother made me a pair of shoes out of blanket material.'

To the Jews the future seemed bleak. 'As I think of it now my mother knew something very bad about our fate . . . She told me that she wanted me to escape from Rivesaltes!' His mother could not read, nobody had a radio but, 'Knowing my mother, she knew.' At first he planned to escape with another boy but at the last minute the boy's parents changed their minds. Henri believed his mother would soon follow him.

He followed her instructions, leaving on 1 May 1941, a holiday when there were fewer guards on duty, wearing a double layer of clothes to avoid carrying baggage – 'But I was already very skinny by then.' He pretended to gather firewood, and sneaked through a hole in the barbed wire, crawling and running, and hiding in the ditch, until he found his way to the road to Perpignan, and walked the 10 kilometres into town. He found the railway station, bought a ticket to Marseille and hid in the toilet till the train was due, hours later. In Marseille he found the headquarters of OSE, close to the station, where he was warmly welcomed. He was sent to an OSE home in St-Raphaël, and the following year was one of the lucky few chosen to emigrate to America.

A contemporary photo shows him so smart, in a white collar and dark blazer, his hair short and well brushed, his eyes like an old man's. His mother had signed him on to the list to go to America but he had to understand that she could not come with him. She and other parents were brought from Rivesaltes to say farewell. 'When we said goodbye, I had it in my mind that my mother and I would be reunited, wherever that might be. It did not occur to me, it did not register in my soul that this could be our last goodbye. It was a little more than a decade later that I learned that with this visit I had seen my mother for the last time.'

Only much later did he learn that his mother had been sent to Auschwitz on 14 August 1942. She was about forty-one when she died, though Parens says he has not yet been able to take the final step of finding out exactly when and how she died.

One of the most precious records of that tragic time is the *Journal de Rivesaltes, 1941–2* by Friedel Bohny-Reiter a young nurse with the *Secours Suisse aux Enfants*. Friedel came to Rivesaltes from Switzerland in December 1941, and stayed until the end, keeping a regular journal, written in German, in two big school notebooks. The notebooks stayed in a drawer for fifty years afterwards, until she was persuaded to publish and to make a film about her memories of the camp.

Friedel herself was Austrian, born in Vienna in 1912, orphaned by the 1914 war and fostered by a Swiss family. She trained as a nurse, and joined the SSE (*Secours Suisse aux Enfants*), who sent her to Rivesaltes. No doubt her own experience made her especially sensitive to the suffering of others; she often expresses the deep satisfaction she finds in her work, gruelling and sad as it often was.

She arrived at Rivesaltes in a howling gale in November 1941, and was horrified by the squalor of the camp, the immense misery and desolation. 'All I can see are the huge eyes of starving children, their faces marked by suffering,' she wrote in her journal late that night. The barracks allocated to the SSE had five rooms, where a kitchen was set up, and which became a haven for the people in the camp, and especially the children, who were encouraged to paint murals on the walls to make it more cheerful. Friedel said she felt guilty to have a room of her own, even though the window had no glass and was covered only in an old blanket.

Friedel's responsibility extended only to the children, and she observes the conditions of the rest of the camp with frustrated helplessness, occasionally able to offer a little extra food, medical care, or sometimes support for the dying.

'My first job of the morning is to distribute the rice' – a supplement to the inadequate rations. 'We take it in buckets from barrack to barrack, in wind so strong it almost upsets the cart.' She serves the rice to eager children, huddled in blankets, clutching enamel plates or jam jars to receive their portion.

She tries to help the sick children in the infirmary, 'little skeletons with pale old faces – I try to find a way to wash them, and find a bath, towels, even soap, but then there is no wood to heat the water.' She says she feels powerless. 'I can do so little to help the sick, covered in layers of filthy clothes, often without sheets, on dirty mattresses.'

There is a constant stream of desperate people. 'A young girl of 16 is sent to me, her father died 3 weeks ago, her mother 2 days ago . . . What can I do for her. Only give her a little bit of food.'

Another woman comes to the door. 'A mother with bare legs, cloths wrapped round her feet, comes to see me – she has not been able to get permission to send her children to one of the "homes" and begs me to help.' Friedel goes to see the commandant, who grudgingly signs the necessary papers to release the child. One woman has tried to commit suicide. Another has escaped with her two children, 'But what will she do on such a hard winter night?' Often prisoners who had escaped, or even been released, come back because they are unable to live outside without money or papers.

Friedel's photos bear out her words, a row of beds with mothers and children huddled together, wearing all their clothes, swathed in shawls, their bags of possessions hanging from nails on the wall; children, hair tangled, wrapped in blankets; a hungry crowd of anxious faces gathered around the soup kitchen; a row of children's feet, in ruined sandals, tied up with cloth and string.

*29 November 1941.* 'It is raining and raining. We need boots to go outside. The water comes in everywhere. It is terrible weather for our people. Their shoes, already in bad shape, are completely soaked. The children's feet are blue with cold. It is terrible not to be able to help. But we have no shoes to give them.'

*5 December.* The cold arrives. 'Glacial wind, crystalline skies, moonlit nights, and so very cold. In the barracks they are freezing, shivering in their beds. I am full of impotent rage at such misery.'

They celebrate Christmas with tiny presents and chocolate for the children, and sing carols in all their different languages. They even manage Father Christmas. And the Jews celebrated Hanukkah, as Vivette Samuel, the aid worker with the OSE Jewish Children's Rescue Network, described:

> With a trembling hand, one of the veteran inmates lights the first small flame of the gigantic Menorah built by the detainees. And the traditional song borne by hundreds of voices ascends in the night that falls on the camp. For a moment the suffering recedes, and I allow myself to be invaded by an immense hope.

But by the end of December they face a grave problem: there is no more firewood. 'I could not even distribute the rice today,' writes Friedel. And the rats are a constant nuisance. 'When I pass out stores I see them strolling peacefully all over the sacks. They never touch the poison. I must get a cat.'

The men are starving in their barracks. 'Some of them can't even stand up, but I can do little for them.' Sometimes the wind is so strong they can barely walk to the outside latrines. One man has been knocked down by the wind. 'He cannot get up, he is so thin and hungry. His wife is beside him, but she does not complain, she just fixes her eyes on my pot of rice, and says "I am so hungry."' One image Friedel cannot forget, 'A Russian man pulling old spinach leaves from a dustbin, devouring them roots and earth, with the eyes of an animal. These poor people have lost all dignity.'

And yet Friedel still finds inspiration in her surroundings, joy in a fine morning, clear sky and sunshine, glimpses of the blue hills beyond the barracks. 'When I see the Pyrenees in their immense purity . . . Mont Canigou rising up beyond the plain, green and fertile, the peaks stretching to the sky. I feel strength there.' And she recalls that well-loved line of scripture, 'I will lift up mine eyes unto the hills, from whence cometh my help.'

In spring she planted a garden, rejoicing in the sight of carrots, tomatoes and lettuces growing in the grey desert of the camp. She describes an evening spent with the children, Spaniards, gypsies and Jews, singing with them, and says, 'It would be hard to find a life more beautiful.' For her the camp has become another world. When she pays a visit to Perpignan she says: 'It is so strange to see all these people in coats and hats and real leather shoes . . .'

Though many children were rescued from the camp, it was at great cost, since their parents never knew if they would ever see them again. Sometimes their last communications were practical. Estelle Sapir, for example, a seventeen-year-old Polish Jew imprisoned in Rivesaltes, managed a final conversation with her father, Joseph, through the prison fence. 'Don't worry for money,' he said. 'You have plenty of money in Switzerland.' He named the different cities where he had stored his family's savings. Reaching through the barbed wire with a single finger to touch his daughter, he made her repeat the information to be sure she would not forget. The day after this exchange, Joseph Sapir was transported to the Majdanek death camp in Poland and was never heard from again.

Estelle survived the Holocaust. In 1946, in accordance with her father's wishes, she went to the Crédit Suisse bank in Geneva and enquired about the family accounts. The teller returned with a folder labelled 'J. Sapir', but even though it was obvious that Estelle was the rightful claimant, the bank manager took refuge in formalities, coldly insisting that she provide her father's death certificate, a known impossibility. Estelle visited the bank several times, twice in 1946, once in 1957 and once in 1996. The Swiss bankers refused to budge.

In her *Journal* Friedel describes four children sitting in a truck ready to leave. 'Their mothers wait with them, force themselves to be brave even though the tears are coursing down their cheeks. The little children hardly know what is happening, and then the truck disappears at the turn of the road.' More infants are sent to a home in Banyuls. 'I find an incredible resistance. The mothers do not wish to separate from their children. When they finally leave, the mothers weep, they have lost the most precious thing they have left.' Yet the children are keen to go. 'Their experiences of the camp must be so bitter that their joy of leaving is greater than the sadness of leaving their mother.'

Donald Lowrie recorded in his book, *The Hunted Children*, the agony of separation, 'No one slept the night before the children were to be moved . . . Those hours remain an ineffacable memory. Some groups, both Christian and Jewish, spent the night in prayer. Some parents passed hours writing out final admonitions for their children; many wrote wills, disposing of property they had left in Germany, for the youngsters to take with them. The terrible morning came, with the military trucks drawn up before the office. Families clung to each other – many cried out in wild affliction and others stood dry-eyed and tense as children were loaded into the trucks. We would never forget the moment when the vehicles rolled out of camp, with parents trying in one last gaze to fix an image to last for eternity.'

Most at risk were the babies born in the camp, and there are heart-rending photos of tiny children who look like famine victims. If she could, Friedel would take them to the Maternité d'Elne, though it was always a struggle to get permission from the camp doctor because he didn't want people to see evidence of the camp's maltreatment. Friedel got them there any way she could, riding her bicycle with its little Swiss Red Cross flag, or once wrapping four or five babies and tucking them in with the milk churns to be delivered to Elne. There, a Swiss teacher, Elisabeth Eidenbenz, had organised a maternity hospital in the dilapidated Château d'En Bardou just outside Elne. She had arrived in the Pyrénées-Orientales in the spring of 1939 after working in Spain as an aid worker, and was horrified by the conditions for pregnant women and new mothers in the camps. She had taken photos of them in the camps and threatened to send them all over Europe if the French government did not do something to help.

The château has recently been rescued from ruin and has opened as a memorial. It is a fine pink stuccoed building with big French windows and views to the mountains, and must have been a wonderful place to find respite, albeit brief, for mothers who were allowed to spend a few weeks there with their new babies. There are photos, some taken by Friedel, of the women sitting on the sunny terrace, knitting or cuddling their babies, a row of infants on a rug with their bottles warming in a big saucepan, a cluster of cradles made from fruit crates under the trees in the garden. Over 600 babies were born there, before the château was requisitioned by the Germans in 1944.

On 27 April 1942 Friedel herself took a group of fifty-six children to Chambon, leaving their mothers with tears in their eyes. It was a long journey on freezing trains to Lyon, the children utterly wretched, trembling with cold, but not complaining. 'They knew after the terrible voyage a new life was waiting for them.' At Chambon, Gusti Bohner, director of the colony, welcomed the children, telling them they must feel at home, they could play in the garden, sleep in clean sheets, and their eyes widened with delight and astonishment. Friedel wrote: 'I felt such gratitude to be able to bring them out of their misery and I prayed that their future would be brighter, that they could experience the world of childhood each had a right to.'

Friedel and Gusti found time for a walk together. 'We stopped to listen to the birds. How could the world be so beautiful, so peaceful.' Ten days later she returned to Chambon. 'Around me the forests, the fields, the peace. Rays of sun shine through the branches of the pine trees . . . I feel such light, a true happiness in me, as I have never felt before. It is as if I have come home . . . I would never have thought I could find such a feeling of peace in all this chaos . . . To be no longer alone.' Gusti and Friedel saw each other in snatched moments after that and wrote letters, both remaining profoundly committed to the work they were doing. For Friedel the thought of Gusti was sometimes the only point of light in her life. After the war they married.

But at Rivesaltes conditions were deteriorating even further. 'The situation of the camp is getting worse every day. There is less bread, no more milk for the old or the children, just half a litre for the sick.' More and more people are dying and more barracks given over to the sick. The camp doctors suggest that only the most desperate need extra rations, and propose giving experimental vitamin injections instead of more food. Friedel is angry. 'It is absurd – according to their logic we need only feed those who are close to death.' Eventually they are given permission to feed the most hungry, but are not allowed into the barracks of the dying, where the doctors are carrying out their experiments.

Friedel describes a disinfectant process.

The men are sent outside, though many of them can barely walk or even stand up straight, while the barracks and beds are sprayed with disinfectant. Before they can go back in they have to remove their clothes to be disinfected, each one must raise his arms to be sprayed front and back, you see their skeletal bodies with loose wrinkled skin.

Many of the internees have been taken off to labour camps.

They took all those who seemed to be able to stand up. All from 16 to 55, women and girls too. How will they be treated? The Spanish are indignant, better to return to Spain and be shot, than join the work groups. Today I had nothing to give, no consolation.

The Jews meanwhile were scheduled for destruction. In March 1941 the Vichy government created a special agency, the Commissariat General aux Questions Juives, to co-ordinate the deportation of the Jews. This was run between May 1942 and 1944 by the appalling anti-Semite Louis Darquier de Pellepoix, as he styled himself, the subject of Carmen Callil's 2006 book, *Bad Faith*. Mass arrests of Jews, carried out by French police, had begun in earnest in Paris in August 1941 when 4,000 were seized and sent to the Drancy transit camp, a holding camp in a half-built municipal housing estate 10 kilometres north-east of

Paris. The first deportation train, with 1,112 men aged between twenty and forty-eight, half of them French Jews, left for Germany on 27 March 1942. The French were among the first to be killed when the gas chambers began operating at Auschwitz in July.

From June 1942 all Jews over six in the Occupied zone were obliged to wear a yellow star; this was not required in the *Zone Libre*, but there they compiled a detailed census, and stamped identity cards with the word Jew in large red letters. It made them much easier to find when the time came.

At the Wannsee conference on 20 January 1942 the Nazis had decided on the Final Solution. There was no other way to rid Europe of the Jews; they were to be exterminated; gassed or worked to death in the camps. Officially the Vichy government was informed that they would be transported to the East for work and resettlement. According to a German embassy assessment of Vichy anti-Semitic measures thus far, in February 1942: 'The French government would be happy to get rid of the Jews in any way whatsoever, without too much fuss.'

Assessments were made of the potential number of Jews that could be deported from France, with an initial quota of 40,000. The Vichy government offered to include 10,000 foreign Jews from the Unoccupied zone, eager to get rid of the welfare and security problem they represented. This was also far preferable to French police arresting French Jews, which was 'embarrassing' and might have caused a public reaction. The Germans had no inclination either to stir things up. It was better to allow the French to police themselves, without the need for further military reinforcement.

Until then only adults had actually been deported, but now it was decided that children should be deported with their parents, to make up the numbers. Pierre Laval had proposed sending the children, and presented it as a humanitarian move. Keeping families together was after all Vichy policy. 'They must all go,' he said. Vichy had no desire to look after abandoned children if the parents left without them.

On 16 and 17 July 1942 came the *Grande Rafle* in Paris, when as many as 9,000 French police arrested over 13,000 Jews. The total would have been higher had not many French police refused to obey orders and forewarned their prey. About 6,000 were sent to Drancy, the rest were locked up in the Vélodrome d'Hiver, Vél d'Hiv for short. Seven thousand people, including 4,000 children, were held there for five days in terrible heat and squalor, with almost no food or water or sanitation. There were only six lavatories. What happened there, in the country whose revolutionary leaders had been the first European nation to emancipate Jews in 1791, was finally acknowledged in 1995 by President Jacques Chirac, who said: 'These dark hours have sullied our history for ever and are an insult to our past and traditions.' From the Vél d'Hiv they were interned in Drancy, and then French gendarmes escorted the convoys of cattle trucks to the frontier. They must at the very least have wondered whether their desperate and starving prisoners were likely to see any improvement in their treatment. At the same time as the *Grande Rafle* in Paris in July, a German commission toured the camps of the South to assess the numbers to be deported, and found to their regret that there were fewer than they had expected. Many had been released or helped to escape, often smuggled across the Pyrenees with the help of Jewish underground movements, the escape networks or the aid of ordinary French people.

Friedel watched the Germans arrive, though she remained innocent of their true purpose. (Alice Resch's account, written after the war, suggests that they did know, but I wonder if this was hindsight.)

*16 July 1942*. 'Today the black cars of the German commission came to the camp. The exiles and refugees from Germany have the choice to return there. There are not many candidates. But the temptation to return to a regular life must be great.' Then the convoys began in earnest from the South. More Jews began arriving at the station of Rivesaltes, some transferred from other camps, some who had escaped from the Occupied zone and been arrested crossing the demarcation line. In August 1942 Rivesaltes became a regional centre for gathering Jews for deportation.

Friedel: 'It is like a nightmare, so many new faces, more miserable, more hungry than ever. I will see these unhappy people in front of me for the rest of my life. I am here and I can do nothing.'

Then the screenings began. The process of deciding who should go, and those who were exempt, was carried out by the police, the local Préfecture and the camp commanders. It was presided over by Jean Latsha, then the secretary general of the Préfecture. (He washed his hands and joined the Resistance after that. Then he became prefect of the Pyrénées-Orientales after the Liberation.) They apparently did all they could to find reasons for exemption, but still there were quotas to be filled.

*3 August*. Friedel: 'Today there was a roll call, everywhere I go there are anxious faces, "Where are they sending us?" Their nightmare is to be sent to Poland. What can I tell them, what do I know? I try to console, them, "Be brave it can't be worse than here." '

She photographed them waiting for deportation, huddled in groups or slumped on the ground, clutching their bags and cartons. 'They have been told to take only strictly necessary baggage . . . Despair mounts day by day. The sick stay here, but their families must go, paralysed, war invalids, old, all the world must go.' She lists their provisions for five days: 1,375g bread, 500g sausage, 3 tins sardines, 2 kilos tomatoes, 1 kilo fruit, 250g jam.

She expresses astonishment at their passivity. 'The majority accept their fate.' Still there have been several suicide attempts and two of her German volunteers escaped during the night, in a terrible thunderstorm, the lightning flashes illuminating their silhouettes in the fields as they fled.

Worst of all was the fate of the children, the children they had tried so hard to protect. One nurse in another camp, during feverish preparations for deportation, recalled hearing convulsive sobs and finding a little four-year-old hiding in a dog kennel. 'But what are you doing there, my little man?' 'I'm a dog. They don't deport dogs!'

The aid organisations struggled even more desperately to save people, especially the children. Numerous delegations including Quakers went to Vichy to plead for the deportees, to no avail. Many thousands of children were nevertheless rescued, hidden in orphanages, schools and convents or 'adopted' by French people. Louis Malle's film *Au Revoir, les Enfants* tells the story of one Jewish boy hidden in a Catholic school, but eventually taken away by the Germans.

The relief workers eventually managed to obtain the release of children under sixteen whose parents agreed to be parted from them. A leaflet addressed to Jewish mothers read: 'Your maternal instinct must instruct you to part with your children and not, as usual, to hold them close to you.'

At Les Milles, near Marseille, the children were taken away in buses, leaving parents who were to be deported that evening. An aid worker Raymond Raoul Lambert, head of UGIF-*South recalled the scene: 'The fathers and mothers must be restrained when the buses leave the courtyard. What cries and what tears, what gestures of poor fathers who caress the face of a son or daughter before the final deportation, to retain the impression on their finger tips.'

Since only unaccompanied children would be left behind, the only solution for some was to abandon them. 'I am sad and furious,' wrote Friedel. 'How many mothers have come to me in tears. We agree to leave with courage, but we want to leave our children behind.'

---

* Union Générale des Israélites de France.

'Thirty children were found abandoned one day,' said Anne Boitel, pausing in our tour of the camp, her clear young voice breaking with emotion for the first time. 'It was the only way their mothers could save them. That was the reality of Rivesaltes,' she added fiercely.

*19 August.* Terrible heat. I have watched them come out in long lines from their barracks carrying all their belongings, the guards beside them. They line up for the roll call, waiting for hours exposed to the sun. Then the trucks come to take them to the station. I can still hear the wails of people on the air . . . They come out of the trucks between two lines of guards, some hesitant, some apathetic, some with a defiant air, head held high. It is hours till all are in the wagons, where the heat is stupefying. I look at their faces, mournful, ruined faces, not even showing despair . . .

Friedel may have been innocent of the full horror of their fate, but some of them seemed to know they were condemned. Numerous messages bear witness, scribbled in haste, thrown out onto the track or given to the charity workers assisting their departure. The last communication Hedy Epstein ever received from her mother was a postcard dated 4 September 1942. The message said: 'Travelling to the east . . . Sending you a final goodbye.'

The mother of twenty-four writing to her three-year-old son whom she has left behind:

My dear little only baby,
I hope you will read these words one day, when you will understand the gravity of these events.
You are our only thought and we must tear you from those closest to you, at the moment when you really need them, I don't know if we can keep hoping that we see you again one day, if we will be lost or dead.

Even then the numbers were not enough, and in the southern zone still the *Zone Libre*, before the Germans occupied it, on 26 August 1942, there were massive round-ups, including manhunts looking for Jews hidden away in the forests and mountains. Seventeen were taken from Prades early one morning. The round-ups took place at 4 or 5 a.m. so as not to attract the attention of the rest of the population. Even the children's colonies were raided by the French police, who took away children to be deported with their parents. Still the numbers were disappointing. On 9 September in Toulouse they caught only 10 per cent of the Jews they were trying to arrest.

*13 September.* Friedel was on the station at Rivesaltes, a station like

any other French station, watching the wagons being loaded with terrified people.

> It is 12.30 and we have only just got back from the station. We have
> been there since 3 p.m. It was horrible today. Such scenes. The people
> were left standing up for the roll call under a leaden sun, from 7 a.m. to
> 11 a.m. Then they separated those who had to leave from those who
> stayed. I can still hear the cries of the women. I managed to free the
> children of one of the mothers. When I wanted to take them she pulled
> them to her. I lifted the children in my arms and took them to our
> quarters. When the mother refused to get into the truck the guards
> pushed her in.
> Wagon after wagon was filled. Two were still empty, and they had to
> find more to fill them. A woman who was a Belgian Protestant had
> come to the camp with her two children to look for her Jewish
> husband. Three more were needed to make up the convoy and they
> seized her and her children. The guards held her down as they took her
> to the wagon, and shut the iron door behind her . . . 'I am not a Jew,'
> she screamed.
> Sometimes I feel afraid that we who are here are implicated in this
> terrible betrayal.

There was another witness that day, 13 September 1942. Sylvia
Gutmann was speaking at the camp during the open day and I sat at
the back of the tent to listen to her. She spoke in an American accent, a
smartly dressed woman of sixty-seven, with well-cut grey hair and a
gold star of David round her neck.

She had been born in Antwerp in 1939 of German-Jewish parents
who had fled there with their two elder daughters, Rita and Suzy. After
the German invasion of Belgium they sought refuge in France and
planned to cross the Pyrenees into Spain. At the last moment however
the *passeur* told them that the children could not accompany their
parents, so they stayed hidden in France. In August 1942 the family
was arrested, and the mother and daughters were sent to Rivesaltes.
Their sick father was left behind in Nay, a small village near Pau in the
western Pyrenees. On 13 September 1942 their mother was selected for
deportation.

Although Sylvia had been only three years old on that terrible day
she carries the burden of all their memories. She described the roll call
to the listening audience, her words translated into French as she
spoke.

'Our mother was asked: "Marka Gutmann. Do you want to take your
children with you?"

'She looked at us, and said: "Go back to the barracks." I climbed out of my baby carriage and ran after her. "Mama take me with you, take me with you!"

'But they would not let me go near her.'

She shouted out in German to her older daughter: 'Rita! Promise you will take care of the baby.'

Sylvia was weeping, and the translator cleared her throat.

'They put her on the train. In a cattle car like an animal with a hundred others. And she was sent to Drancy. With no food, no water, no milk, no hope.

'They took her to Auschwitz. Aged thirty-four on September 16th my mother died. All she was guilty of was being a Jew.'

The children were returned to their father, but he was soon arrested and sent to Auschwitz, where he too died in 1943. The children escaped to Switzerland, from where they were taken by an uncle to the USA in 1946. There they all tried to forget, and Rita looked after her little sister devotedly.

'But when she died in my arms with Alzheimer's I promised her I would never forget. Two months later I tried to commit suicide. It was as if I had lost my mother again.'

Sylvia decided to explore her memories, visiting Rivesaltes in 1998, where she was disappointed to find no memorial for the camp, and finally she went to live in Berlin, where she talks to schoolchildren about her story.

'I am so grateful that you are all here. You have brought my mother here. There must be a memorial here! And maybe one day there will never be another Rivesaltes!'

I found my English self squirming at her histrionic manner, as she tried to convey her horror and sadness, the damage she had suffered. But then I felt deep chagrin, as I looked around me and realised she had touched people deeply; people were weeping, including several men clearly holding back tears. Several went to talk to her afterwards. She was telling their story for them and they needed to hear it. It was not for me to judge.

Between 27 March and 11 November 1942 over 40,000 Jews were sent to Germany from France, including 6,000 children, most of whom were gassed on arrival. Ten thousand Jews were deported from the South, including over 2,300 from Rivesaltes, sent to Drancy and on to Auschwitz. By the end of August Rivesaltes had become the main collection centre in the Unoccupied zone, receiving convoys of Jews from all the other camps. It has thus been described as 'the Drancy of the South'.

How much did local people know of what was happening? They certainly knew about the camp in Rivesaltes and must have been aware of the conditions there, and they must have known about the round-ups. But there is no mention of any of the round-ups or deportations in *L'Indépendant* during any of that period. The question of who knew what and when is still a matter of anguished debate, but there was information about the annihilation of Jews in the Resistance press as early as July 1942 and news on the BBC about the annihilation programme in July and August. For most people, though, the idea was literally unthinkable and it was dismissed as anti-Nazi propaganda.

To this day some of the French prefer to think that Pétain was only a dupe and had no idea of what was happening. But Paul Webster in his book *Pétain's Crime* says: 'the round-up of Jews in the free Zone, an entirely French responsibility, has remained obscure even though it involved at least 10,000 police. From the beginning it was a Vichy decision and was discussed by the Cabinet with Pétain present.' He refers to a letter discovered by Serge Klarsfeld, the Romanian lawyer who devoted his life to searching out Nazi war criminals and re-membering the Jewish dead. The letter was found in German archives, written in 1943 by Pétain's devoted doctor and influential confidant Bernard Ménétrel, speaking of his admiration for 'the resolution with which the Germans are implementing the final annihilation of the Jews'.

But there was one courageous voice raised against the treatment of the Jews. Jules-Gérard Saliège, the elderly archbishop of Toulouse, defied the prevailing attitude of the Catholic Church, generally a great champion of Vichy's new moral order. A woman Catholic social worker had been to see the archbishop describing the appalling scenes at the camp of Récébédou, near Toulouse. Saliège wrote a pastoral letter that was read in all the churches of the region, on Sunday 23 August, protesting that:

> The treatment of children, women, fathers, and mothers like herds of cattle, the separation of members of a family from one another and their deportation to unknown destinations, are sad spectacles which have been reserved for us to witness in our times. Why does the Church's right of asylum no longer exist? Why are we defeated? Lord have mercy on us ... Jews are men and women. They are our brothers. A Christian cannot forget that.

His letter was highly influential, and the protests that followed from a handful of religious leaders, Catholic, Protestant and Jewish, did help bring the deportations to a temporary halt. There were also protests from the gendarmes who objected to escorting the trains, and were shocked at the appalling conditions suffered by those in the cattle trucks. The knowledge of the deportations created a significant shift in opinion against Vichy, with many ordinary French people hiding and helping the hunted Jews.

Friedel wrote on 22 October:

> I have been to Rivesaltes. The peasants were going home, one after the other on their little carts. A faint pall of woodsmoke floated over the town. The mountains are blue and far.
>
> Then I came to the station. A train was ready for a convoy, troubled faces, and tears. I can't stand it any more.

It was the last convoy from Rivesaltes, but not the last of the war. They began again in February 1943, and continued throughout France, especially after the occupation of the southern zone, right until the end of the war. Over 14,000 were deported in the last eight months, bringing the total in two and a half years to 75,721 Jewish men and women and including over 10,000 children. Over 56,000 were foreign Jews. Only 2,567 survived the death camps. About 4,000 died in French camps or were executed in France.

In November 1942 when the Germans invaded the southern zone the camp was emptied. Friedel and the other aid workers were given forty-eight hours to pack up. Friedel describes the empty desolate barracks, silent now, remembers the faces of the unhappy Jews waiting to leave, the proud Spaniards she had come to love so much. 'They have all gone now. Even the hills are grey. Mount Canigou seems far away, cold and distant.'

After the war the camp was used for German prisoners of war, who did not get very good treatment either, and then in 1962 it was used to accommodate the Harkis, the Algerians who had supported the French in the Algerian War and were unable to return to Algeria.

On our tour of Rivesaltes we arrived at the Swiss Cross barracks where the murals had been painted by children to decorate the walls. But they are not there. In 2004 these were desecrated, chiselled off the wall, in what was assumed to be an anti-Semitic protest, though the perpetrators have never been found.

# CHAPTER 11

# OCCUPATION

'It was a big solidly built stone house, the door closed only with a latch. Inside all the family were gathered around the hearth. Suspended over the burning logs was a big black pot full of promising smells. The master came to welcome me, and the old folks by the fire looked solemnly at this strange boy from the city. Soon I was sat at the table and once everyone was sitting down, the mistress brought a steaming bowl of soup, filling the house with good smells. I looked at my plate full of unfamiliar things, potatoes, beans and other vegetables garnished with pieces of salt pork to which everyone added as much warm milk as they wished. "Do you like the ragout?" they asked. "If not we will make you an omelette." You would have to be very delicate and difficult not to like this good peasant cooking, all natural ingredients from the farm and the land. I have never tasted anything so good, and once my plate was empty they filled it again.'

Michel Perpigna, *Les Mossetans*

Michel Perpigna arrived in Mosset as a boy of ten in January 1942. 'I will never forget the moment I first came to Mosset,' he says now. 'In Perpignan there had been nothing to eat!' Since he retired here he has become the poet of Mosset, and his novels and poems about his beloved *pays* have given me much insight into the local history; the story of his time as a shepherd boy, the love story set in the little iron-mining village of Valmanya, high up on the side of Canigou, where his grandfather had been a miner. And most of all this village, which welcomed him as an evacuee in the bitter winter of 1942.

I went to see him in his house just a few minutes' walk outside the village, and he welcomed me into his study, dominated by a giant blown-up photo of the *Pessebre*, a Mosset production of the nativity story written by Perpigna, that became so popular that the amateur Mosset choir performed it at the church of La Madeleine in Paris and the Sagrada Familia in Barcelona. An achievement of which Michel Perpigna is justly proud.

'I had spent a month in hospital after being operated on for appendicitis,' he said, explaining his evacuation to Mosset. Aid organisations in Perpignan, primarily the Red Cross and the Quakers, had appealed for villagers to take in children from the towns. 'So I set off in my short pants and wooden-soled boots, beret over one ear,' he wrote in his book about Mosset. When he arrived in Prades he was put on the bus to Mosset, crowded with people after market day. 'They all looked so alike, almost the same height, with skin tanned by the dry wind and sun of the mountain.' He describes the men in their Sunday best corduroy suits and big hats, the women covering their faces with black scarves against the noise and smell of the gazogene fuel carried in a giant tank at the back of the bus.

It was an uncomfortable bumpy ride, over the icy rutted road, but the little boy was more interested in what he could see. 'I stood on tiptoes to try and see the amazing landscape. I had never seen the mountains covered in snow before! The stone houses of the village above us and the smoke from the chimneys looked just like a Christmas card.'

They arrived at the square in front of the church where a crowd was waiting for the post. 'Then Madame Fabre came to meet me, wrapped in a thick woollen shawl, stepping carefully on the thick ice.' He showed me her photo in his book about Mosset, a plump woman with a big smile, swathed in black, headscarf and all. He had introduced himself. 'Bonjour Madame, I have been sent by the Secours National.' But she looked confused and puzzled.

'Was it the pallor of my face or the thin bare legs, shivering in my shorts, my feet frozen in my galoshes? She tried to take my case and I told her in Catalan that I was big enough to carry it myself. Her expression changed instantly. With great relief she smiled. "Ah you speak Catalan, that's good, at least we will be able to talk." '

The meal he was served was the best moment of the day. 'I was so hungry!'

He leaned forward, his tone serious. 'In Perpignan life had become more and more difficult, people spent hours queuing to buy food. It was different in the country, where the produce of the land was enough for the inhabitants to live.' He chuckled. 'In Mosset they never had to eat Swedes or Jerusalem artichokes . . .'

Those two vegetables, which the French until then considered food only fit for animals, became a staple food, and people still shudder at the memory, a symbol of the Occupation. When you ask about the war years, the first response invariably recalls the lack of food, the constant gnawing hunger that dominated most people's lives during those years.

All the old people I talked to had been teenagers or children then, and everyone had a story – one elderly lady told me about smuggling milk for her baby brother under her dress, another described his father hiding a pig from the Germans, and growing a secret patch of potatoes. One of the oldest residents of Mosset, the much cherished Madame Marty, now well into her nineties, born in 1910, still remembers. I met her one day when I passed by after a walk with a friend, to take her a bunch of the wildflowers she missed so much. She was cooking, in a wheelchair, still in her pinafore, a feisty old lady, with a sharp mobile face and white hair rolled up in a loose bun. When we asked about the war, she laughed, picking up the baguette from the table. 'Well, bread was rationed, but this – it is like sand, only fit for animals!' Her husband had been taken prisoner, and she had returned to live with her family in Pia, a small village north of Perpignan.

'I didn't hear anything for three months, then finally just a postcard, to say he was in good health.' It was three years before she saw him again.

They had a vegetable garden, vines, and animals, but the women had to do all the work. 'We had a horse but it was requisitioned, so my mother got a donkey.' They hid as much food as they could. 'We had the seed potatoes hidden under a barrel in the wine *cave*,' she recalled. 'We hid sugar, too, but it was washed away in the flood.' The butcher always looked out for them. 'He used to cut the horse meat extra thin for the prostitutes, so we got more. "That will make them kick less in bed," he said,' and she roars with laughter at a joke she must have been telling for nearly seventy years. But then she shuddered. 'But there were times, when you heard the heavy boots on the street . . .' And she remembered the period when her brother was hidden in the house to avoid being sent to work in Germany.

First food, then concern for the prisoners of war held in Germany, after that the memories fade or are suppressed. The French call the years of Occupation the black years. Even in the Unoccupied zone, without the daily presence of the enemy, they were subject to the constraints of the Vichy government and the increasingly exigent requisitioning of the Germans. Rationing, censorship and fear of arrest for contravening curfews or labour laws, hiding food or even escapees, perhaps for active resistance, loomed like a black cloud over the country.

There are few people left who really know what it was like. Parents rarely talked to their children about it afterwards, and there are only a handful of personal memoirs, like Michel Perpigna's book, or Amélie's letters. Historians and local journalists have tried to piece the story together, but they tread delicately. Local histories very often pass over the war altogether. Perhaps not surprisingly, the history of Mosset written by Colonel Ruffiandis, head of the Legion Française des Combattants in the Pyrénées-Orientales, ends in 1914 with a tribute to the soldiers of that earlier terrible war. But a history of Molitg-les-Bains, the spa village lower down the Castellane valley, extends from the eleventh century to 2002, and makes no mention of the war. (Actually, a passing reference is made to damage to the hotel being caused by the Maquis, but nothing more.) Several books about the *quartiers* of Prades cite the problems of food supplies for the shopkeepers, but the main reference to the war is a full page of photos of the good citizens of Prades dancing again after years when it was forbidden.

A few letters from Amélie survive, giving some indication of life in Prades at that time. There too food was scarce, as Amélie and Pierre discovered when they set up house there, and Pierre re-established his medical practice. They and their relatives were undoubtedly glad of the beans and potatoes they continued to grow at Corbiac, particularly the cousins in Marseille, where food was especially insufficient. Amélie's grandmother in Arles had died and her mother had moved into the house, managing to feed herself from the produce of the garden but with little to spare.

A handful of letters from Amélie to her sister Mimi in Sisteron gives some indication of their lives. The maid has left, so Amélie has to do most of her own cooking and cleaning – not too successfully. 'I am so slow,' she writes. 'I have to be careful not to read instead of doing the housework.' She thanks her sister for sending knitted clothes for the baby. 'Without soap I have damaged some of his woollens,' she admits. Scrubbing clothes that are fast wearing out takes hours of work; the lack of soap is constantly bemoaned. A second child was expected, a daughter, born in August 1941. But despite the difficulties many said how much hope for the future a new baby represented.

Though rather reluctantly, Amélie was fulfilling the Vichy ideal of the woman at home, breeding more children for France and feeding and caring for her family. She was also now trying to raise two pigs (clearly Pierre won that particular argument).

In January 1941 she wrote.

I read in the newspaper that it is cold everywhere. Here it has snowed, and it is too cold to go out. There are a lot of very sick people because of the typhoid epidemic. This morning we buried a young girl . . . all due to the water it seems. It has been restored in the houses now but we still have to boil water to drink.

Henri is eating well and learning to sing Frère Jacques.

They have asked if we can send any dried vegetables to Marseille but we can find nothing here. There is hardship everywhere.

She struggles to send parcels to Clo, still a prisoner of war in Germany.

We have sent two parcels to Clo, but who knows if he will get them, with this new procedure. We are happy you have received some news.

A later parcel was delayed, she explains, 'because the espadrilles are not ready'. She describes the contents in detail, as if every item is a sacrifice:

The parcel weighs 5 k. As well as two pairs of espadrilles, there is a kilo of haricots, a kilo of sugar, half a kilo of almonds, a single tablet of chocolate plus one bar, one little tin of sardines, and a jar of rillettes, one tin of tomato sauce, two heads of garlic, to season the beans, 2 cubes of Kub, three little dry black boudin sausages, one soft black boudin sausage, one saucisse and one little saucisson.
It does not deprive us.

Henri is not well, she says. 'But we hope the air at Corbiac will bring the colour back to his cheeks.'

They are still hopeful for the release of the prisoners, and in May Amélie writes: 'Today we were happy to read Marshal Pétain talking of the return of prisoners. Yesterday they were even citing numbers, 700 men a day will be returned, they say. At least it will give you a bit of courage . . .'

At first many believed that Pétain would succeed in bringing prisoners back, hopeful particularly for veterans of the last war and men with large families, but by the end of 1941 the prospect was beginning to fade. A few categories were repatriated, including sick prisoners, medical workers, postmen and gendarmes. Some managed to wangle their release, others escaped with false papers. After the first few months regular parcel distribution was established by the Red Cross, and sending food to the prisoners became a critical concern for the families at home.

No doubt due to possible censorship – hundreds of thousands of letters were intercepted and read by the Vichy government – there is no indication of Amélie's politics in the letters (though her daughter told me she was a communist all her life). But a note of ambiguity emerged in another letter, describing the trip of some cousins to the St Joan of Arc festival organised by the Légion Française des Combattants in Carcassonne. Joan of Arc was a favourite symbol of the Vichy government, and Pétain's sacrifice of himself for France likened to her heroic martyrdom.

There they had butter in the morning, good steak and as much bread as they could eat! Now everybody seems to be in the Légion . . . but since Pierre was only in the war behind the lines, he was careful about the entry requirements and was not admitted as a member . . . I prefer to be in Prades where the talk is of seeds and cultivation – our potatoes are growing well.

The ambiguous note was typical, I began to realise. Two very different books gave me some insight. *Les Forêts de la nuit* by Jean-Louis Curtis, published in 1946, is a bitter account of a small town in the western Pyrenees just inside the Occupied zone. The cast of small-town characters – the penurious aristocrat, the town slut, the snobs, the agonised intellectual – are portrayed with all their squalid compromises and occasional heroic gestures in what Curtis calls 'the maudlin comedy' of France at that time. Most are keen supporters of Pétain, some are active collaborators who believe in the New Europe that Germany promises, happily socialise with the Germans in their midst and hold virulently anti-Semitic views. A working-class communist is cynically convinced that nothing will change whichever way the war goes. One idealistic youth joins the Resistance and suffers a terrible end. Another becomes one of his depraved torturers. One pillar of the community discreetly supports the Resistance with no risk to himself, well positioned for future power. Most simply wait, go to the cinema, negotiate for food supplies with the 'millionaire peasants' and dig deep into their wine cellars. When the time comes they take down the portrait of Pétain and replace it with de Gaulle's.

*Les Forêts de la nuit* won the Prix Goncourt, but I was shocked by the moral bankruptcy of the community described. I asked a French friend from that region if it could be considered realistic. 'Oh yes, it is the town of Orthez. It was just like that in the war.'

For me the best rendering of the atmosphere of those years in the South, what she calls 'the demoralizing ambiguity of the Occupation', came from a Scotswoman, Janet Teissier de Cros, in her book, *Divided Loyalties*. Teissier de Cros was married to a Frenchman, and after he joined his regiment in September 1939 she ended up stuck in the mountains of the Cévennes, north of Nîmes, until 1944. She stayed in their summer cottage with their two young children, struggling to cope with the wartime rations, cooking, cleaning and washing with only wood as fuel, in the old way, and bicycling for miles in the Cévennes hills to search for food. She was torn between her loyalty to Britain and to the country she had married into, and was very aware of the divisions of loyalty for the French themselves – to Vichy, to de Gaulle's Free French abroad, and to the Resistance in France.

Her in-laws remained staunch Pétain supporters to the end, and this became increasingly difficult for her. Yet she describes Papa, her father-in-law, with great sympathy: his total confidence in the French army, the biggest in Europe at that time. Even in June 1940, like so many other old soldiers, he still saw the war in terms of 1914–18 and was devastated at the collapse of France. She describes the shame, for some, of the armistice, but at that point she herself was still reassuring them: 'Surely we could trust Pétain.' She conveys their fear that:

> the Apocalypse had been loosed upon us and that we would all be torn asunder and deported separately to concentration camps, and then the profound relief to hear that part of France was to be left free . . . the conciliating tone of Hitler's speech bewitched us into believing that perhaps after all he had been maligned, we dreamed for a moment that he was after all human enough to respect all that France stood for.

Almost all believed then that Britain's defeat was only weeks away, forced to the conclusion that no country could stand up against the strength of Germany. She describes the breath of hope from de Gaulle's first speech from London, 'the magnificent absurdity of the course he chose, setting out with for sole baggage, France's honour', yet somehow crystallising the aspirations of those who refused to submit.

She recalls the sudden fear of friends with Jewish grandparents, the arrest of a local communist peasant, the problems of communication between Occupied and Unoccupied zones. She records her joy, and the complicit smiles with covert sympathisers when in June 1941 Germany attacked Russia, and Russia was forced to join the war. They thought that finally there was some hope, and in the end they would be proved right. But this went unmentioned in their local newspapers.

'We lived cut off from all news of the Allied world.' How could they know what to believe? 'Was Pétain perhaps the saint and martyr his admirers took him for? Did I identify de Gaulle with Britain or with France?' For Papa it was impossible to believe in the details of concentration camps. 'We were so poisoned with lies during all the years of the Occupation that he soon formed the habit of disbelieving everything as pro or anti German propaganda.' Looking back she makes a critical distinction: 'I can understand Papa's being a Pétainist; he was never at any moment a collaborator.'

For almost three years France was a country bewitched, like a rabbit caught in the spotlights of a car at night, not knowing which way to turn to save itself. Even now historians do not agree about the level of support for the Vichy government. Even now you can kill a French dinner party by asking whose side they were on in the war. It is a commonplace now that all French people claim to have been in the Resistance, and that in fact only a small percentage were truly active. But it is equally true that not being active Resistants did not mean that people were pro-German, or even pro-Vichy, and the two, for people at that time, were not the same thing.

Some insist that the French remained supine to the end, *attentiste*, waiting, only really supporting the Allied war effort when success seemed certain. Others (such as the French historian Philippe Burrin) say that after the autumn of 1940 most of the population wanted victory for England, and were sceptical or hostile about collaboration. From mid-1941 the German invasion of the Soviet Union, the execution of hostages as reprisals for attacks on Germans, the *Relève* of 1947 calling for volunteer workers to go to Germany, discredited collaboration. In the *Zone Libre*, however, many did remain loyal to Pétain, still believing that he provided a shield between them and the Germans, and that perhaps he was even working secretly with the British.

As far as the South was concerned Pétain could do no wrong. Some people still think that. One woman I interviewed in Prades, the daughter of the Vichy-appointed mayor, said: 'Pétain I am sure was sincere. He was manipulated by the Germans and that wretched fellow Laval.'

It is hard to understand now the devotion inspired by the old soldier with the piercing blue eyes, even harder to understand people's loyalty to what historian Richard Cobb describes as his 'dishonourable, equivocal and ludicrous regime'. Cobb calls it a 'regime born of defeat' and thus paradoxically obsessed with emblems of nationhood, flags, medals and uniforms.

Devotion to Pétain reached its apogee in the Pyrenees when in August 1941 a group of Légionnaires and members of the CAF (Club Alpin Français) climbed Canigou and rechristened one of its peaks Pic Pétain. And in 1943 there was an even more bizarre pilgrimage, when a group of Scouts, some barefoot as an act of penitence, spent several days dragging an iron cross weighing 112 kilos, plus 200 kilos of cement, to erect it on the peak.

It is difficult now to really understand that epoch, but nor was it easy to see what was happening at the time. Between Frenchmen in the two zones there was almost total ignorance. In the *Zone Libre* they would say they didn't know how the Occupied zone put up with the Germans; in Marseille they called it the defeated zone. Conversely those in the North accused the Unoccupied zone of leading an easy life, lying about in the sun all day, playing pétanque and drinking pastis.

Since the Vichy press and radio were heavily censored propaganda, more and more people listened to the BBC and Swiss radio, despite the risk of arrest. (Even in Vichy it is said the hotels fell silent as the 9 o'clock news came on.) '*Radio Paris ment . . .*' – Radio Paris lies – became one of the best-known jingles of the entire Occupation. Later as Resistance grew, clandestine tracts and newspapers offered alternative versions of events.

The tiny village of Mosset has its own library, and Marie-Jo Delattre, the dedicated librarian, rescued a cache of the local newspaper, *L'Indépendant*, from 1942, destined for the dustbin. The level of propaganda is abundantly clear. News from the Eastern Front in 1942, where Hitler was suffering his first major setback, was overwhelmingly positive, with daily reports of Russian casualties and prisoners taken by the Germans.

On 15 April 1942, for example, there is news of the emotional reunion of Pétain and Pierre Laval (the Germans had insisted the collaborationist Laval be brought back into the government, after he had been fired by Pétain), a piece about the RAF attacking Normandy, and a report of twenty-five communist terrorists condemned to death in Paris; it ends with congratulations to the French police for their cooperation with the Germans. At the bottom of the page is the daily photo of French prisoners in a German camp.

At such a distance it is impossible to read between the lines, though no doubt many did. Pablo Casals condemned *L'Indépendant* as mere propaganda, but it must have had some integrity, since the paper's director, Georges Brousse, was denounced by the Milice, the Vichy political police, in March 1944, and deported to Buchenwald, where he died.

But turning the single broadsheet page to the local news and classified section on the back reveals a different picture. An incongruous normality rules, with property for sale – even an ad for an estate agents – and a column for car sales, though there is only a single van on offer. Then, along with the birth, marriage and death announcements, there are congratulations to families on the return of a prisoner. There are regular benefits held in different villages to raise money for POW parcels and appealing for donations of books to be sent. An event in Mosset raised 2,942 francs. 'Thanks to all the organisers, in particular the curé, and all the young artists.' Sometimes apparently the soirées became dances, with forbidden dancing around a wind-up gramophone.

Often these meetings were organised by the Légion Française des Combattants, which seemed to be very active. Colonel Ruffiandis is described attending many events in villages throughout the region, giving rousing speeches urging people to join the Legion and support Pétain. After each event they sing the Marseillaise, still permitted in the Unoccupied zone, and rather less often 'Maréchal Nous Voilà'. At first this seemed to emphasise the popularity of the Legion, until I read that by this time, mid-1942, its membership was already declining, so Ruffiandis was presumably trying to whip up support.

One of Ruffiandis's visits was to St-Laurent-de-Cerdans, high in the Vallespir near the Spanish border, now the last place where they make traditional espadrilles. The emblem of the Legion was blessed by the local curé, Abbé Bousquet. There is a photo of the abbé in 1936 presiding over a group of tiny choirboys in lace-trimmed vestments and polished black boots, their hands piously folded in prayer. By the time of Ruffiandis's visit in 1942 some of the choirboys would already be in the Resistance, and the abbé himself was by then deeply involved in aiding illegal escapes across the border.

The newspaper has a regular column at the top of the page, with information about the latest rations and supplies, and the opening days for local boulangeries. There is no doubt that in the South many truly suffered from hunger. You can see it still when you look at some of the old folk, how small and stunted they are as a result of undernourishment. The southern zone was much poorer than the North, dependent on the Occupied zone for everything except wine and fruit. Before the war the Occupied zone had produced 70 per cent of French wheat, 85 per cent of butter, 65 per cent of meat and all the sugar. Although the peasants survived by growing most of their own food, people in towns in the South came closer to desperate hunger than many in the North.

Rationing began in September 1940, and people were categorised according to need – pregnant women, young children, adolescents, sick, old and agricultural workers. (The category J3 for a teenager is a usage that persists to this day, as a recent reference in *Madame Figaro* bears out.) The first restrictions affected the boulangeries most. The manufacture of croissants and brioches was forbidden, and by March 1941 the boulangeries were only open three days a week. Next it was milk, then meat, oil, coffee and wine. Schoolchildren were bidden to collect acorns, which were used to make ersatz coffee. According to a school project produced by children in the neighbouring Aude department in June 1941, almost everyone in the town had killed their dogs because there was no food for them. Between them the pupils had been known to eat hedgehog, grass snakes, a fox, frogs, a squirrel, a cat, a falcon and a badger.

The newspaper announced when rations would be distributed. When long queues became the norm, it was forbidden to start queuing before 5 a.m. in the morning. As the war continued rations were further reduced. The black market flourished for those who could pay, but most survived by bartering with neighbours – potatoes for milk, charcuterie for beans, butter for espadrilles. These and other such transactions were what the French called *système D*, from the verb *se débrouiller*, to get by, to look after yourself. The system is captured in the first scene of Jean-Pierre Melville's 1969 classic film about the Resistance, *L'Armée des ombres*, where gendarmes, with their prisoner in a car, stop at a deserted farmhouse to pick up a basket of provisions. 'We all have to look after ourselves these days,' they grunt as they drive off.

There was also textile rationing, with wool very hard to come by. Leather soles on shoes were replaced with wood. The children in photos of the time often seem to be wearing clothes that are too small for them, the sleeves above the wrists, the skirts high above the knees. Boys under fifteen were forbidden to wear long trousers.

The Lost and Found column summed it up.

> Lost: 5 ration cards; a purse with 50 francs; ration cards for bread, potatoes and meat; a girl's dress; a brooch; a bread card; a notebook with tobacco card in the name of Montgaillard; another bread card; a woman's hat.
> Found: a dog; a child's glove; a military identity badge; a scarf; a meat ration card; a bicycle pump.

Further issues of *L'Indépendant* that month describe the continuing failure of the Russians, more vicious attacks by the RAF in the north of France, and the arrest of communists for distributing tracts. School gardens are encouraged, to train future agricultural workers. In Prades there is a call for land that can be used for family gardens. There is information on the rationing of meat and carrots, restrictions on the sale of jam, and the distribution of figs to families – 'Bring money and a bag and don't be late.' Advice is offered on the use of tree bark as vehicle fuel, and on the control of lice (warm vinegar and a fine comb are recommended), with a warning that any children found still infested would have their heads shaved.

There is a column for criminal proceedings, with arrests made for stealing cauliflowers, for watering milk, and for selling fresh bread. A young fellow from the mountains was fined for transporting a fine 14-kilo ham without permission. In Céret a woman was arrested for stealing China vases and artificial flowers from the cemetery. As restrictions tightened the atmosphere in the small towns and villages soured. People grew suspicious and jealous of each other, constantly muttering about *les autres*, what shady deals they had done to acquire much-needed essentials. Even close neighbours did not trust each other and families turned increasingly in on themselves.

The newspaper always has a strong sports section, with news, of boules, bullfights and especially rugby which was wildly popular. One of the photos from the German POW camps features a prisoners' Catalan rugby club. Cinema was the other great form of entertainment, providing a welcome distraction from hunger and anxiety, and warmth too in the cold winter months. French cinema was encouraged by the Nazis, who wanted French film to be part of the New Europe, an antidote to Hollywood. Although some film directors left France, others like Pagnol continued to make films in the southern zone. Over 200 feature films were produced during the Occupation, among them Marcel Carné's *Les Enfants du paradis*, Children of Paradise, one of the most highly regarded French films. Many celebrated Vichy ideas, but others were more subtle. Henri-Georges Clouzot's *Le Corbeau*, The Crow, in particular drew big audiences; a *film noir* set ostensibly just after the First World War, about the scandal and hypocrisy of a small French town when its citizens become victims of a wave of poison-pen letters. Perhaps it struck a chord – certainly many thousands of letters of denunciation were sent during the Occupation. When the Germans left Perpignan they destroyed most of the archives, but they left their files on collaborators and letters of denunciation intact. There they remain, unopened. *Le Corbeau* was considered so controversial and subversive that it was banned until 1969.

In Perpignan a wide range of films was shown, *Jud Suess* (The Suspect Jew), Goebbels's pet project about a nefarious nineteenth-century Jew, drew considerable audiences, though not as many as films starring Raimu and Fernandel, Pagnol's much-loved duo. Less popular were the German newsreels shown alongside French films. The whistling and stamping that greeted them got so out of hand that the authorities at one point insisted the lights must be left on. In Perpignan three people were jailed for six months for whistling at the appearance of Pétain on the screen, and another woman was arrested for calling Pétain a 'dirty collabo'. In October 1942 the audience applauded at news of El Alamein and sang 'God Save the King'. Later on cinemas became places to avoid when the Germans began to make mass arrests for forced labour.

On 19 April 1942 in *L'Indépendant* there was a boxed appeal to the farmers to deliver their wheat, 'to save the country from hunger' and feed the undernourished and old in the cities. 'A bread crisis in the towns will have repercussions in the country,' they were warned. There were offers of pigs to buy, chickens and even a convoy of mules available. There was a report of an outbreak of mildew on the vines, and in the local news section congratulations offered to the hunters of Caudiès-de-Fenouillèdes on the killing of a 60-kilo wild boar, to be divided between them all.

On 18 May the headline announced that 68,000 Russians had been captured by the Germans, and that Laval had gone to Paris to talk to his 'collaborators' – the word used, which by then was not entirely without negative connotations . . . It was announced that all the potato crop that year must be kept for seed potatoes. And a woman had fallen into the canal while doing her washing, but had fortunately been rescued by the other washerwomen.

There are big events in Prades, with important changes to names of streets, the *route nationale* taking the name Avenue Maréchal Pétain. A huge Légionnaire meeting had taken place, with Ruffiandis making a speech to an enormous crowd, including several local mayors, and the *sous-préfet* of Prades. Schoolchildren and teachers – often dragooned to swell a crowd – sang a resounding Marseillaise at the end, apparently.

On 20 May after more disinformation on the Russian Front, the fishing season opened and there was a story about a cart pulled by two cows going over a cliff. One of the cows was strangled by the yoke harness, and the vet authorised that the meat could be eaten.

June the 18th 1942 headlined a speech by Pétain marking the dolorous anniversary of the armistice. The manufacture of biscuits was forbidden in order to keep all the flour available for bread-making. Four foreign internees from the camp at Rivesaltes were given prison sentences for trafficking tobacco, cigars and condensed milk.

Then on 23 June came Laval's most famous speech: 'I wish the victory of Germany, because without it there will be Bolsheviks everywhere.' It was he who had announced the *Relève*, the scheme whereby French workers were encouraged to 'volunteer' to work in Germany; in return for every three workers one prisoner would be released.

Thenceforth every day there were reports of willing volunteers going off to Germany from all over France, and photos of smiling Frenchmen waving from the trains as they set out. In the end the scheme proved another disappointment, with only about 90,000 prisoners in total released. The *Relève* was perceived by the French as punishment, and words like deportation were used. Peasants in particular proved extremely reluctant to take up the offer. One prefect complained that the average worker was '*fermement attaché á son clocher*' (metaphorically 'attached to his bell tower', his own neck of the woods), which was ironic considering the Vichy drive to return to the land. People became increasingly disillusioned with the government claptrap, and the less gullible saw that the commitment to supply French workers to aid the German war effort was a further step in Vichy collaboration.

Locally, according to the newspaper reports, the weather that summer of 1942 was terrible, first very dry so that all the crops were failing, followed by dramatic hailstorms, with hail as big as pigeon's eggs. There were quarters of Perpignan without water and a front-page petition appealed for daily water distribution. Dried vegetables and soap had been distributed and there were more arrests for the theft of vegetables, beans, chocolate and sugar. There was a ban on sending butter in family parcels, and a reminder that letters were not allowed in parcels for prisoners. In Prades there were complaints about the lack of fresh vegetables in the market. There is also a small item about a police investigation after a wagon of charcoal destined for Prades schools was found to have two blasting charges and a detonator hidden inside it. It is the only clue to the presence of any Resistance. I wonder if it was there for that reason. Or were they merely pointing up the inhumanity of the 'terrorists' in targeting schools? Who knows?

The last newspaper in my bundle is dated 16 November 1942. The front page deals with events in North Africa. On 8 November Anglo-American forces had landed in Morocco and Algeria (Operation Torch), still under Vichy control, but there had been not a word about it in the official French press. Only those who listened to Radio Londres knew anything about it. The front page is taken up with dramatic condemnations of the treachery of General Henri Giraud, who had escaped from Germany and joined the Allies, and of General de Lattre de Tassigny. When the Germans crossed the demarcation line on 11 November 1942 the armistice army had been dissolved and ordered to surrender its arms. General de Lattre, previously commanding Vichy's 16th military district in Montpellier, had tried to organise military resistance in the Montagnes Noires. He was arrested and imprisoned but escaped to join the Allies. And there is a telegram for Admiral Darlan, ordering him to defend North Africa against the Allied aggression and to take no action against the German forces. But Darlan agreed to a ceasefire with the American forces (and was later assassinated, apparently with some British connivance, which just goes to show the opaque depths of military strategy outside France as well).

Only a small piece lost in the middle of the front page and date-lined Berlin mentions that the Germans have taken over the Unoccupied zone:

> and have announced that all the important strategic points on the Mediterranean coast of Southern France are now under the protection of the German and Italian army. The passage through France was effected in an astonishingly rapid way and without incident. Life and business continue everywhere without any problems.

This was something of an understatement. On 11 November between 11.30 a.m. and 12 motorised German troops arrived in Perpignan. Most of the population was taken by surprise. The teenage Henri Goujon was there, with his camera, and Dr Goujon proudly described to me the corner where he had hidden so as to take the pictures. They are blurred but have real immediacy: two helmeted Germans on motorbikes powering past the boy's hiding place, a huge tank bristling with guns seen from a low angle, and a convoy of open cars and officers in their long-peaked caps, passing an old lady on a cart pulled by an emaciated donkey.

There are other pictures: German motorised transport marked with swastikas travelling along the coast road; Germans on the quays of Port-Vendres; positioning artillery along the coast; a German soldier driving a cart loaded with hay, clearly just requisitioned for the horses; two smartly dressed officers studying a local map; others shaking hands with Franco's troops on the Spanish frontier; three spruce German soldiers at Le Perthus checking the papers of an elderly agricultural worker in threadbare espadrilles and beret. Another shows a soldier off duty, sunbathing and reading a German newspaper, the sea gently lapping in the cove below.

In Perpignan German signage was imposed. The 1st Regiment of the 7th Panzer division occupied the Citadelle, the barracks, the arsenal, the post office, the station and the airport, where the first Messerschmitts landed. The Todt Organisation, responsible for building fortifications, took over the Chamber of Commerce, with its eagle displayed over the doorway. There were machine-gun posts set up on the main bridge over the river and at the entrance to the old town, in front of the Grand Café de la Paix and the Castillet, the one remaining tower of the old city battlements. By the end of the day the swastika floated over Perpignan.

In the days that followed the Germans took over the whole region, from the coast to the mountains and the far reaches of the Vallespir, Cerdagne and Capcir. The Spanish frontier was declared a forbidden zone 15 kilometres deep and henceforth patrolled by the Germans. German troops moved into barracks and towns all along the frontier, in towns like Bourg-Madame and the citadel of Mont-Louis and even small villages like St-Laurent-de-Cerdans. The Germans trudged all the way up to the tiny hamlet of Mantet in order to patrol the escape route over the frontier, and built a barracks high up there on the mountainside. It remained till quite recently, providing a useful refuge for walkers, but sadly burnt down after a chip pan fire. When the Germans arrived, the village itself was evacuated to Py, a few kilometres further down. This however meant that the Germans were dependent on Py for their supplies, which proved to be unaccountably erratic. They soon left. Looking down on the village of Mantet from the other side of the valley, I imagined the grey uniformed soldiers with their black helmets winding their way like insects down to the village from the ridge above, I could fully understand why the locals nicknamed them *doryphores*, after the Colorado beetles that plagued their potatoes.

The Germans' main objective in invading the *Zone Libre* was to defend the Mediterranean coast from Allied attack. Access to the coast was forbidden and they rapidly began constructing the *Südwall*, mining the beaches and building defences of ditches, barbed wire and concrete barricades, reinforced by artillery, especially along the flat part of the coast at Canet, St-Cyprien and Argelès, which seemed to offer an ideal place for an Allied landing. Only a few months before, Pat O'Leary and his charges had escaped from these same beaches.

The harbour at Port-Vendres was heavily barricaded, and concrete blocks installed along the beaches of the fishing villages of Collioure and Banyuls and the frontier town of Cerbère. People close to the beaches were evacuated, and bigger houses and villas requisitioned. A canal was constructed leading to the St-Cyprien beach, to avoid the defensive walls being submerged in case of flooding. It is still known among the old folk as the 'Canal des Allemands'.

Limited fishing zones were permitted, but the fishermen had to be accompanied by a German soldier to see that they declared all the fish they caught. There is a photo of a boat full of fishermen at Collioure with a German soldier aboard. All look very cheerful, and he is obviously helping them with their catch – they had nicknamed him the *charcutier* because he had been a sausage-maker in Frankfurt.

For the soldiers, who numbered among them Poles, Austrians and Czechs as well as Germans, posting to the Mediterranean coast was a relief, especially for those who been fighting on the Eastern Front, and had suffered frostbitten fingers and feet. Some of them seem to have been as hungry as the local population, and there are stories of Germans soldiers stealing rabbits, chickens and vegetables, even, once, a dog. (They demanded a pot to cook it in from its owner.)

There are many accounts of people risking their lives to return to the mined fields near the coast to forage for vegetables. My friend Renée Castellas was a small child living near to the coastal village of Mèze near Montpellier, and she remembers that on Friday mornings at school after the usual Thursday off there always seemed to be an empty chair, another child missing, blown up by a landmine after straying into the forbidden coastal zone, to look for mussels to eat. Later the entire coastline and villages were evacuated, though in St-Cyprien this proved rather inconvenient for the occupying Germans, since four days after the evacuation the troops found themselves without drinking water. They had to send a car and three soldiers to fetch the *fontainier* (responsible for maintenance of the village drinking water) from his new residence and take him back each night. No doubt the *fontainier* failed to satisfactorily explain the complexities of the water system.

Visiting Banyuls one day, I went into the town hall to enquire about the coastal occupation. It was a very casual town hall, with most of the staff in shorts and sandals. I was almost immediately whisked into the office of the mayor, Roger Rull, a typical Catalan, small and forceful, in a short-sleeved check shirt and square-framed silver glasses. Beyond a large model of a Catalan fishing boat the windows gave on to postcard views of sea and mountains.

He suggested we visit the town, talking as we went. As we wove our way through the shoppers carrying their baguettes for the midday meal and the tourists surveying espadrilles in the shoe shop, it was clear he was a popular fellow. He was greeted left and right, a car tooted as he passed, kisses were bestowed and he reached up to a garbage man sitting in his truck to shake him by the wrist as he passed. He pointed out the house where Lisa and Hans Fittko had lived and the path they took with the refugees they helped escape. Then we stood on the promenade, looking onto the bay and the horizon of the sea, and he explained where the concrete walls and fortifications had been built along the edge of the beach.

He was only a small child when the Germans occupied their village, the original settlement of Banyuls, Puig-del-Mas, about a kilometre inland. 'But I can remember the column of troops appearing, followed by the horses and trucks. In front was a little Mongolian, a Russian POW who took care of their mules. We used to give him fag ends through the door in the *cave* where he looked after the animals.'

The Germans were quite friendly, it seems. 'To us they were just Philippe and Paul – there was one who had a sort of mincing step' – the mayor demonstrates – 'the villagers called him "Demoiselle".' He recalled them being kind to the village children. 'They gave us soup with butter in it.'

Most of the 25,000 German troops in the department were stationed in Perpignan, commandeering hotels and of course brothels, *maisons closes* as they were called. There was one for officers in rue de l'Horloge in the old town – it was later blown up by the Resistance. Soldiers were billeted in the surrounding villages and there was a German presence in most of the towns of the region. They usually took over the finer houses, or requisitioned accommodation from the local inhabitants. (Madame Marty said her mother had claimed to suffer from TB to avoid it.) Even tiny villages might have just one German stationed there, and they often ended up with quite friendly relations. In Prades the Germans officers took over Villa Lafabrègue, a splendid colonnaded mansion on the outskirts of the town, with a big garden full of palm trees. You can stay there now; a cheerful young English couple run it as a bed and breakfast.

Pablo Casals, then aged sixty-five, was still in Prades when the Germans came. 'From the moment Hitler had come to power in Germany I had refused to play in that country – that birthplace of Beethoven and Bach which had been so dear to me – but now the Nazis had come to me,' he wrote in his autobiography. He had been urged to leave, and offered large sums of money to play in the USA, but had felt his place was with his fellow Catalans.

He and the Alavedra family had moved into the Villa Colette, a small villa on the outskirts of the town. Casals describes it surrounded by trees and gardens, though now there are houses built all around. In the garden though you can still see the old washhouse, rabbit hutches and a big shady cherry tree.

It was rented to him by M. Four, who ran the local bus company. His daughter Annick lives there now, and she kindly showed me round one day. The Alavedras had lived on the ground floor, and Casals and his companion Señora Capdevila (their relationship is never entirely clear) had the upstairs floor, accessible by a staircase at the back. Casals had the front bedroom with a view of Canigou, and a small room at the back where he worked. It is a tiny room, but here he crammed in his piano and cello, and practised every day.

They shared their meals – such as they were – continued their support of the Spanish refugees, and were visited by other Catalan refugees, exiled poets and musicians like themselves. They followed the progress of the war like so many others via the BBC nightly broadcasts, sometimes hiding under a blanket to muffle the sound.

Musician Casals and poet Joan Alavedra continued their work. Casals started each day playing Bach suites, first on the piano, then on the cello. It was important he said to begin with the most basic things. From time to time Casals gave benefit concerts, including concerts in the church in Prades, but he says, as the war progressed, living in the town became more difficult. 'The atmosphere grew more strained, some of the townspeople were openly hostile, others turned away when they passed me on the street.' Many suspected him of communist sympathies because of his support for the Spanish Republican cause.

One particular gesture did not help his reputation. Casals with another Catalan refugee, Ventura Gassol, who had been minister of culture in the Republican Catalan government, no less, had the bright idea of ringing the bell of St-Michel-de-Cuxa, as a patriotic Catalan gesture. Cuxa is a magnificent tenth-century Romanesque abbey which is the pride of Prades (and now the location for the annual Casals festival). Then it was still in a fairly ruinous state, but inhabited by a small community of Cistercians. Some restoration had been attempted by the esteemed Catalan architect Josep Puig i Cadafalch in the 1930s. There is a photo of Joan Alavedra and Cadafalch inspecting the roof together and Alavedra went regularly to talk to the monks and find a refuge to write. (The monks were not particularly picky about those they gave sanctuary, it seemed. After the Liberation they were tried for sheltering members of the Milice.) The citizens of Ripoll in Spain, site of another Catalan monastery, had sent a bell to be installed in one of the towers.

'It was,' recalled Casals almost gleefully, 'an unforgettable moment, there, in the serenity of those old pillars and arches . . . when the rich sounds of the bell pealed forth to the surrounding mountains!' But the gesture provoked a scandal and the perpetrators were denounced as Reds and anarchists. It was probably worth it.

Madame Alavedra recalled their time in Prades when we talked in Barcelona; how she gave piano lessons in exchange for milk, and became the first piano teacher at La Coûme. But they were always hungry. 'We once had a *fête de l'eau chaude*,' she recalled, 'a hot water celebration – we had nothing else!' But still for her it is a happy memory, the poetry and music compensating for deprivation. 'The Maestro adored the children, and took them for walks, and helped with their homework.' She showed me photos of them all, up in the mountains, the children in their shorts and boots, Casals with his hat and stick. 'For my son's first communion in the church in Prades, the Maestro went back on foot to the Villa Colette to collect his cello and play for him. Somehow we managed to transform suffering into happiness.'

It was during his sojourn in Prades that Casals wrote the music for *El Pessebre*, the oratorio that later became popular all over the world. It was August 1943, and Casals saw that there was a Catalan poetry competition with a money prize due to take place in Perpignan. They were so short of money that he encouraged Alavedra to enter. Alavedra decided to submit the *Pessebre* poem he had written for his daughter in Barcelona, 'but he couldn't find it anywhere,' said Madame Alavedra. 'We were sure it must have been lost when we left Barcelona.'

Then his daughter Maria, aged fourteen, announced: 'But I have it!' She rushed off to find the little black case she had refused to abandon when they made their epic escape through the mountains, and there was the poem, one of the precious objects she had been obstinately determined to keep. The poem won first prize in the competition, and Casals began to set it to music, asking Montserrat Alavedra to sing each section as he completed it.

When the Germans arrived in Prades in 1942 life had grown harsher, and both Casals and Alavedra were placed under constant surveillance, suspected of being in contact with the Maquis and the Spanish refugees who had joined them. Periodically the Gestapo came to search the house, and they were told they were on the list for possible arrest or execution. It became even more of a struggle to survive, as rationing became more drastic. 'At Villa Colette we existed for the most part on boiled turnips, beans and other greens. Milk or meat was an unheard-of luxury.' Potatoes by then were as great a cause for celebration as hot water.

In the winter it was terribly cold, with no coal and little wood. Casals recalled: 'Every day I would go out and limping along with the aid of my cane, gather sticks and branches that had fallen from the trees.'

They wore their overcoats indoors and out, and for Casals playing the cello became increasingly difficult.

One morning Casals was in his room working on the *Pessebre* when a car pulled up outside the house and three German officers got out and knocked on the door. Worried that his friends might get into trouble if they were refused entry, he said: 'Send them up.'

'As I heard the footsteps on the stairs, I thought that perhaps this was the moment that I had feared.'

The Germans entered the tiny study, immaculate in their uniforms and gleaming boots, clicked their heels, and gave the Hitler salute. 'We have come to pay our respects. We are great admirers of your music.' They asked if he was comfortable. 'Perhaps you could use more coal, or perhaps more food.' Casals replied that he had everything he needed.

They asked why he stayed in Prades, why not return to Spain? And Casals explained that he was opposed to Franco. 'If there were freedom in Spain I would go.'

Then they came to the point. 'You know you are loved in Germany. You are invited to come to Germany and play for the German people.' When Casals refused, saying he had to take the same attitude to Germany as to Spain, they tried to persuade him.

'The Führer loves music. If you come to Berlin, he himself will attend your performance.' And they even offered to lay on a special train. Eventually they gave up, asked for an autographed photo, and pleaded with Casals to play some Brahms or Bach for them. But Casals refused, blaming his rheumatism. Finally one of the officers sat down at Casals's piano and played a Bach aria. They asked to see his cello, which Casals took from its case and laid on the bed. 'They picked it up and touched it . . . It made me feel deathly ill . . .'

It is one of the most often cited stories about Casals's time in Prades. His position seemed resolute, his anti-fascism unquestionable. Watching a film of Casals talking, giving a speech about peace, and his love for Catalonia, at the age of ninety-seven, I recognised him as a Catalan peasant. He has been described as a mix of seigneur and peasant, and the description seemed apt. The way he pursed his lips and jutted out his chin reminded me of the stubborn local farmers I had sometimes confronted. I could imagine him refusing to play for the Germans.

But then I had one of those experiences that summed up for me the ambiguities inherent in the Occupation period here. Several people had said to me that Casals was not much liked in Prades, and I had assumed his left-wing sympathies were the reason. But then I went to talk to Madame Monique de Decker, the daughter of the wartime mayor of Prades.

Madame de Decker received me in her house tucked away in a cul de sac in the old town of Prades, with a façade of green shutters and lace curtains, rooms crammed with massive wooden furniture, paintings and family mementoes. She showed me the house, stressing that it was much as it had been when she lived there with her parents during the war: the patterned tiled floor, 'Deus vos Gardes' in Catalan over the door, the kitchen with its big pink marble sink. A Napoleonic medal awarded to her grandfather hung over her bed.

From a large armoire full of linen and glassware she produced two small glasses, and served local muscat and a delicious cake made according to her mother's recipe. Unlike so many, she was keen to speak, to explain her father's actions during the war. She sat facing me beside the table, a woman of eighty-five, still vivacious, in a blue denim dress, with fine red hair and pearly lipstick.

Her father, Colonel Victor Pyguilhem, had been appointed mayor of Prades by the Vichy government in 1941, when many of the left-wing mayors were dismissed and replaced by special delegations. He was a career military man, who had fought in the 1914–18 war, and been imprisoned for nineteen months in Germany. 'So he was no friend of the Germans,' stressed Madame de Decker.

Pyguilhem was pure Catalan, brought up in the high mountain plateau of the Cerdagne by peasant parents. His horsemanship was so accomplished that in 1922 he joined the Ecole de Gendarmerie. He became captain of the gendarmerie in Romainville, a communist suburb of Paris – 'That was purgatory for Papa,' said Madame de Decker – and La Rochelle. There he became great friends with the novelist Georges Simenon, who lived nearby. 'Simenon liked to talk to my father about his work, the crimes, the prisoners, he was a great source for Simenon.'

Madame de Decker disappeared upstairs to fetch a folder bulging with photos, letters, invitations and press clippings, and a framed picture of her father, splendid on horseback in full dress uniform. One of his proudest moments was as part of the guard of honour for the visit of the British Royal Family to Paris in 1938. 'He was on the right-hand side of the Queen!' (The French gendarmerie are responsible for policing the countryside and small towns, and ceremonies involving foreign heads of state.)

Pyguilhem was in Paris when France collapsed in 1940. Dismissed, he decided to return to Prades and the family. 'I may as well go fishing,' he said. Fishing apparently had never been so popular, as the only leisure activity available after the confiscation of firearms. One writer describes the Paris Métro filling up each morning with fishermen loaded down with rods and tackle.

But Pyguilhem's appointment as mayor of Prades in 1941 changed all that. 'He was appointed by Pétain himself, he could not disobey the orders of a superior officer,' said Madame de Decker firmly, adding her comment about the sincerity of Pétain.

According to a local history of Prades, Pyguilhem appears to have been an exemplary mayor, establishing a sports ground, in line with the Vichy emphasis on healthy sports. When the *Relève* for prisoners was proposed, he even sent his own son to Germany to set an example. (An experience that permanently damaged her brother, says Madame de Decker.) The same history bemoans Pyguilhem's treatment after the Liberation when he was tried and imprisoned for his loyalty to Vichy. 'He suffered terribly then,' said Madame de Decker, wiping her eyes. 'But he was not a collaborator.' She insisted he had always behaved impeccably and had helped fugitives to cross to Spain.

'The Maquis humiliated my father, they even came and searched the house.' During the days of what is called *l'épuration*, the purge, the colonel was imprisoned and even paraded through the streets. 'He was marched down the Route Nationale between *maquisards* with machine guns. But my younger brother and my husband, both in their Resistance armbands, rescued him from the procession, and everybody clapped. Everybody respected my father.'

In Prades she had met a Belgian, a musician and engineering student. 'I fell totally in love with this blond blue-eyed boy.' They were married in 1943 in the Grand Hôtel of Prades by her father as mayor. 'Even though there was so little food, friends supplied a duck – and I even managed a long white dress,' said Madame de Decker, 'which was very difficult then, when cloth was rationed.'

But when I asked what it was like to live in Prades under German occupation, I drew a blank. Madame de Decker said: 'But I have no idea. We left for the Corrèze.' Her new husband went to work on an engineering project, 'and we both joined the Maquis there. I carried messages and that sort of thing. I could have been killed!' She recalled meeting parachute drops of arms from English planes, and smoothed her dress down. 'I even had a skirt made of parachute silk!'

'But what did your father think about you being in the Maquis?' I asked curiously.

'Oh, he didn't know anything about it.'

All she could remember of Prades were the food problems, which she tried to solve by working on a farm owned by friends nearby. 'You couldn't take anything away with you, so you had to eat as much as you could while you were there. It was always hard riding my bicycle back! But I usually managed to smuggle milk back hidden under my dress. We would hide it in the *cave* for my brother. Papa never knew about that.' She did remember a round-up of Jews in Prades. 'They took a poor woman who was working as a cleaner for one of our neighbours down the street. We never saw her again.'

After a Resistance attack on Prades – 'The wrong kind of Maquis, communists,' snapped Madame de Decker – Colonel Pyguilhem apparently volunteered himself as hostage to the German authorities in Perpignan, to avoid reprisals against the town. The attack had happened on his watch. I recalled this incident from Pablo Casals's autobiography. The chronology of events was wrong, but the action seemed to be confirmed by Casals. According to Casals the Germans were impressed by the mayor's honourable gesture, and Prades was spared. There was indeed no reprisal against Prades. Revenge was exacted elsewhere.

The connection with Casals intrigued me, and when I asked Madame de Decker she produced another folder of correspondence between Casals and Victor Pyguilhem. 'They were great friends,' she said. She explained that when she came to Prades at seventeen she enjoyed visiting all the grand houses and châteaux, and playing tennis. That maybe was how she encountered Casals, who adored tennis. She showed me a photo of Casals and Pyguilhem together after Casals had been made a citizen of Prades in 1941, sharing celebration aperitifs in the shady garden of the Hôtel Hostalrich. (Behind them French and Catalan flags are flying – no swastika yet.) Madame Alavedra and Señora Capdevila are also smiling in the photo. Next to Casals is General Paul Galy, President of the Légion Française des Combattants, and in March 1941 Casals gave a concert in Perpignan for a benefit organised by the Legion.

Madame de Decker showed me long handwritten letters from Casals to her father up until the 1960s, full of personal news, with affectionate messages for all the family. And a letter dated 1953, written in support of Pyguilhem as part of an amnesty application, expressing Casals's admiration and respect for Pyguilhem and his conduct during the Occupation. Then I was puzzled. How could Casals the anti-fascist, the great man of peace and justice, be friends with a Pétainist mayor? In the end I think both were Catalans, with peasant backgrounds, a shared loyalty that eclipsed all other politics. I listened again to Casals playing Bach. I could not believe that Casals was somehow a fake, on the wrong side, so where did that leave Pyguilhem?

In February 1943 the most disastrous Vichy policy was launched, the Service du Travail Obligatoire (STO), which required men normally eligible for military service to do two years' forced labour, mainly in Germany. Thenceforth evading STO became the goal of many young men. They became known as *réfractaires*, and historians estimate that there were about 250,000 who escaped STO. Many took jobs as miners or woodcutters, exempt from forced labour quotas. Some, but by no means all, took to the Maquis. And others joined the Milice, the paramilitary arm of the Legion, created in February 1943 expressly to crush the Resistance. Virtual civil war was around the corner.

In February 1943 in Prades, Pierre received a letter from the Ministry of Labour, dated 25 February, which required him to carry out medical checks for STO, insisting that he was rigorous in his examinations. He was required to pass as many men as possible as fit for work, assessing their strength for different levels of labour. Only severe infirmity should be exempt. A further letter was sent the next day, 26 February, from the Préfecture in Perpignan, stressing the urgency with which he must proceed. It was an unenviable, invidious position to be put in. Some mayors resigned rather than enforce the forced labour laws, either on principle or because they feared Resistance reprisals. Doctors could not save everyone by failing them medically, and since they had a quota to fill, if they saved some then others had to go.

The next day, 27 February, Pierre was dead. He had been riding his motorbike – how one thinks of Amélie's warnings – after attending a birth in Mosset, and just where the steep road makes a tricky bend before approaching Prades he was thrown off his bike and over the side to the steep rocky canyon below. He had apparently run into the back of a lorry, unexpectedly stopped after the bend because it had run out of petrol. His daughter tells me that her mother always said it happened because he was in such a state of rage over the STO requirements he was expected to enforce.

More sinister, however, there are suggestions that a wire had been stretched across the road, deliberately to overturn his motorbike. And both sides have been accused of setting the trap. Was he suspected of Vichy sympathies by the Resistance? Or was it the Milice who decided he was a traitor to the cause?

Poor, poor Amélie. She was awaiting their third child, and must have been still reeling from the news that the Germans had totally destroyed the old port of Marseille; at a few hours' notice the Vieux Port had been evacuated: ten thousand inhabitants, their cows, goats, chickens, geese and rabbits. And almost as many huge rats swimming out to the harbour. Then the Germans blew it all to pieces, systematically, street by street. It must have seemed to Amélie as if her world was coming to an end.

# CHAPTER 12

# RESISTANCE

'Do you want the truth, or just the usual stuff?'
*Ancien Résistant*, Fillols

In March 1943 there was another tragic death, though no one knew about it at the time. Today in Perpignan there is an avenue Rosette Blanc, but she is not there. Like her friend Odette Sabaté, Rose Blanc had been an early Resistant; they went together to greet the International Brigade at Cerbère in 1938, when Rose was nineteen. Rose worked hard to support the Spanish refugees, inspired by her communist ideals, and by 1940 she was a key personality in the embryonic local Resistance.

Communist leaders had supported the Hitler–Stalin pact in 1939, and after the declaration of war in September the French Communist Party had been made illegal. It was even suggested that the workers of France should fraternise with ordinary German soldiers after the invasion. But despite any political dilemma, at a local level many communists were active against Vichy and the Germans long before the invasion of the Soviet Union allowed them to officially switch sides.

I discovered that Rose's sister was still alive and went to see her in Vernet, a working-class suburb of Perpignan. I was greeted by her husband, Jean Rostand, a big pale man with a little blue knitted cap on his head. Marcelle Rostand was hanging out the washing in the tiny dusty garden, and we sat at the oilcloth-covered table in the dim interior, blinds drawn against the fierce sun outside, to wait for her. Among the children's portraits and childish drawings on the wall, the photo of Rose Blanc took pride of place. It was a photo I knew well by now, the dark hair looped back, the serious brown eyes and full upturned mouth.

While we waited for his wife to finish her chores Jean Rostand told me about himself. He too had been in the Resistance, directing actions in the Prades area for the Francs-Tireurs et Partisans Français (FTPF), the armed wing of the Communist Party, towards the end of the war. He had still been at school in 1941, aged seventeen, hoping to become a teacher, but was already involved with the nascent local Resistance, and was soon arrested by the French police. He was sent first to prison and then to a work camp in the Cantal. He explained how he managed to escape.

'We were moving camp, and three of us, all in our uniforms, a seminarist, a teacher and a student of German, just walked out of the gate. We just seized our chance, and started running till we got to the demarcation line. We told the Germans we were off to build the *Südwall* and we made it back to Perpignan.'

He soon became involved with the local Resistance. 'We kept moving, never stayed in the same place. You had to know how to survive in the wild.'

I thought of the forests and rivers here, and asked inanely: 'Did you fish?'

'We didn't have time for fishing,' he snorted. 'It was a dangerous life!' (Actually the Maquis were more likely to fish with the aid of grenades once they had some.) He began explaining to me the difference between the groups of Maquis in the region, the FTPF being the armed wing of the communists, reinforced by Spanish guerrilleros. 'They already knew how to fight.' Then there were the Gaullists, who were informed and supplied by the Allies (who were reluctant to supply arms to the FTPF since they didn't much fancy a communist future).

At this point Marcelle Rostand came in with her laundry basket. M. Rostand explained that she was very deaf, and I wondered how I was going to talk to her. By then I was quite lost in the complexities of the Communist Party and the Soviet Pact, and said that I really wanted to hear about her sister Rose Blanc. Then Marcelle brought a low stool to the table, and leaned close to me. I could see clearly the resemblance to her sister, the delicate features and big brown eyes behind her glasses. I repeated my question loudly in her ear. She frowned and nodded and began to talk. I didn't need to ask questions, she knew what she wanted to say.

'We were a family of eight children, Rose was the fifth and I was three years younger.' They were poor farmers but managed to buy a property in Soler, near Perpignan. 'So then we could sell vegetables.' There they went to school. 'We walked two kilometres to school, and knitted on the way!' But Rose, though a good student, had to leave at the age of twelve to work in the canning factory of Ille-sur-Têt.

'But when she was fourteen Rose was sent to Paris. Mother wept to see her go.' Marcelle too was weeping, and took off her glasses to wipe her eyes with a large practical man's handkerchief. I wondered if we should stop. But she wanted to continue.

Rose worked as a maid, but soon fell ill, far from her family, and deprived of the light and air of the South. She was rescued by an uncle who sent her to typing school, a skill she would put to good use in typing innumerable Resistance tracts. (Marcelle proudly showed me her certificate.) 'Eventually Rose came back. We met her off the train. She was wearing a hat!'

By then, in 1937, Rose had become involved with the Young Communist movement, inspired particularly by Danièle Casanova, the Pasionaria of the Resistance, the charismatic, militant young Corsican who had already travelled to the USA and Moscow as part of an International Young Communist delegation protesting against the growing threat of fascism. Casanova had created the Union des Jeunes Filles de France, the women's branch of the Young Communists, and soon Rose was organising the local branch in the Pyrénées-Orientales.

'I was only thirteen then,' recalled Marcelle, 'but I wanted to follow my sister, so I went with her to meetings, and helped her collect boxes of milk for Spain. I was as Red as she was.' Marcelle laughed, indicating the scarf knotted around her neck.

In June 1937 Rose went with Danièle Casanova to take supplies to Madrid, visited the trenches and returned with a Republican bullet as a souvenir and a determination to fight fascism, whatever the cost. She continued to support the Republicans, once helping to smuggle parts of an aeroplane engine across the border, and after the defeat, typing innumerable tracts, often working right through the night. Then in December 1939 the party called her back to Paris to continue the struggle there, along with Danièle. Two women, with their shared southern roots, became close, and Danièle treated Rose almost like a daughter.

After the fall of France in June 1940, Rose cycled from Paris to Perpignan, with bags full of tracts condemning the Nazi occupation. But she soon returned to Paris, where she began a clandestine existence, changing her name, and living illegally in rue Chabrières, Porte de Versailles, in the 15th arrondissement, where there is now a plaque in her honour. As well as producing Resistance tracts, she continued to take part in protests and demonstrations, risking possible arrest and execution.

Marcelle brought a scrapbook to show me the rest of the story, told in a few photos and photocopies of the last letters Rose wrote, each page of the scrapbook carefully embellished with pictures of flowers. There were grief-stricken poems written by the family; Rose's story had deeply marked them all.

Rose was arrested in Paris in 1942 as a communist and imprisoned along with Danièle and other comrades. Each week her uncle brought a parcel of supplies and thus Rose managed to write letters, folded up tightly, and secreted in the parcel boxes when they were returned, hidden in crusts of bread. After five months they were transferred to the prison of Romainville, living in fear that they would be selected to be shot as hostages. Rose wrote to her family that there was little hope of her release, expressing her disgust at 'the French police who are serving the Germans so obsequiously'.

They were sent to Auschwitz-Birkenau in Poland, the first convoy of non-Jewish Resistant women to be deported there, 230 women between seventeen and sixty-nine years old, only forty-nine of whom would survive. During the three-day journey without food or water, some died on the way. According to those who survived, Rose remained cheerful, encouraging her companions and singing songs for them in her strong Catalan accent. The convoy was famous for entering the camp singing 'La Marseillaise'.

It was cold January when they arrived, confronted by dogs, barbed wire, the smoke rising from the crematoriums. They were shaved and tattooed and forced to stand naked for hours in the cold. Marcelle shows me the photo of Rose in a striped prison uniform, numbered, hair roughly shorn with scissors. They were put to work draining the swamp around the camp, but Rose fell, hurt her leg, and untreated it became infected. She suffered gangrene and dysentery, and though Danièle tried to take care of her, she died on 15 March 1943. Danièle Casanova died less than two months later, of typhus, on 9 May.

There were not many like Rose Blanc, either here or anywhere else in France. Resistance at the beginning of the war was extremely limited. A handful of those already committed, like Rose and Odette, continued their struggle. Some, like the young Pierre Solanes, were inspired by de Gaulle's first broadcast, but most people were reeling from the shock of defeat and resistance seemed impossible.

Most remained passive, seduced by the propaganda of the Vichy regime and wrapped up in the mounting pressures of daily life. Only gradually did people come to understand that their invader was not just German, but specifically Nazi, a realisation exemplified in the first clandestine novel of the Resistance, *Le Silence de la mer*, by 'Vercors' (real name Jean Bruller), published in 1942, in which an idealistic cultured German is billeted on a French family, and comes to realise for himself the true nature of his masters.

But there were a handful of men and women, officers, teachers, working-class communists and priests, who did not accept defeat and did grasp the full implications of Nazi ideology. In the Pyrenees region there were also the Spanish Republicans, ready to continue their struggle against fascism, experienced fighters who had little to lose. They were often the first members of the escape networks and Maquis groups that developed and they played an important role in Resistance in the region. They also had an impact elsewhere in France in places where they had been sent as forced labour.

There were early pockets of resistance and secret initiatives by small groups, though a very small percentage of the population was involved. Local movements nearly all grew from below, more in the towns at first than in the country. Eventually German requisitions and the forced labour laws alienated the peasantry as well, so they were more inclined to offer sanctuary to Resistants, if not to become actively involved themselves.

The groups were necessarily covert and rarely had contact with each other. Some knew nothing of de Gaulle. As late as July 1942, the journals of three different movements, calling for a demonstration on 14 July, were distributed secretly during the night in Prades unknown to each other.

There were a few secret signals, such as carrying two fishing rods, *deux gaules* – and later a craze for displaying safety pins, which were known as *épingles anglaises*. Newsreels in cinemas became occasions for whistling and roaring abuse. There were public demonstrations and the 14th of July, Bastille Day, the national festival which had been abolished by the Vichy government, became a favourite date, communicated by the regular Radio Londres 9 p.m. broadcast.

There is a plaque now in Perpignan to commemorate the first 14 July demonstration in 1942, when despite Vichy police and barricades the Place Arago in Perpignan slowly filled with participants. More than three hundred people came out of their houses and down to the square in the middle of town. Each wore a rosette of red, white and blue, some carried banners, 'Bread for the workers! Milk for our children!' They looked at each other for the first time, curious to see who was on the same side of the barricades. They sang the Marseillaise. Vichy police, the Service d'Ordre Légionnaire (SOL), jostled the crowd shouting 'Death to the Gaullists', and some fighting broke out, but otherwise it was peaceful. However several days later thirty people were interrogated by the police, three teachers were fired, and several communists arrested.

In the early days resistance was about information and influence, countering the propaganda and misinformation of Vichy by disseminating tracts and newspapers and keeping alive the idea of liberation and freedom. As Jean Rostand put it, 'Part of our purpose was to give hope to the population.'

Local people, like Odette, her mother and her sister Francine, produced anti-Vichy propaganda, forged and supplied false papers and provided hiding places. Others acted as *passeurs* across the mountains. There were also people in ordinary jobs, doing their bit to subvert the new regime; town clerks copied key documents, garages serviced vehicles to transport the Maquis and supplies, doctors and nurses treated wounded escapees and Resistants.

The first clandestine networks in the region had developed to aid escapees across the frontier to Spain. They would later provide intelligence to the Allied forces outside France. In reality the most effective resistance in the Pyrenees continued to be in helping people to escape. It was certainly the most valuable local contribution to the war effort. They saved the lives of refugees who would otherwise have been transported to Germany or executed, and they guided soldiers and aviators on their path back to the Allied camp to fight again.

Many came through Perpignan, where there were safe hotels and bars like the Continental Bar on Place Arago. Some of the houses in the warren of streets in the old town had doors to the streets on either side, invaluable escape routes. There was a sweetshop, the Confiserie Vivant on rue de la Barre, which was a key location. Behind the shop was a courtyard, and another building with access to the street behind. There they hid the refugees, who included by all accounts two of de Gaulle's brothers, Xavier and Pierre; the father of General Giraud; and the painter Albert Marquet and his wife. The elegant little shop is still there, and you can buy expensive hand-made chocolates carefully wrapped in exquisite beribboned little boxes.

Increased patrols made escape by sea more and more difficult, especially after the German occupation, when the beaches were mined. By 1944 the coastal strip was evacuated and totally inaccessible. The coastal frontier crossings were also much more heavily patrolled, and there had been many arrests. The *passeurs* and their charges had to head further into the mountains, crossing at various remote cols along the ridge of the frontier, or over the high plateau of the Cerdagne, or through Andorra. These vital links between valleys on each side of the border had sustained the life of these remote regions for centuries, providing passage for trade, smugglers and shepherds.

Many of the *passeurs* who knew the mountains best were Spanish, and risked arrest and execution if they were discovered over the border in Spain. Some *passeurs* took escapees across out of political commitment, as the Fittkos did. Others did it for the money. They had to eat like everybody else. The rate for a crossing became more and more expensive as the war progressed and it became more dangerous. The highest rate was for Jews. A few of the *passeurs* were known to take the money and abandon their charges, and stories abounded of their perfidy.

Many though were like Henri Melich, people who knew their own bit of mountain and wanted to play their part. Melich, a spry, dapper little man with silver hair and moustache, came to meet me in the small village of Ponteilla outside Perpignan, and took me to his house. At first we talked rather formally in the living room (his wife made coffee and stayed in the kitchen), but he kept referring to books I should read, so we went into his study. There he came to life, twinkling up and down his library steps like the passionate autodidact bookseller he had always been. He showed me his oldest book, an ancient school history book, sniffing the pages with great satisfaction.

He also found his own (unpublished) account of his war experiences which he kindly allowed me to use, and then began to explain his background. He and his family had left a small village near Barcelona during the Retirada. 'How long were we on the road? Maybe eight or ten days. I was thirteen, I don't remember much. But I remember the French reception at Le Perthus. That was terrible. My father made himself look older, hunched over and unshaven, so he wasn't sent off with the men to a separate camp.'

Eventually they joined his sister, who was already living in Quillan, in the Aude near Limoux, just over the departmental border from the Col de Jau and Pyrénées-Orientales. 'I wanted to go to school but I was told I was too old. But I was too young to work either, so I ended up in the forest woodcutting and making charcoal in the Corbières. I loved reading so I really taught myself.'

The family began sheltering other refugees, and in 1943, aged seventeen, Melich began to work as part of a chain aiding escapers through the steep gorges and valleys of the Aude, and then handing them over to a *passeur* from Spain or Andorra. Usually he collected the refugees in Quillan, where they stayed in a safe house, the local brothel run by Madame Raymonde Rousset. 'I remember the first time, a couple in their forties who were so exhausted we had to wait a day for them to recover. We followed the railway tracks to Belvianes, but the woman was wearing high-heeled shoes and they had to stay another night to find shoes more suitable for walking.'

He had to be careful. Once his father was warned by the chief of the gendarmerie in Quillan, fortunately a sympathiser, that he had been noticed in Belvianes coming through the village with suspicious-looking people. And his brother-in-law was a pro-Vichy gendarme. 'According to him we were all bandits and terrorists. If he had known what I was doing, would he have denounced me? At that time I doubted it. Now I'm not so sure . . .'

Sometimes the *passeurs* he handed over to were rogues. 'We knew of one group who paid 30,000 francs each and then were abandoned in the middle of the mountains. They were lucky to be discovered by another expedition. We heard of others who never arrived.' Melich hesitated at this point, gave me a quizzical look, then produced a magazine. 'Later on we found the Andorrans were charging money, stealing stuff, jewellery and so on, even killing some of them. Much later many bodies were found in Andorra. But we were doing it for free, we had the idea we were all in the same struggle.' He showed me an article in the Spanish magazine, *La Reveue Reporter* written in 1977: 'The mountains of death', a journalistic investigation that described the discovery of skeletons in shallow graves. 'From the photos there was no doubt of their origins,' said Melich grimly. 'But the article was soon suppressed.'

The Royal Escaping Society had put me in touch with Reg Lewis, a British aviator who had escaped across the Pyrenees via Quillan in March 1944. He told me the details when I went to see him in Gidea Park, in Essex. He was a Londoner who joined Bomber Command in 1941. He still has pictures of planes all over his walls, an enduring passion. By 1944 he was dropping secret agents all over France. On 7 February, 'in absolutely bloody awful weather' as Lewis put it, the Halifax took off again. But by the time they were crossing Central France, headed for Marseille, the plane had iced up completely, and finally they had to abandon the aircraft and bale out. 'I can still remember that awful crack when you tumble over and the parachute opens,' Lewis recalled.

He landed in deep snow in the hills above the Rhône valley, and tramped off to the nearest farmhouse, explaining that he was 'RAF – Anglais' to the old lady who answered the door. They took care of him, and he made contact with the other members of his crew who were all hidden in a barn.

Then an American turned up, in full Marine battledress. 'He had hand grenades strapped to him, knife, guns, every bloody thing! A real tough guy.' This was Peter Ortiz of the Office of Strategic Services (OSS), forerunner of the CIA, who became famous for strolling around occupied France in full uniform. The next time Reg saw him, he had swapped his captain's insignia for those of a major; the badge had apparently been dropped down to him with supplies for the local Resistance. The air crew were kept hidden, although some of the maquis group unwisely got drunk in the village and reveal the foreigners' presence. The maquis were summarily dealt with, court-martialled and shot by others in the group.

Lewis and his crew were very anxious to get away. 'We had our escape maps, of course, of folded silk, and realised the only way back home was to get down to the Spanish border.' After three weeks Ortiz arranged transport to Valence, and they were crammed onto a train that rapidly filled with German troops. 'Thank God, they couldn't speak French either. They even offered us cigarettes.'

They arrived in Carcassonne and made contact with a priest on the platform as arranged, and were then taken into the Pyrenees on a small local train. 'Then we walked all night, through disused railway tunnels, past waterfalls. We walked for hours. Then we saw a bonfire and found a field full of people, American airmen shot down, people on the run from every corner of Europe: Czechs, Poles, Greeks, a right unholy mixture.' Lewis shook his head in wonder at the memory.

That evening they started walking again, escorted by three Spanish guides. 'We were given a couple of loaves of bread and a great hunk of roast meat, so we guessed some serious walking lay ahead of us.' They walked for a week through deep snow, with only one night's rest, forty people huddled in a stone shelter. Happily for him Reg had kept his escape pack so could supplement supplies with chocolate, condensed milk and benzedrine. Though when the benzedrine wore off he almost collapsed and was close to being abandoned, until the guides were persuaded to give him another chance.

They climbed ridge after ridge, until finally they were told: 'You're in Spain!' But they still had two more days of walking, and a couple of nights in a barn full of sheep, until they were finally picked up by truck and delivered to the British consulate in Barcelona.

Later Reg sent me a map of the route he reckoned they must have followed, from Quillan via Belvianes, Quérigut, through the Capcir, skirting Mount Carlit, at 2,921 metres the highest peak this end of the Pyrenees, to Latour-de-Carol, Puigcerda and into Spain. He added a note: 'I don't think that we walked in such a straight line!' He also sent me a copy of a letter he had received from Señor Guardia Socada in

1985, written in French: 'Bien cher Monsieur Lewis, Without doubt you were part of that expedition, the biggest our team made across the frontier.' Señor Socada confirmed the route they had taken with a group of thirty-eight escapees. The two men finally met again, in Barcelona, guide and escapee, forty-one years later.

There were clearly many untold stories about these mountain escape routes, and I had become intrigued by the story of Abbé Ginoux, a priest in the small village of Dorres in the Cerdagne. This remote mountain plateau, divided between Spain and France by the Treaty of the Pyrenees in 1659, was an ideal place for refugees to try to cross the frontier. Abbé Ginoux had smuggled many across the border, only 2 kilometres from the village, lodging the refugees in the presbytery, or with sympathetic peasant neighbours, and sometimes even hiding them in the church. He slipped their brand-new false identity papers under the church prayer mats so that they were rubbed and worn by the faithful to appear more authentic. Abbé Ginoux clearly had a sense of humour.

I drove up to the Cerdagne in early September, with blue skies and sun so bright it hurt, up the helter-skelter road of the Têt valley, the villages clinging like limpets to the valley sides, the river flowing down its rocky bed to the coast. Beyond the great stone citadel of Mont-Louis, an important guard post in wartime and still headquarters of a parachute regiment, the landscape opened up, a broad vista of pastures dotted with cows, surrounded by mountain peaks, misted by cloud. This is not gentle country, mind: any wind would make it a howling steppe. The farms already had their wood stacked ready for winter and the thick snow that would inevitably come.

I stopped in Saillagouse, hoping to visit the gendarmerie. Here one brave gendarme, Raymond Botet, had been a key element in the escape network. But in Saillagouse the gendarmerie only opens three times a week. In the small village of Osséja I bought bread before the boulangerie shut for lunch. Here the sanatorium had once provided shelter to refugees making for the frontier.

The main frontier town of Bourg-Madame is now merged with its Spanish counterpart, Puigcerda. There is a sign to say you are entering Spain, but the border post is empty, a dusty remnant. The contrast between the two towns is astonishing. Bourg-Madame is a classic small French town, with its boulangeries, blue shutters and geraniums. It was after midday, and everybody had shut up shop for lunch.

Across the border the roads were terrible, the parking worse, the driving more flamboyant, Spain in short. I was in a Catalan town with a

Ramblas, a Modernista theatre, a Placa Barcelona, a market still bustling in Spanish and Catalan and no one ready for lunch till 2.30 at least.
These days the main problem in crossing the frontier it seems is to be
sure you are heading the right way for lunch. Go in the wrong direction
and you miss two nationalities of lunch.

Returning to France, I followed the railway line along the border, the
crucial crossing for escapees, and went up to Dorres via the sanatorium
of Escaldes. Dorres is a village of stonecutters, with high-quality stone-
work around even the simplest window. The church, a fine tenth-
century Romanesque building, was firmly shut, though, to protect its
precious statue of a Black Virgin.

Happily the hotel next door was not, and although they had told me
with some satisfaction over the phone that there were no vacancies, I
tentatively approached the elderly Madame behind the bar. She observed me critically for a moment, but I was soon installed in a small
room overlooking the street, the school, the town hall, and the silvery-
grey slate roofs of the village.

Then I put on my boots and set out on a pilgrimage to the Chapelle
de Belloc, the route where Abbé Ginoux had led his charges. From the
little stone chapel, high on the hill, I could see the long blue outline of
the Puigmal, bare of snow now but still forbidding. Several small towns
are scattered across the plateau, divided between countries by the
straight lines of road, rail and frontier. After the sun the day had
darkened, a storm threatened, and low leaden clouds were massing to
the west over the hills. There was a rumble and I shivered, suddenly
chill. I was glad I had a bed for the night and would not be sleeping on
the hard ground with a blanket, and only stone-dry bread to eat.

At the hotel I enquired if anyone knew about Abbé Ginoux, and I
was directed to Madame Marty, the stern old lady behind the bar.
When I mentioned the abbé, a smile lit her eyes and softened her
features. She explained that her family had lived next door to the abbé,
running a hostel for patients of the sanatorium. They had helped him
look after the refugees hidden in the presbytery, or up in the attic of the
church, snug among old confessional cushions.

'My mother cooked for them,' recalled Madame Marty, 'and I would
take them the food.' Sometimes they stayed in the hostel. 'They stayed
in a room at the back of the house,' she said, 'where there was a
window onto the street at the back and then straight out into fields and
mountains.'

'What was the village like in those days?' I asked.

'We were *paysans*, everybody was afraid.'

'So what made your family willing to take the risk of sheltering refugees?'

'Ah, that was Abbé Ginoux.' She smiled fondly. 'He did so much good, so much good, he was like a father to all the world. My aunt used to cook for him – that was how we got to know him.'

Ginoux was from the Gard, a southerner though not a mountain dweller, and had come to Dorres with tuberculosis. Cured by the mountains, he decided to stay and became curé of the tiny village and chaplain to the sanatorium. Dr Goujon could remember him – a big man, asthmatic, who smoked too much, he said. A black and white photo shows a man with a shiny pate, big nose, shy smile and warm eyes. His remote parish was to prove very useful. He was involved in the Resistance early, in contact with anti-Franco Spanish clergy and the Toulouse escape network after 1939.

The mountain sanatoriums in the Cerdagne provided discreet sanctuary for those wanting to cross the frontier. Many patients came for long stays to cure the tuberculosis that was increasingly common during the war, and they were often accompanied or visited by their families. Ginoux worked with the curés of Latour-de-Carol, the international station where trains from Toulouse and the Petit Train Jaune converged before heading down to Barcelona, and with the curé of Puigcerda, across the frontier. He was also involved with the monks of Villa Roselande in nearby Angoustrine, a monastic TB sanatorium. Visible from the Villa is Llivia, a Spanish enclave in the middle of French territory. When the treaty of the Pyrenees was signed in 1659, all the villages on the border were designated French. However, it was afterwards discovered that Llivia was officially a town not a village and thus remained Spanish. To this day it is resolutely Spanish, and it is hard even to find because it is so grudgingly signposted by the French. If refugees could make it into Llivia they were technically in Spain, and there was an international road through French territory which connected them to Spain itself. The brothers found many pretexts to visit their confrères in Llivia. They had their cemetery there, which provided endless excuses for visits. Thus they managed to smuggle the refugees across.

Eventually one of the brothers was entrapped and arrested. He had been out walking and had been accosted by a German soldier, who had said he wanted to desert to avoid the Russian Front. 'Spain is not far,' said Brother Nectaire. 'You can see it over there. You just have to follow this little path.' The monk was arrested, and deported to Dachau and Buchenwald. A year later the German commander of Bourg-Madame ordered all the brothers out, 'for helping terrorists flee to Spain', and they were summarily ejected.

The refugees, many of them Jews, came by various routes, from Toulouse though the Ariège, from the Aude through Quillan, Limoux and Carcassonne or through the valley of the Têt from Perpignan and Prades. Some went by way of Mosset and La Coûme, where the Krügers' farm was remote enough to provide a staging post on the escape route. Various ingenious methods were devised to disguise their identities. The names of patients housed in the psychiatric hospital of Limoux were borrowed; a sympathetic bishop in Toulouse devised religious identities that helped qualify them for treatment in the sanatoria. They set off, dressed in a priest's soutane, breviary in hand, to take the train.

Once installed in Dorres, they had to be careful of patrols so near to the frontier. Madame Marty explained: 'We had a signal. In case of any problem we would bang three times on the wooden floor, and they could climb out of the window and escape to the mountains.' It was used only once, she said, when in March 1943 the German border patrol arrived to make a check at 6 o'clock in the evening. 'Two English flyers were hidden in the bedroom downstairs, and they jumped out of the window as arranged. Abbé Ginoux went to find them in the fields once the danger was past.'

Ginoux himself often guided them to the frontier, leaving Dorres at nightfall or before daybreak, ostensibly taking the mountain path to the Chapelle de Belloc but then veering south to come down above the cemetery of Enveitg, near the border. There the group waited hidden behind the wall. Ginoux went into the cemetery as if to pray, from where he could spy out the route. If all was clear he gave the signal to cross the road and a stone bridge as fast as possible and make for the railway line, where there was a gap in the fence for cows to cross into the pasture. Then they would head for a farm (half of it was in Spain and half in France) where they were met to make the forty-minute walk to Puigcerda. Among those who escaped this way was the Grand Rabbi of Brussels, who crossed in February 1942, and Rabbi Mordoch, leader of the Jewish community in Perpignan, who fled in 1942. Other distinguished escapees via the Cerdagne included the daughter of General Giraud, and the wife of General de Lattre de Tassigny, disguised as a peasant selling milk.

In the cemetery at Enveitg there was a monument to the Spanish refugees who died crossing the frontier the other way in 1939, and a resinous scent of cypresses in the air. Above the graves with their wrought-iron crosses and enamel nameplates stands the tall granite column, topped by an iron calvary, where Abbé Ginoux pretended to pray. From here you can still see right across the road, now a two-lane highway of fast cars, and beyond it the railway tracks to Spain.

Before I left Dorres I finally visited the church. The villagers were bustling about with a copy of the Black Virgin (the real one was behind bars in a side chapel), due for one of her regular processions up to the Chapelle. She was wrapped in lace, placed on a cushion between wooden poles. Then they put her in the back of a car, quicker than walking but no doubt as prayerful. Somehow their practical ministrations echoed those of the abbé.

After the German occupation of the South in November 1942 repression was intensified, and the lists of suspects for arrest grew longer: Spanish refugees, anti-fascist refugees like the Fittkos, all immigrant Jews not yet arrested, all known communists and anarchists. The French Milice, an extreme development of the SOL, the Service d'Ordre Légionnaire, which had sprung from the Légion Française des Combattants, was created in January 1943 with the express purpose of rounding them all up. They specialised in the capture and torture of Resistants. Although originally loyal to Pétain, the Milice increasingly allied itself with the Germans, and was supplied with German arms. Many in the Legion were repulsed by their activities and renounced the oath of allegiance they had given to Pétain.

The first assembly of the local Milice, with their signature black uniform and black berets, took place in the Paris cinema in Perpignan at the end of February 1943 and included the Milice chief, André Cutzach, the prefect of the Pyrénées-Orientales, and Colonel Ruffiandis, as departmental president of the Legion. Their mission was to combat treason and communism, and their aims were listed as follows:

Against bourgeois selfishness [egoïsme]. For French solidarity.
Against apathy. For enthusiasm.
Against scepticism. For faith.
Against individualism. For community spirit.
Against egalitarianism. For hierarchy.
Against democracy. For authority.
Against anarchy. For discipline.
Against Bolshevism. For Nationalism.
Against Gaullist dissidence. For French unity.
Against the Jewish leper. For French purity.

The Milice were well paid, and many of the new recruits were young and poor. Joining was seen as an alternative way to escape STO and immediately conferred a dubious kind of status. Louis Malle's film *Lacombe Lucien* portrays one of them, an ignorant teenager who knows little else than how to catch rabbits and set traps for birds. Rejected by the Maquis, he joins the Milice instead. When he sends money to his mother, she takes it, but she also shows him the little coffin with his name on it, courtesy of the Resistance.

In June 1943 the Milice turned its attention to the Sabaté family, still producing false papers and tracts, typewritten and hand-lettered from their Perpignan attic, hiding escapees and even arms and explosives in their cellar. I asked Odette Sabaté to tell me what happened during our meeting in Ria.

'All three of us were arrested by the Milice. My mother at home, my sister and I at work – I was working for the post office by then.' They had been located after someone was arrested with one of the identity cards they had made and, after some persuasion, had confessed their names. 'We had been warned that if they got us we would be in big trouble,' said Odette. All three were imprisoned and interrogated. Then Odette was allowed to return home to pick up some clothes. 'I was accompanied by a regular gendarme who said to me; "What did you do – Steal a cake?" I told him I was going to my aunt's house to leave our key, and I managed to slip out of the back entrance into the next street.'

Odette knew she had to get away as fast as possible, and she managed to reach Montpellier and make contact with the Resistance there. She ended up in Lyon, a liaison between the Occupied and Unoccupied zones, a slight girl looking even younger than her eighteen years, she was rarely suspected. She recalled carrying parts of a machine gun in her shopping bag – 'I had no idea how to use it!' But it was a hard and lonely time. 'It was better we had no contact with each other, and no one knew where we lived, so I found a room for myself.' She ate her meals in front of a mirror, telling herself stories for company.

But after the landing in Provence in August 1944, Odette was arrested by the Gestapo, and imprisoned. 'The Spanish had always said to me, If you are arrested, you mustn't start to talk. If you start they will never stop. They will want more and more.' She was tortured, forced to drink water till she lost consciousness. She clasped her hands together on the table. 'What helped me was to think there have been others before you who have held out. They are going to kill you anyway, the main thing is to hold out another hour, another day.' What mattered was to hold out long enough for a warning to reach other comrades. Each morning she and the other prisoners were called out for a roll call never knowing who would be condemned to die that day.

After the Liberation she was freed and she returned to Perpignan. She had known nothing of what happened to her mother and sister until May 1944. They had been sentenced to prison by the French court in Montpellier, where Francine, a tiny, handicapped young woman, had given a speech justifying her actions, her determination to liberate France from the Nazis. They had been delivered to the Germans and sent to the Ravensbrück women's concentration camp. 'I knew then I would never see them again.' Odette looked at me. 'Returning to the house in Perpignan was the worst day of my life.' She heard the appalling details of their incarceration later from another returned prisoner, Louise Horte.

Francine had suffered particularly because of her handicapped hip. It was hard to get up in the morning without assistance from others, let alone stand for hours for the freezing roll calls. Her mother, Josephine, was selected on 29 March 1945 and sent to the gas ovens, then cremated. Watching her mother go destroyed the last hope for Francine. She may have died before the Russians arrived on 25 April, or she may have been part of the column of wretched prisoners that the Germans took with them when they fled the camp. Unable to walk far, she would have been killed along the way. She was twenty-five.

Odette showed me the last letter received from her mother, written in the train transporting them to Germany.

We have been put into cattle wagons, and have now passed Châlons-sur-Marne. But before we left Paris, I want you to know we all sang, 600 women, for an hour as we waited on the platform. For punishment we have been deprived of water for 24 hours since then.

But our courage is the same, and we still hope to be soon free and with you again . . . Amédine should take the sewing machine and the big photo of Pierre.

Big kisses for all and Vive la France. Josephine

As the war intensified the Resistance movements gradually made contact with each other. De Gaulle sent Jean Moulin to try and unite the distinct factions that had emerged, each with its own particular motivation and goal. There were significant differences between the Free French in London and local Resistance groups, in particular the communist FTPF. Moulin achieved a great deal travelling and negotiating between the different factions to create the MUR, the United

Resistance Movement, but after he was betrayed, tortured and executed (in July 1943), the communists still kept their distance.

In the Pyrenees Spaniards had started many of the first Maquis groups, although some of the Spanish kept themselves separate, and the deep political divisions among them remained, with anarchists and communists still at bitter loggerheads. One group stayed well hidden on the frontier above Prats-de-Mollo throughout the war, appearing only to kill a German guard from time to time, and poised to return to the fight in their own country as soon as they could.

As resistance grew, the call for weapons became more urgent, and the internal Resistance was dependent on the Allies for parachute drops of arms and supplies. These went overwhelmingly to the MUR and its active wing, the Secret Army, not to the communists, whom no one wanted to encourage. It had become a tradition for the BBC to play the national anthems of all the Allies every Sunday night before the news at 9 p.m., but after the German invasion of Russia in June 1941 the British government could not bring itself to permit the playing of the Internationale. They insisted that to call the Internationale a national anthem was a contradiction in terms. But the Russian ambassador refused to substitute other Russian music, and after six months the government finally gave in.

The strategies in France were opposed. The Gaullists aimed to hold back for the Allied landing, while the FTPF believed it was better to continually harass the Germans with ambushes and sabotage. They were effective in blowing up railways and depots, and with more arms and explosives could no doubt have done more. They were particularly keen on explosives, especially the Spanish, and would blow up a telephone exchange even if the damage could just as easily have been done with a pair of wire cutters.

Meanwhile all waited eagerly for the promised Allied landing, which many believed would happen on the Languedoc coast. As indeed did the Germans, feverishly constructing their *Südwall* defences. After the success of the Allied landings in North Africa, the German defeat at Stalingrad and the fall of Mussolini in July 1943, *Le jour J*, D-Day, was expected to happen at any moment. But it did not come, and '*débarquement*' became a word snorted ironically, a future that would never arrive. Meanwhile everything seemed to get worse. The Germans became more brutal and the Vichy government and the Milice more committed to collaboration with the occupier.

It was not until 1943 that the local Resistance really began to emerge, though there had been isolated incidents of sabotage before, such as cutting the telephone lines of the German headquarters at the Hôtel de France in the centre of Perpignan in November 1942. But throughout 1943 the sabotage intensified: the iron ore transport cable from Canigou was cut, interrupting transport for a month; a convoy of guns and tanks was held up in the station of Rivesaltes by railway staff who interfered with the brakes. Often the actual damage may have been quite minor, but it meant that the Vichy government and the Germans had to deploy more and more personnel to guard railways, mines, depots, public buildings and industries that were producing goods for the Germans.

The most significant factors in the growth of the Resistance were the actions of Vichy itself – most of all the launch of STO in February 1943, the forced labour policy, which caused widespread rebellion from the start. The southern zone began turning its back on a regime which had appeared to promise them a kind of immunity. The little villages and towns of the South which since 1940 had been relatively quiet and unmolested suddenly found themselves threatened with forced labour and what they saw as deportation. Until then the Resistance had been largely urban, with networks and safe houses mainly located in the towns. Now it took to the hills.

Although some of the young men determined to avoid forced labour in Germany disappeared across the border to Spain, and some simply lay low – one peasant family in Mosset kept their son hidden in a barn outside the village for the rest of the war – many escaped to the woods and hills of southern France. Another Vichy policy helped: foreign labour, in particular the Spanish refugees from the camps, had been formed into small rural work gangs, labouring to supply the huge demand for lumber, and particularly charcoal, the essential substitute for petrol. Their remote forest encampments provided ideal locations for the fugitive *réfractaires*.

Though at first their motives were as much to save themselves as to save France, this emerging rural Resistance became increasingly significant. They found hiding places in the forests, and refuge in the crumbling stone buildings of abandoned farms in the depopulated uplands. Again not quite the 'Return to the Land' that Vichy had envisaged. This growing phenomenon – a mixture of *réfractaires*, antifascists and communists on the run, and Spanish Civil War veterans – became known as the Maquis, after the Corsican word for the pervasive scrubland that cloaks the island. Taking to the Maquis acquired a certain mystique as the idea of revolt took root. The possibility of armed combat began to seem more realistic.

They were encouraged to see themselves as special and set apart, Stern instructions were issued by the leaders of the United Resistance movement to anyone wishing to join the Maquis, which made it sound like a spiritual mission. They must expect to submit to tough discipline, to obey orders, and to 'renounce all links with family and friends until the end of the war', to expect no regular wage or certainty of arms, 'to surrender all egoism and individualism for the common cause'. There are echoes of the Cathars, the 'pure' religious dissidents of the thirteenth century who also found sanctuary in the Pyrenees, and sacrificed themselves for their beliefs.

But the Maquis – which eventually totalled about 500 active participants in the department of the Pyrénées-Orientales, although the figure of about 2,500 is estimated by Jean Larrieu for all Resistance members in the department – had to survive, to establish themselves with supplies and shelter, and enlist the sympathy of local peasants in the farms and villages on whom they were largely dependent. They needed arms and ammunition, and had to have access to an open area remote enough to receive parachute drops.

Their identity and solidarity was further consolidated by the determination of Vichy and the Germans to hunt them down. Massive search operations were organised throughout the South, often with tragic outcomes. A poorly armed camp in the Cévennes was betrayed and surrounded by German forces in July 1943. Three *maquisards* were killed, fifteen wounded and forty-three taken prisoner and deported to Germany, including the local mayor. The camp had included thirty-two *réfractaires* from the region. The bodies of two of those killed were thrown from the back of a lorry into the main street of St-Jean-du-Gard, and their burial expressly forbidden.

Such brutality only increased the bitterness of the population against the government and the Germans, and more and more people, previously '*attentiste*', began to discreetly support the Resistance. An FTPF list of its Catalan members, including their *noms de guerre*, offers a gloriously diverse range of occupations: accountant, doctor, Spanish refugee, railworker, retired, student, chauffeur, agricultural worker, mason, nurse, printer, painter, cook, winemaker, teacher, plumber, electrician, miner, woodcutter and *dactylo*, typist – a woman, of course. In November 1943 the chief of the local Milice reported gloomily:

A wind of revolt is blowing . . . the population rejoice at clandestine crossings of the frontier, they weep when Jews are arrested, the

Maréchal is defamed . . . The magistrates are apprehensive about judging the communo-gaullistes . . . we are near the end of our tether.

There were plenty of opportunities to support the Resistance apart from direct action. As well as supplying the outlaws with essential food and clothing, women in the villages could frustrate house searches or misdirect the hunters, local mayors could warn people of forthcoming attacks. Teachers played a key role in the networks, and the local priests were as likely to be loyal to their own population as to their bishop. Gendarmes could slow down operations, and even French bureaucracy played its part, sometimes delaying enquiries about specific individuals for months. Sympathetic officials, or at least those who saw which way the wind was blowing, allowed themselves to be tied up to look as though they had been forced to hand over ration books. Some town hall secretaries waited for the *maquisards* to come and rob them at the end of each month when the ration books arrived. In places the *maquisards* even installed electricity in their camps, routed from nearby power lines. People began to refer to them as our Maquis, our boys.

I was told the story of the Germans arriving to requisition food at a farm in Mosset where there were *maquisards* and weapons hidden in the barn, and how the farmer's wife had managed to see them off. Then I was told the story again, about another farm, and when I saw the film *Army of the Shadows* I realised this was one of those Resistance myths. It certainly happened to somebody.

The winter of 1943 was tough. The Maquis dug in, but it was harder to hide than in summer; the leafless trees revealed their camps, rising smoke could be seen, and tracks and footsteps were easily visible in the snow. The gazogene-fuelled lorries were more likely to break down in winter and sometimes could take as long as an hour to get started. When they had supplies of meat, a sheep or cow stolen preferably from the herd of a collaborator, they discovered it was better to stew the meat than roast it because the cooking smell was less noticeable. They were often extremely hungry – one Resistant in the Aude remembered living on a few large onions for over a week.

Getting supplies became a time-consuming part of their activities. At best they were supplied with food by sympathetic farmers or villagers, offering them IOUs in exchange, debts that they promised would be repaid when the war ended. A few of the old people in Mosset can remember the Maquis coming down from the Col de Jau to the village square and calling for the villagers to bring them potatoes and other essentials. But they also talk about two sorts of Maquis, the real

Resistance and the '*faux Maquis*', the 'False' ones, their fear of a knock on the door in the middle of the night, and their anxiety that they would open up to the *faux Maquis*, who would rob them of all their food.

When spring 1944 finally arrived, the rivers flowing with the melting snow of the mountains, tender green leaves screening the trees again, the tension rose further. The Germans terrorised rural areas with arrests and reprisals, even public hangings. They warned the population that patrols would shoot out windows lit up after curfew and open fire on cars with headlights. They began to round up everybody, Jews who had thus far escaped, Resistants or *réfractaires*, and deport them straight away. Over 1,000 men were arrested in Perpignan in June 1944. When the Vichy administration and local officials protested, they too were threatened with deportation. Local officials resigned wholesale. Rewards were promised to anyone who arrested or helped to arrest enemy soldiers or agents, or revealed the site of a downed aircraft.

The Resistance fought back, with attacks on railway lines, bridges, the power station in Arles-sur-Tech, the German bookshop in Perpignan and hotels used by the Germans, and ambushes of German soldiers patrolling the frontier. They killed the deputy head of the Milice in Perpignan. Many people were arrested, and the streets of Perpignan and the surrounding towns now have plaques honouring their names: teacher Louis Torcatis, who set poems of Resistance to music for the school orchestra to play, and had been one of the earliest Resistants, mercilessly tortured for days and days and finally killed; Gilbert Brutus, a famous Catalan rugby player, tortured and killed; Brice Bonnery, hospital administrator, deported to Buchenwald, where he died, and so many others.

Climb to the top of Canigou and it is easy to see how the geography of this region dictated the nature of the local Maquis, though walking on the lower slopes on a peaceful summer's day, lulled by birdsong and a light wind, passing a tree hung with red apples and an elderly couple out picking blackberries, it takes effort to believe that these hills were sites of such bloodshed, brutality and treason. But not only were the Pyrenees a frontier, albeit heavily patrolled by the Germans, but the valleys and plateaux provided a wealth of hiding places and potential sites for receiving parachute drops. I was discussing this with Roger Chanal, who had been part of a Canigou-based Maquis group, during lunch one day. He picked up his napkin and folded the linen into an impressively accurate model of Canigou, an extensive massif with two peaks and numerous valleys surrounded by lower hills and a maze of twisting gorges and valleys. Canigou stands proudly alone at the end of the Pyrenean chain, not surrounded by a mass of other peaks. It is eminently visible, dominating the landscape and the towns and villages scattered around it, a beacon even for mariners on the Mediterranean.

Tucked into the steep sides of Canigou and the surrounding hills are old mine workings, natural caves, the stone shelters of the shepherds, and walkers' chalets. Just above Prades, to the south of the river Têt, rises the plateau of Ambouillas, a remote redoubt that was one of the first places where the local Maquis took refuge. On the other side of the Têt valley you can see up the valley of the Castellane. With binoculars you can even discern the bell tower of Corbiac, and beyond that the village of Mosset. The Col de Jau above Mosset soon became a location for the Maquis.

Embedded in the sides of Canigou were small mining villages like Valmanya and Fillols, where most of the population willingly sheltered and supported the Maquis, and gave refuge to escapers. They knew the mountain well, all its secret mule paths and hidden caves. Ultimately the mountain itself was seen as a place of refuge, for the Catalans in particular a symbol of freedom. In his book *In Search of the Maquis*, the historian Rod Kedward describes climbing up into the hills of the Cévennes with a former member of the Resistance. They had a magnificent view of the Mediterranean coast in the distance. 'We'll have balcony seats for the Allied landing,' they had believed. In the Pyrenees many believed the landing would be further along the coast, near the lagoon at Bouzigues; then they would have had the balcony seat. Perhaps one of the Canigou *maquisards* climbed up to the peak of the mountain to view the coast and imagine their liberation.

When I began studying photographs of the Resistance, I was most struck, of course, by their youth – many 'took to the *maquis*' at sixteen or seventeen – but also by their jaunty style: the trousers high-waisted and tightly belted, the berets perched on the side, the kerchief knotted round the neck. There is a picture of one group at the chalet of Cortalets just below the summit of Canigou, with their berets and knapsacks, hand-knitted sweaters tucked tightly into trousers with leather belts. They have just finished a meal at the wooden table outside the refuge; one is still holding a bottle of wine, one smokes a pipe as he fills his pack with food, another is rolling a cigarette. They look young, cheerful, a little wild.

Everybody had been in the Resistance it seemed, but it was not easy finding anyone willing to talk or able to remember. I realised that contacting anyone directly would not work. Letters were regarded with deep suspicion and never answered. I had to be personally recommended for them to talk at all. Anyone who had been in the Maquis, even very young, was at least eighty, and some survivors were over ninety. Some were still known only by their Maquis names. Others only spoke Catalan. Sometimes the encounters were frustrating – I went to see one elderly chap in the camp site he ran, assured that he had many tales to tell about the Resistance. Indeed he did, but they were not his own. He had been only eleven when the war ended. I went to Collioure to interview an elderly fisherman about his underground activities, but my difficulties with his thick Catalan accent were further compounded by his lack of teeth.

In Arles-sur-Tech I went to see José Molina, a Spanish *passeur*, a mason originally from Andalucia. He is now over ninety, small, with a pair of large pointed ears and a twinkle in his eye, making him look like an antique pixie from one of his own carvings for the abbey. He slipped often into Spanish, and again I missed a great deal, though he told me about leading the fugitives from Amélie-les-Bains up to the frontier, and how his wife had to call on his boss when he did not get back the same day. After our talk we went out to his terrace, a shabby corner hung with washing, but transformed by the glossy leaves and red flowers of a single magnificent camellia bush. M. Molina selected several perfect blossoms and solemnly presented them to me with a courteous bow.

I drove up to Cassagnes, a small village lost in the vines in the high hills above the valley of the Têt, where I knew there had been a dramatic German attack on the Maquis. I wondered if there was still anyone left who would remember. Here civilisation is quickly left behind. In only a few minutes there is nothing, only dry *maquis*, dusty pungent herbs, rocks, spiky aloes and patches of vines. In the vineyards, each with its own little *casot*, the stone shelter for the vineyard workers, the vines are turning brown, the grapes heavy and ready to pick. Below lies the plain, stretching towards Perpignan and the sea beyond the white limestone hills of the Corbières. It is *maquis* country in every sense of the word. I drove through Bélesta, a steep village, which calls itself Bélesta-la-Frontière, a reminder that we are now on the border of Roussillon (Catalonia Nord) and France. Three people chatting beside the road, one woman in a pinafore, turned their heads slowly as I drove by. An old man in his nightshirt looked down suspiciously from his balcony.

Outside the village of Cassagnes is the inevitable *Monument aux*

*Morts.* I counted the names, twenty for 1914–1918, two for 1940–1944, one of them François Masse. In the village there was a familiar somnolence. It was already 11.30 a.m. Almost lunchtime. The *mairie* was closed, the post office had been open between 9 and 10.30. The bar did not open till 9 p.m. each evening. As I wandered the streets, from behind half-closed shutters I could hear loud conversations, the clatter of saucepans as food was prepared. Then I found the boulangerie still open, and enquired if they knew anyone who might remember the war . . .

'Well there's M. Cabrie. He is one of the oldest inhabitants.' I was directed to a house with closed brown shutters, and rang the bell. M. Cabrie came downstairs, tall in blue overalls, with a full head of silver hair under his checked cap. He opened the big double doors to the *cave*, and when I explained my business, waved me inside and indicated the other chair. We sat in the dim coolness, the door ajar for light, next to a few crates of peaches.

'I don't remember much,' he began. 'People here don't talk about the war, they like to keep it under cover . . .' He grinned, pulling his fists towards him as if pulling a carpet. 'I was at the Ecole Militaire in Paris when the war began, and after the *débâcle* I came back here.' His family were wine-growers and there was plenty of work to do. 'My father had died. My brother was a prisoner. My uncle was the curé here. He did what he could, hiding Jews . . .' He shook his head. 'I remember going to Perpignan with him to ask the commandant to excuse five young boys from forced labour in Germany. That was frightening, all the soldiers there with their guns . . . The commandant said: "But they will like Germany, it is a beautiful country!" My uncle said: "I think they would enjoy it more after the war!" When he came back he helped them all to escape.'

'There was a German attack on the Resistance here?'

'Yes, eight hundred soldiers! It was terrible. They were in a ruined *mas* near Pleus, but they were all surrounded on the Col de Bataille . . . But the Maquis – they made some mistakes and poor Masse was killed, and his son wounded.'

I had read some of the story. In March the Germans and Milice attacked the Maquis of Pleus, based near Cassagnes. Eight hundred Germans and Milice surrounded them, and it turned out later they had been betrayed by one of their own members, Jean Martinez, known as the Mascot. He had been injured earlier in an accident and returned to his family to be looked after. But then he was recruited by the Milice and gave away all the Maquis hiding places. Fortunately the Maquis were forewarned and managed to escape, but two innocent people, one of them François Masse, working in the vineyards were killed. 'My uncle intervened to get permission to rescue the body and we went up there with my van to get him,' said Cabrie. In May five of the Maquis were arrested and deported. After the war the *milicien* who betrayed them was condemned to twenty years in prison, but escaped a death sentence. He had been under sixteen.

What else could he remember?

M. Cabrie chuckled. 'I remember Xavier de Gaulle in Ille-sur-Têt!' The brother of General de Gaulle had apparently spent most of the war as a tax inspector in the little town in the Têt valley below us. But the church clock was chiming noon and his wife came down to tell him lunch was ready.

Henri Melich, the young *passeur* from Quillan, joined the Maquis as soon as he could, with the group at Salvezines in January 1944. 'I was a bit of a solitary dreamer but I knew I had to take part. Though my father was sceptical about taking up arms for France. We're still foreigners here, he said.' Melich joined the Maquis Jean Robert, named for two young *maquisards* who had already died. 'It was communist-led, but we didn't know that.' He set off with a group of four *maquisards* in an old Renault with machine-gun barrels sticking out of the windows, arriving at dusk at the village of Salvezines. Salvezines was well situated for the Maquis, on the border between the Aude and the Pyrénées-Orientales, safely tucked away in the forest, canopied by beech and chestnut, rivers rippling over great mossy boulders. The high hills around made any German attack difficult, but they were still near enough to the main routes to Carcassonne and Foix for the Maquis to ambush Germans.

The linchpins of the Salvezines Maquis were the Riberos, both teachers committed to Resistance, Madame Ribero in Salvezines and her husband in the nearby village of Gincla. They kept the Maquis informed of parachute drops and German movements.

'We arrived first at the Nicoleu farm where there were already twenty *maquisards* preparing an evening meal. Then we left the car to walk into the forest – we had a dynamo torch which you had to keep pressing. We got to the second camp, a cabin covered in tarpaulin. We ate cold pasta and a handful of dried figs. My first night another *maquisard* shared his blanket with me.' Melich was only seventeen. 'I thought about my parents at that moment, my father coming back from the garden with his wheelbarrow, mother doing the dishes before sitting in front of the fire, and my father reading to her. I missed him very much.' Next day he was given his Maquis name – Sans – and a gun. 'It was an old Mauser, a cavalry musket. If I wanted anything better that was up to me.'

Melich still remembers his comrades; the chiefs Lazare, Firmin and Michel, Lorrain who played the violin, Caplan, a well-educated Jew who talked a lot, Soulie, killed a few months later on the Alsace front, Moïse, Pistolet, Jonquille, Samson and Tito. There was another Spaniard, who had been part of Durruti's column on the Aragon front, then interned in France in 1939, and taken by the Germans and enrolled in the German army. In 1943 he had escaped and joined the French Maquis.

'I still find myself using their Maquis names today . . .' said Melich. Another was a medical student, who called himself Dr Richard, with whom Melich had a falling out. They were sitting round the fire one night – they usually shared a cigarette, with extra puffs for that night's cook – when: 'I had the bad idea of comparing Hitler to Napoleon, both ambitious brigands, I said. But Dr Richard was outraged. "Napoleon was a great patriot and very intelligent!" he insisted. I realised that to criticise Napoleon in France went down very badly. We ignored each other after that!'

They were involved in several operations, the first an attack on the gendarmerie of Limoux, to take weapons and ammunition, but this is what Melich remembers most.

'I remember sitting in the back of the truck with Pistolet, our guns on our knees. We stopped to see my father, but I said I didn't have time to visit Mother. His eyes were wet as we left and he watched us go until we disappeared. At the villages we passed people who knew us raised their hands, and the younger kids ran behind us. What did we represent to them? Heroic fighters? We were not much older than they were!'

Later they caused the derailment of a train at Quillan, which was on its way to pick up supplies from a massive German depot at Couiza. 'It was set up by a railway worker from Sète, who climbed on the locomotive and sent it in the direction of the tunnel, jumping off just before it derailed.'

There were Maquis high up on the Col de Jau, accessible from Prades via a steep winding road. The Col de Jau is on the border with the Aude department, and as far as the Catalans are concerned, with France. Anyone from the other side is *gavatch*, a foreigner. Above Mosset the road climbs out of the village past houses and farms that today look almost derelict, the roofs gaping with holes, shutters hanging off, yards full of rusting machinery, pigsties, chicken coops. Smoke rising from the chimneys indicates occupation nevertheless. They probably did not look in much better repair in wartime. There were just more people then dependent on their produce, the vegetables, the chickens, the goats, the precious pig. Twenty-five kilometres or so of hairpin bends and vertiginous drops brings you to the col, 1,500 metres above sea level, one of the high passes of the Pyrenees, often closed by snow during the winter. As you climb, fields and flowers give way to pine forest, dark slopes penetrated by shafts of sun slanting through the branches.

There were several different encampments of Maquis up there at different times, though attempts made to amalgamate the groups seem to have been unsuccessful, and some of the *maquisards* seem to have been rather shady characters. But then Mosset has always had a rather louche reputation – it wasn't for nothing that it was called a den of bandits and thieves in the Middle Ages. There was one group at La Molinasse, a large abandoned farm on the other side of the col, where there is an immediate change in vegetation and climate. Here the red roofs and pungent herbs of the South are left behind, giving way to cool chestnut woods and tumbling rivers, leading down to the spectacular gorges of the upper Aude valley, ideal for ambushes. From there they could be in contact with the Aude Maquis and link up with the escape route to the Cerdagne.

Another group was established in 1944 at Le Caillau, in the stone barracks of the old talc mine near the col, now a basic but welcoming walker's refuge with a big wooden table and log fire. The building sheltered a group of about fifty, including *réfractaires* like Henri Goujon. 'I went up there in the spring of 1944, to escape STO. I was given false papers as a miner, supplied by the Resistance in Perpignan,' Goujon told me. I found a photo of him there with a companion, both bare-chested in shorts and espadrilles. 'We spent our time cutting wood for mine supports. But it wasn't very well organised, we didn't get much to eat. A little bit of bread for a fortnight plus a few potatoes. First time I got it, I ate a little piece like that every day.' His finger and thumb met in a circle as he showed me the amount. 'But then for the last few days it was all mouldy. After that I ate it all in the first couple of days, and waited to see what else would turn up.' Fortunately they could forage for wild berries, bilberries and blackberries, in the woods.

They were sent to check the wood supplies of the *charbonniers*, the Spanish and Italian charcoal-burners in the forest, watching their *meules*, the domed woodpiles they constructed, covered in earth, and left to smoulder slowly, carefully tended for several days until the charcoal was ready. The great advantage of the charcoal thus produced was that it was much lighter to transport than the original wood. 'It was a really dirty job,' said Goujon, 'but the *charbonniers* were great. We made friends with them.' Sometimes the youths would be put on guard, standing watch from a rock overlooking the access road. 'If the Germans or Milice had come I don't know what we would have done,' Goujon chuckled.

Or they were sent to Perpignan with messages, a five-hour descent to Prades. They passed by the lane up to La Coûme. 'I had no idea what was happening there then, though later after the war I became their doctor.' Returning at night was hazardous. 'We had to avoid the Germans in Prades after the 9 p.m. curfew. If they caught you . . .' Goujon shuddered, pulling on his fingernails.

There were some tragedies during that time. The *Monument des Morts* in Mosset has a long list of names of those who died in the First World War, but only two '*Morts pour la France*' in 1939–1945. One of them was Joseph Soler. Aged seventeen. Died 1944. A photo of him from 1942 shows a young boy in a short-sleeved check shirt, hair neatly brushed. Most accounts of Soler's death say he was killed accidentally in the course of an 'engagement', but Mosset poet Michel Perpigna remembered what really happened.

Perpigna had returned to Mosset in 1943 with the rest of his family, evacuated from Perpignan. He was working as a shepherd boy up on the mountain looking after 180 sheep. (He took provisions for the week wrapped up in old pages of *La Revue Tramontane*, a literary journal, copies of which had been left behind by one of the Mosset teachers and pragmatically utilised by the villagers. It was reading his sandwich wrapping that inspired Perpigna to begin writing poetry.) 'I was used to seeing the Maquis pass by. We always said *Salut*.' One day he was with two other boys also working as shepherds, one of them Joseph Soler. 'He brought a grenade with him, we told him to be careful . . . then half an hour later he opened it, it exploded . . . that was how he died, I saw it all, he was blown up by a grenade.'

There were other similar accidents. In Caudiès-de-Fenouillèdes is a plaque to another young Resistant, *mort pour la France*. I was told he had tripped over his own gun and shot himself through the nose. They were all so young, so inexperienced.

In June 1944 the running battle between the Milice and the Resistance came to Mosset. Apparently a group of Maquis had come down to

Mosset from Sournia to investigate a member of the Milice; they had searched his house and taken him away, but released him later. Then a group of forty or so Milice – and Germans according to some accounts – surrounded the village, ostensibly as a show of force for their comrade. But he refused to tell them where the Maquis headquarters were and was himself thrown into prison. A no-win situation: men who signed up for the Milice and then refused to join their attacks seemed to be particularly unpopular with their fellows. This was probably the occasion when people remember the Germans coming to Mosset, and all the young people of the village fleeing up the steep hillsides. Louisette, my elderly informant on the village, recalled it thus: 'I was guarding the cows at Corbiac when fifty Germans came past on motorbikes, armed to the teeth!' She hid in a ditch. 'Everybody fled to the hills. The village was empty.' Another remembered hiding outside the village, and then realising she had forgotten the baby's bottle and having to sneak back to get it. It sounded so trivial at first, but how to feed a small baby without a bottle, and perhaps more important, how to keep the baby from making a noise?

The Milice also came to Catllar, another Castellane village just out-side Prades, and took away two people. They were never heard of again until after the war their corpses were discovered in shallow graves on the outskirts of the village. Three inhabitants of St-Paul-de-Fenouillet, in the Agly valley between Perpignan and the Aude, were taken to Perpignan, where they were tortured. One of them was found hanging in his cell. The Resistance took their revenge. A few days later, the chief of the local Milice in Caudiès-de-Fenouillèdes was discovered in a vineyard with two bullets in the head.

Then in June 1944 they came for Pitt Krüger. Pitt always insisted that it was the curé of Mosset who had denounced him, the same curé with whom he had argued about sending the Spanish children to catechism. His daughter Jamine is equally sure. She was thirteen by then. Michel Perpigna still remembers her. 'I saw her about two or three times a week, when she came down from La Coûme on foot, with her violin. She would wait for the truck collecting milk from the Mosset cows, to give her a lift to her music lesson in Prades, sitting on top of the milk churns. How brave she was!'

'I will never forget the day my father was arrested,' Jamine Noack told me, when I went to visit her again in Prades. She found a photo of the farm at that time. 'He had a hole in the bedroom wall so he could escape into the hayloft, and to a cabin hidden in the forest, no one else knew where it was. He always had a bag ready with books and papers.'

The children were expected to act as lookouts when they were not working in the garden. 'There were two big rocks we could see the road from – there were no trees then, all the terraces were used for agriculture, for maize and potatoes.' It took fifteen to twenty minutes to come up to the farm, plenty of time to hide. 'But that day Pitt was looking for animal bedding, with some of the Spanish children. We were weeding the vegetable garden when the Milice arrived sent by the Gestapo from Perpignan. They gathered all the children, some of them tiny, and held them at gunpoint. Then he asked Yvès where Pitt was – because he was with children she had to tell them, so they found him and he said *au revoir* and they took him away.'

Pitt remembered it thus. 'There'd been letters denouncing us since 1940, but up to 1942 we were protected by the village. Then after 1942 the local gendarmes would alert us when there were Germans around.' La Coûme was a stopping place for Resistants and for foot-sore refugees on the way to the frontier, offering them soup, fresh supplies of bread and sausage and advice about which villages were safe. 'We had three hundred sheep being grazed at La Coûme and they had just been shorn, so they needed bedding. I had gone to look for ferns to keep them warm.' The Milice came and surrounded the house. 'Two guys with revolvers ordered me back to the house, taking me in handcuffs in front of the children, and took me to Perpignan without allowing me time to arrange my affairs.'

He spent about a month in the Citadelle of Perpignan, and was then sent to the infamous German military prison Cherche-Midi in Paris in a cattle wagon. 'At each stop the railway workers tapped on the wagons and said give us your addresses. In Lyon the *chef de transport* came to see me. "You are M. Krüger, you are Aryan, but you have been chained up with Jews," and he moved me down the wagon.'

Less than a month before the liberation of Paris, Pitt Krüger was deported and shunted between prison camps and military prisons in Saarbrücken, Berlin-Spandau, Frankfurt, Halle, Potsdam and Prague.

Jamine, her mother Yvès and her little sister were immediately spirited away from La Coûme by the Resistance, fearing for their lives. They were sheltered in the stables of a château near Toulouse, where the main building was still occupied by the Germans. The Germans were not there much longer. 'We'd been able to hear them playing music. When the end came and they fled, my mother found a broken violin. She always kept a piece of it. Somehow it summed up all the sadness.'

# CHAPTER 13

# LIBERATION

Beside the road between Quillan and Carcassonne, just outside Alet-les-Bains, is a monument to a fallen soldier, Lieutenant Paul Swank 1921–1944. He was an American from Missouri, a promising student of literature. He arrived in the Pyrenees on 11 August, a week before the liberation of the region, and died here in a firefight with the Germans. He had said that he wished to be buried where he fell, and though the American government shipped his body back to the USA, his family later honoured his wishes and brought him back to be buried here. There are two subtly different inscriptions on the tomb. The French inscription reads: '*Ici est tombé glorieusement pour la libération de la France . . .*' The other, in English, says: 'Here fell for the cause of freedom and liberty . . .' Each 17 August there is a ceremony to remember Paul Swank. In 2006 I joined them.

There were flags raised and speeches, a minute of silence, followed by the Last Post, the Star-spangled Banner and the Marseillaise. Two French captains in their képis and gold braid saluted solemnly. Then, just as everyone was about to disperse, an elderly man came forward and insisted on a chance to speak, the words spilling forth in a fierce emotional rush.

He wanted to bear witness to his own experience as a boy of thirteen in the little town of Couiza that day in August 1944. 'The Germans came to get their food supplies from the big depot in Couiza. They summoned the entire population to the village square. By now the villagers had surely heard of the reprisals elsewhere, especially the horrific burning of the Canigou village of Valmanya. What were the Germans going to do? They went up to the church bell tower with a machine gun, and then they demanded seven hostages, including the mayor and the curé, and forced them to walk in front of the German truck so the Maquis couldn't shoot at them.'

As we left the monument even more subdued than before, I was invited to join the annual reunion lunch of the Maquis of Salvezines, or what was left of them. We dined at the Hôtel Canal in Quillan, a traditional hostelry with shutters and lace curtains and white table-cloths, not much changed since they celebrated the liberation of the town there. We had a fine meal, including two sorts of foie gras, duck and goose, and a large *magret de canard*. There were a lot of jokes comparing the grim rations they ate as *maquisards* in the forest. Pasta, because they had liberated a very large quantity, and potatoes if they were lucky, gathering nettles and berries to supplement the meagre diet.

One of them recalled setting off to join the Maquis with a bag, a blanket, and several loaves of bread donated by the *boulanger* of his village. Another talked about the parachute drops, the huge torch they borrowed to light the plane to the right spot, the cigarettes, chocolate and chewing gum that arrived. And the weapons of course – they had so few, some of them so old they dated back to the war of 1870 – and all the dynamite. 'The Spaniards loved dynamite,' they said. (How they must have regretted the arms destroyed when the Spanish Republicans retreated.)

It was such an honour to meet these men – here were all the names I had heard from Henri Melich: Montcalm, Samson, Marseille, Cazals and Jonquille, oldest of them all, a wiry little man with pure white hair and such a twinkle in his eye. Most of them were small, affected permanently by the deprivation of their youth, wartime rations and especially the starvation rations of the Maquis. Maybe Resistance activity in this region was limited, maybe their achievements were exaggerated, but it made a profound difference to them and to their community, for these men to have made the moral choice for Resistance.

I was introduced to one who identified himself as Lapebi, and when I seemed puzzled he explained he had named himself after his bike. He showed me two photos he carried with him always, one on his bike in Limoux before the war, with greased-back hair and an American bolo tie. 'I adored that bike,' he said. 'I went everywhere on it, over all the mountain cols. It was my great passion.'

As I drove back through the deep gorges and tiny villages of the Aude valley, past trucks loaded with hay and wood, a butcher unloading a side of beef, people harvesting tomatoes and beans from their kitchen gardens and fishing in the rivers, I imagined the young American, Paul Swank, arriving here in 1944, dropped into this France of the Middle Ages.

Marc Belli, airline pilot for Airbus and a passionate amateur historian and geologist, has created a website devoted to the Maquis de Salvezines, and I went to see him to learn more about what happened the day Paul Swank died. Belli himself is Italian, and looks like an ancient Roman with his aquiline nose and fringe of grey hair. His

parents fled from Tuscany before the war, escaping the fascist government of Mussolini, and his father became a charcoal-burner in the
Corbières, where Belli was born. Now he spends his weekends in
Bessède-de-Sault, his wife's small village in the Pays de Sault, in the
Aude on the other side of the Col de Jau. The road up here winds
through gloomy Gothic gorges, overshadowed by sharp bleached limestone crags, and it was impossible to imagine from the road below
where parachute drops could possibly have taken place here.

It made sense once we drove up to Le Clat in Belli's battered old
Land Rover. Le Clat is a secret plateau of grassland surrounded by
limestone peaks, to the south the bulk of Madres and in the distance
the familiar outline of Canigou. As we drove Belli described the region,
this remote little corner of the Pyrenees, a secret place of fields and
forests where throughout the war the inhabitants of the few small
villages kept themselves to themselves. They saw few Germans and
would have preferred to see no Maquis either. They had an easy war, it
seems. 'They always had enough to eat here,' Belli explained, slowing
down for a herd of caramel-brown goats to cross the path. 'They grew
lentils and potatoes, had their gardens and animals.' They were not
particularly pleased when the parachutes arrived.

From early 1944 there had been an increase in Allied action, with
attacks by planes and submarines on the German coastal defences.
There were a number of parachute drops, even more after the
Normandy landings in June, which were received at several different
local landing grounds, including Salvezines. Crates of weapons,
ammunition, cigarettes and American banknotes began to fall from
the skies. They were eagerly awaited, and though most of the material
went to the Secret Army, the Gaullist faction of the Resistance, sometimes the FTPF got lucky. On at least one occasion so did the Germans.
The canny local peasants carted the containers home too, and they
finished up as irrigation conduits. (They used the strips of tinfoil Allied
bombers had dropped to distort German radar – called 'Window' by the
British, 'Chaff' by the Americans – as Christmas tree decorations.)

There was a sizeable landing of men as well as supplies near Sansa
on 2 August, located high above the valley of the Conflent; at 2,370
metres, it was the highest parachute landing staged in Europe. The
leader of this mission from the Free French headquarters in Algeria
was Captain Jacques Pujol, who came originally from Prades (though
he had an American mother), accompanied by Jean-Marie Félip, whose
family owned the Prades shoe shop, and a radio operator. Their
mission was apparently to arm the Maquis in case of an Allied landing

on the Languedoc Mediterranean coast. They actually landed at a rather higher altitude than intended, and Pujol injured his knee when they came down among the rocks of the *pic* itself. He struggled down the mountainside, meeting an old shepherd on the way who reassured him there were no Germans in the village. In Sansa he found an old friend he could trust, and the parachute supplies were recovered.

A Maquis group was established in Sansa, with the precious radio hidden in a cave. It was supported by the local gendarmes, the chemist and garage owner from Olette in the valley below, and the rail workers of Villefranche-de-Conflent. Among the group in Sansa was Pierre Solanes, who after his boyish gesture of defiance in support of de Gaulle had joined the Resistance as soon as he was old enough.

But the first parachute drop destined for Le Clat actually missed the plateau. 'It landed on the village itself, the containers smashed through the roofs in the middle of the night,' Belli told me. The inhabitants were terrified, and while it was still dark, transported the entire load by cart into the forest, wrapping the cows' hoofs in dusters to muffle the noise. There they hoped the material would be found by the Maquis and they would not be involved.

In August 1944 another parachute drop from Algeria was planned, destined for the Maquis of Picaussel, a large Gaullist group in the Ariège. But that venture did not go to plan. There is a detailed account of the landing written by one of the parachutists, Jean Kohn, a French Jew who had escaped to America with his family and had volunteered for service in France; his perfect French made him an invaluable candidate for the operation.

Fourteen parachutists set off in a big four-engine Halifax bomber with all their gear: arms, knives, carabines, sub-machine guns, plastic explosives, the works. Kohn recalled:

> We also had maps, 10,000 French francs and twenty 20-Francs gold coins. In addition we were given a note signed by U.S. General Benjamin F. Caffey saying:
>
> 'Secret
> To All Whom It May Concern
> This soldier is a fully accredited representative of the Supreme Allied High Command. He has been instructed to join forces wherever possible with resistance units to wage unceasing war against the German invader for the liberation of France.'

The plane was manned by a mixed crew; the pilots were British, the dispatcher Australian. 'We of course were American boys,' wrote Kohn.

'But on that trip, that night, we did not jump. We came back. Why? Because (we learned later on) the place we were supposed to land on was under attack by the Germans.'

The original drop had been planned for the Maquis of Picaussel, in the Aude a few miles west of Quillan, but when the plane arrived it was clear that something was wrong. There were no agreed signals to be seen, and they could make out fires on the ground. The Picaussel Maquis had been surrounded by Germans and had fled.

So the parachutists set out again on 10 August to land at Le Clat instead. As we stood there in that big solemn place with only the clouds and wind (and goats) for company, Belli explained the plane's trajectory, pointing out the direction of Algeria and showing me the flight path on the map, a view from the sky that only a trained pilot could have. 'Le Clat was the obvious alternative – as close as they could get to the Picaussel Maquis.'

Belli stressed the historical context. 'It was just before the landings in Provence on the fifteenth of August. The Resistance in the Pyrenees was led to believe that the landings would take place along the Golfe du Lion. Americans arriving would make the Germans think the same.' This was Operation Peg, one of twenty teams of parachutists sent into southern France, their objective to cut enemy lines of communication, attack installations, train the local Resistance, and collect intelligence for the Allies.

With the Maquis of Picaussel in disarray, the Salvezines Maquis had been alerted by the local teachers, Ribero and his wife, to go and meet the rescheduled drop. They arrived at midnight with a truck and a car (no lights) to transport the supplies that landed. 'Imagine what it was like, at night, setting the fires to guide the plane, waiting till they heard the noise. It was a Halifax, and they make a LOT of noise,' said Belli, conjuring the scene. 'The plane circled before dropping the containers, which the Maquis – maybe ten men – scrambled to collect.'

But then suddenly men too began to float down from the sky. Some landed on the flat grass, others hit the stone terraces of the hillside. The Maquis were astonished, and rushed round in wild excitement. 'The Americans!'

It was far from ideal terrain, as Kohn wrote.

> We landed on a very very rocky type of hill. I think my buddy, Bill Straus, broke one or two ribs, Sergeant Sampson hurt his coccyx . . . this site had been selected to receive equipment only and not paratroopers. The maquisards thought for a little while we were German

paratroopers. It is a good thing they did not shoot at us.

As soon as we landed, we met the FTP maquis. I did not even know what FTP meant at the time nor did we know that this group of 'maquisards' was called Jean Robert-Faïta – for us it was the 'Maquis'. They were communists – they saluted each other with raised closed fists. To me this was not a surprise as I had been through the 'Front Populaire' election explosion in 1936 when long parades of protesting socialists and communists would go throughout Paris saluting with their raised fists.

But to my American buddies who came from 'middle town' United States, this was quite a novelty to say the least. I did explain that these communists and socialists were also very patriotic French boys – to no avail – especially to some of our fellows who came from the U.S. 'Deep South' with good religious background.

In the dark they collected up all the gear, loaded it into trucks and took off for Salvezines, hoping not to meet any Germans on the way. The injured men were taken care of in the village, and the rest arrived at the Nicoleu farm.

There we were greeted by a whole bunch of young men . . . most of them young French boys. But there were others – some older men who were politically 'engaged' – communists, socialists, people who hated Vichy. There were also some Spanish Republic ex-soldiers . . . even some Jews. We slept outside in our sleeping bags in the woods. In case of a surprise attack we could come out of the bags and fight back quickly without being caught in a house.

A representative of the Secret Army soon turned up, claiming that the drop was intended for them and that the Americans had ended up with the wrong Maquis. According to Kohn there was quite an argument, but the Americans told him they were quite happy where they were, and did not care which Maquis they had joined. Kohn acted as interpreter. 'We told all parties that we had to fight one enemy: the Germans. Therefore let's not have a fight between Resistance groups.' They trained the *maquisards* in the use of the Enfield rifles and explosives they had brought, and set to work strengthening the defences around the village, mining the roads and positioning machine guns. 'Right away we started to blow a few bridges,' wrote Kohn. 'It turned out that the destruction of bridges on roads the Germans were not really using was a senseless exercise. One case in particular was especially bad: we half destroyed a railroad bridge which could not be used anyway since there was a derailed train convoy a few hundred feet

down the line.' (This was presumably the one already derailed by
Melich and his railway pals.) Kohn writes:

> We had learnt for months how to use these plastic explosives and we
> were really itching to have a go at a few bridges to show our new
> friends how good we were. One bridge on a secondary road was also
> blown very neatly one night. We forgot to put up a danger sign or some
> branches across the road. In the morning a French car came, the driver
> did not see the bridge had gone. He and his woman passenger were
> killed in the crash.

There were other problems.

> Our radio contact with Algiers did not work. I was told our operator
> sent a danger signal over the air which meant the Germans had
> captured us. Contact was established later on by the Resistance radio
> group and Algiers did learn finally we were all right. I think our radio
> never worked. One thing that did work though was the power gen-
> erator we had to crank while the radio man was working on his
> messages. It took a lot of elbow grease to turn the handles. We all
> took turns in working it. With all the good will of our radio man,
> Algiers did not answer.

They never did establish radio contact. As soon as word got out of the
Americans' arrival, the camp grew and soon there were about 200
*maquisards*. Some even had to be turned away because there were not
enough weapons.

The camp was further swelled by German prisoners. Melich recalled
the incident. 'We were unloading some ammunition near the farm,
when Dr Richard appeared on his motorbike shouting: "The Germans,
The Germans!" ' They rushed to arm themselves and wait for the
attack, when they saw a German car grinding slowly up the path. On
the running board was Jonquille, gesticulating and bellowing: 'Don't
shoot!' Inside the car were nine German prisoners they had captured.
They were Alsatian soldiers, enrolled by force into the German army,
and had put up no resistance. 'We didn't even need to guard them, they
willingly took charge of the cooking and kitchen work,' said Melich.

Kohn wrote of another sombre incident, not mentioned by Melich:

> The maquisards captured a member of the Milice who had done
> horrible things to other resistance fighters. His capture had been
> facilitated as first his girl friend got caught. She was frightened and
> forced to tell him to meet her in a café in Quillan. As he arrived he was
> jumped on by a few maquisards who took him up to our camp.
> There he was 'judged' by what I might call a kangaroo court after

being beaten to a pulp. We were impressed to see what he went
through and still be able to walk and stand up. He was condemned to
immediate death and shot by firing squad the same day in front of all
the maquisards and ourselves. I was a little shaken about the whole
affair since the 'court' was not a real one. But in those difficult days,
revenge was high in everybody's mind against persons who not only
had collaborated with the Germans, but worse, had acted as agents for
the Gestapo by denouncing and killing other Frenchmen. At the same
time, knowing what the Milice had done in that area, nobody felt sorry
for that man. This Milice man turned out to be courageous as he
realised he did not have a chance to come out alive. He was taken to the
execution area where he refused to be blindfolded and before being
shot he did cry out loud and clear:
'Messieurs, Vive la France.'
After this execution, we were served a 'cassoulet.' Believe it or not,
our little OG group did not have much appetite. We were not really at
ease. We had orders not to interfere in local affairs – and we did not.
But this fast court martial followed by firing squad gave us the shivers.

Melich recalled a more cheerful meal with the Americans, after
the *maquisards* had captured a cow from a neighbouring farm. The
motley international group sang songs together, with the Americans
contributing the French song they knew best, 'Alouette, gentille
alouette . . .'
The Mediterranean landing finally happened, in St-Tropez on 15
August 1944. No doubt the Languedoc Resistance were disappointed it
was not on their territory after all. The German High Command told
their forces stationed in and around Toulouse to retreat at all speed
towards the Rhône Valley and go north to avoid being taken in a pincer
movement by the Allies coming from Normandy and the new beach-
head in the South.
The Carcassonne German command decided to move fast and take
as much food as they could from Couiza, a small town between Limoux
and Quillan, where they held a large stock of supplies. There were
100,000 rations there, wrote Kohn. 'In those days food was really
scarce. If we could take that inventory away from the Germans, it
would deprive them of their daily needs in their flight north. It would
also be most welcome, not only by us, but principally by the local
population.' But the Germans were well armed and had infantry
support, and after loading up the supplies they took hostages from
Couiza to walk in front of their trucks and started heading north
towards Carcassonne. (Some reports say the hostages were strapped to
the roof of the trucks.)

'We were supposed to stop them,' wrote Kohn.

I was always a volunteer for that kind of thing. Lieutenant Swank, Sergeant Galley, John Frickey, Rock Veilleux and myself started north from Quillan with explosives. I do not know what roads we took to go there. Apparently we must have gone unnoticed around Couiza and Esperaza. We were guided by our FTP maquisards. We were to blow the road north of Alet where the Aude river flows in a narrow gorge. The large stones falling from the cliff on the road would halt the German convoy who would have to stop to move the stones. Then we would shoot at them.

Swank, the team engineer, placed the explosives near to the road, then took cover, but when he and Sergeant Galley went to check the damage after the explosion, they realised it was not enough. Then the Germans arrived sooner than expected, a troop of about 250. 'A large group of real tough German soldiers came rushing up the road shooting with all they had,' wrote Kohn. 'At that very moment Lieutenant Swank got shot and killed. I do not know exactly how he was immobilised. A German officer finished him with a shot in the head.'

According to the account of the Aude Maquis by its chief, Lucien Maury, Swank had bravely protected the retreat of his men, shooting as long as he could, killing as many as twenty Germans without hurting any of the hostages, before he himself was mortally wounded. According to the OSS Mission report:

During this action Lieutenant Swank was hit four times by enemy machine gun fire before he fell to the ground. Even after he was hit, he made an effort to draw his pistol and continue the fight as long as there was a spark of life left in his body. His action was so brave that it won the praise of the enemy officers who made this statement: 'We have never seen a man fight as hard as this officer against overwhelming odds.' Lieutenant Swank fought even after he could no longer stand on his feet – until a German Officer emptied his pistol into his throat, the bullets coming out behind his right ear. Sergeant Galley saw Lieutenant Swank fall and thought him dead, but he [Galley] continued to fight on alone until his right hand was shattered so badly by an explosive bullet, that he could no longer use his weapons. He also received a bullet wound in the left foot before withdrawing up the hillside under the protecting fire of the other men.

But it was a successful operation. Acording to the OSS Report, 'The enemy was turned back with the loss of nineteen killed and twenty-four wounded, against the loss of one American and two Maquis killed and two Americans and two Maquis wounded.' According to one report some of the Germans retreated via the Col de Jau, where they were attacked by the Maquis based there.

The food rations were distributed to the Maquis and local villages. Melich remembered the supplies in detail afterwards: 'tins of all sorts, meat, pilchards, plus flour, pasta, rice, sugar, jam, chocolate and above all tobacco'.

During the firefight when Paul Swank was killed, Kohn himself had been positioned on the cliff overhanging the road.

> Two Germans came up on the cliff from behind. They wanted to shoot me. One of them said in German very clearly:
> 'Recht fünf meters.' (on the right: five meters)
> That was I they were talking about.
> They threw a potato type hand grenade that landed real close and when it went off, my woollen cap blew off. I was hit on my right thigh (at the time I did not realise I was slightly wounded). Then I had three choices:
> – I surrender – NO
> – I fight back – NO, they were two with a sub machine gun and I was alone.
> – I flee – Yes
> I remembered our orders: Do not fight if 'they' are more numerous than you.
> So I fled.

Belli had been investigating with his metal detector at the site of the combat, and had found bullets, both American and German, which bore out the witnesses' accounts. Then searching higher up the steep side of the gorge, where Kohn had been attacked, he again found bullets, and to his astonishment, a Colt 45. 'I couldn't believe it, it was exactly where Kohn must have dropped it,' Belli told me. He had been in contact with Jean Kohn, who was living in Paris, and took the gun to show him. Later I spoke to Jean Kohn himself, still going strong, 'with all his own teeth and all his own hair', as he put it, and he explained, 'I still had my packing list of equipment from 1944 and we looked at it and checked out the serial numbers. "It is your pistol!" Marc said. I couldn't believe it. We were both astonished and just laughed and laughed. I had been so scared at that moment, I didn't even know where I had dropped it!'

'I did not know I was wounded, even slightly,' Kohn wrote.

> I went up the mountain. I heard some shots during the night. I slept in the mountain, I had been scared, scared, I mean very afraid to be shot, to be taken prisoner or I don't know what. Night had fallen. I was so

tired by then that I ended up in a bush way high on that mountain side feeding on a small roll of mint Lifesavers and fell fast asleep. Early in the morning, I felt good since I was still alive. I figured the best way would be to go over the hill and see what I could do to get back to Quillan.

I went up to the top of the hill and down on the other side. It was a beautiful and warm summer day. The countryside was bare of houses. Not even cultivated fields. Just some trees and bushes. I finally saw a farm or what I thought looked like a farmhouse. I looked at it for a long time to make sure there were no Germans there. I ran a little, approaching it cautiously, stopped for a while, still inspecting it. Then I rushed in and asked quickly,

'Any Germans around?'

'No.'

Then, 'Please give me something to drink.'

They gave me some water and probably some food.

It seemed to me these farmers did not want to be involved in anything that had to do with fighting, especially with so many Germans around. But they did call for help and organised my pickup to have me return to Quillan. Somebody came with a car . . . and put a civilian coat on top of my uniform. This was really extremely dangerous. I was hiding under a civilian coat. Should we have been caught by the Germans we might have been shot on the spot.

Upon reaching Quillan, I found out that Paul Swank had been killed. I was shocked.

Kohn was in time for the funeral of Swank and the other two Maquis who had been killed.

I remember vividly Lt. Weeks kneeling at the open coffin holding the cold hand of Lt. Swank as a farewell gesture. We then all went to the church where a religious service was held and from there to the cemetery where he was buried in a temporary grave.

The killing of my lieutenant really shocked me. It was the first death of one of us that we witnessed. You always hear about death in War, but that was 'it.' We had known him for such a short while before our mission. Yet this was as if we had lost an old time friend. That evening after the burial we were silent. Our little group felt very, very sad.

I was taken to a doctor to see if he could take the small piece of grenade from my thigh. He had what looked like a pair of thin long medical tongs. He tried, without success. Since he could not find it he told me the best would be to forget it and keep that piece of metal in my body as a war souvenir.

Up to that point we were not really motivated, but from that day on, we saw the War with a different eye. We were much more careful and cautious in taking up fighting positions. We did help take a few German prisoners, but we did not hold them, that was not our purpose. I think there was a rumour going around that said we took in 10,000 German prisoners. That's not right. Maybe some Germans did ask to surrender to us, Americans. They must have figured they would receive better treatment from us than from the French as they surely knew of some atrocities perpetrated a few weeks before by tough German units. I do not remember anything about all this. One thing is certain: we were not supposed to take any prisoners. That was not our job. What could a bunch of twelve American GIs do with prisoners anyway. How could we hold them? In chains?

So we 'liberated' Limoux, some other villages and ended up in Carcassonne . . . In Limoux, we were invited to a big lunch by the father of one of our maquisards: M. Balateu. He had a butcher shop next to the church in the center of town. He had a turn of the century type beard, a little like George the Fifth of England. He showed us medals from his service during World War One.

What a lunch. I can remember a beautiful cold veal roast. One of us refused a second or third helping. Mr Balateu pushed one slice off the serving plate and said: 'it already fell, so eat it'.

We were also 'officially' received by the city council – or what was left of it at the Hotel Modern & Pigeon. The 'feast' there was made up of tomatoes from start to end in different combinations. When we came out we certainly were still hungry.

One morning while we set up position on a road, overlooking a wide plain, around noon, we heard church bells ringing all over the place. Somebody told us that Paris had been liberated.

As the Germans retreated at full speed, they abandoned Carcassonne. We moved in behind them. This is the way we 'liberated' the city. We visited the old walled Cité as the first of many future American tourists.

We lived in a hotel next to the railroad station which a few days before had housed the local German Kommandantur. Photos of Hitler, Goering and other Nazis were thrown on the ground, destroyed and burnt as the local people applauded.

We had a parade where we marched with other resistance groups.

During 19 and 20 August 1944 the Pyrénées-Orientales became the first department in France to be liberated by its own Resistance forces, who barrelled down from their mountain hideouts in whatever transport they could muster. There was a huge outburst of joy. The longed-for Liberation had finally come, and Resistance fighters paraded proudly through the streets of towns and villages to great acclaim. But in Perpignan, where there were still many German troops, there was mayhem, and that was when many of the Resistance were killed, so often totally inexperienced young boys, handling weapons almost for the first time.

On the coast the Germans took a heavy toll before they left, blowing up all the quays of Port-Vendres and causing massive destruction to the town. Elsewhere they destroyed petrol reserves and food supplies. What they made sure they did not destroy were files on their collaborators and letters of denunciation. Many of the German troops, especially those stationed near the frontier, turned tail and fled through Spain.

In small towns and villages with little or no German presence, the population were more than happy to welcome the Resistance and there was rarely any fighting. The tiny village of Rabouillet, up in the hills midway between Mosset and Salvezines, was the first village to be officially liberated in the department on 9 August. Since the Pyrénées-Orientales claims to be the first department in France to liberate itself, I wondered if this meant that Rabouillet was the first village to be liberated in France. Certainly it merited a visit. Rabouillet may be the quietest village I have ever been to, lost in the cool chestnut forests, surrounded by great stacks of tree-length logs ready to be transported. In the village chickens clucked busily, a woman was filling water bottles from the fountain, there were soap suds in the communal *lavoir*. It can have changed little in essence since the war. But a proud plaque is mounted on the wall of the town hall, commemorating that day, and in the cemetery the grave of one young man, killed during the bloody liberation of Perpignan.

The joy and relief were inevitably mingled with anger and bitterness, and the reprisals began, with collaborators summarily shot dead and women who had been suspected of consorting with Germans shaved and paraded naked in the streets. Kohn remembered what it was like in the small town of Limoux.

'Collaborators' were caught. The local Gendarme Captain who seemed to have 'collaborated' with the Vichy Government more than he should have, fled and was in hiding. Unfortunately his wife was caught and as was the 'fashion' in those days, her head was shaved. She came to me to ask for protection as she was afraid she would be shot. I told her not to worry. Her hair would grow back. I was an American soldier with orders not to interfere in local politics. The 'resistance' groups told me not to bother since she would not be beaten up or shot. Some other women were also shaved and paraded throughout the city. Many of these relatively young women had 'collaborated' with German soldiers and the jealous French maquisards – husbands, fiancés, friends – took their revenge on those poor girls. Maybe the 'favours' they gave the Germans were to obtain some extra food? Anyway they should not have been so friendly with the occupant.

In Carcassonne it was the same:

The Resistance groups took the city over, young women's heads were shaved. One girl in particular was badly beaten by parents of boys she had denounced and who had been killed by the Gestapo. I was told she had a swastika tattooed on her belly.

Henri Melich remembered a similar incident after the liberation of Quillan, a hysterical crowd surrounding three women who were about to have their heads shaved. Melich protested, since one of them was Raymonde Rousset, the brothel-keeper, who was accused of collaborating with the Germans – 'The same Raymonde who had never hesitated to help us hide fugitives.' In Prades it must have been the same, according to the account from Madame de Decker of the treatment meted out to her father, the Pétainist mayor.

Jean-Louis Curtis captured the atmosphere in *Forests of the Night*: the Germans leaving in the middle of the night, the French flag floating again over the town, the *maquisards* given a rousing welcome by the crowds. But as they jeered at the women led to be shaved, they began to ask by what right the Resistance had appointed themselves the new rulers, what exactly had they done after all,

the forces of interior hostility which had been held down so long, might explode at any moment . . . nobody felt safe. Possibly because nobody had a clear conscience . . . There they were all of them, the small honest profiteers of the war, hilarious, bursting with fat and greed, the peasants of the neighbourhood, those who had exploited the German goldmine scientifically and discerningly. And all the others as well, the thoughtless ones, the neutral ones, and those who had fluctuated from one side to the other . . . Perhaps time would soon show that the greatness and sacrifice of a handful of Frenchmen had redeemed the apathy of the great mass of the exhausted and weary French people?

Perhaps.

According to historians the *épuration sauvage*, the savage purge, was at its most extensive in the South of France, because that area was mainly liberated by the French Resistance rather than by Allied troops, and was also where the Maquis had the greatest presence and where the civil war between the Resistance and the hated Milice was most ferocious. It was an extreme period when all normal laws were suspended, and the violence of the Liberation embittered the relations between neighbours for years afterwards.

Some scores were settled right then, as known collaborators and Milice were dragged out and shot. Then formal courts were established and judgement passed. Some were executed, many sent to prison. Colonel Ruffiandis was imprisoned, and in June 1945 he was sentenced to five years of *'indignité nationale'*, which meant he was deprived of the right to vote or hold office for a period of time.

The real Ruffiandis remained a mystery to me, as did the mayor of Prades, Victor Pyguilhem. A contemporary newspaper article complained that Ruffiandis's sentence was not tough enough, that although he had disassociated himself from the Milice he had still supported Pétain to the end. Much much later, in 2000, the husband of Louisette, Marcel Grau, who had been in the Resistance in Mosset, defended Ruffiandis, saying that he had warned Grau's mother that he had been denounced to the Milice, and that he had helped English airmen escape to Spain. (The mayor of Mosset, Louis Soler, had sheltered two English airmen for a week before they crossed the frontier.) Recalling Ruffiandis's book on Mosset, his love for the village, I was well prepared to believe that in the end his loyalties would lie there.

In Mosset the priest became the scapegoat in a grisly episode that is still spoken of in hushed tones. Isidore Pailler had never been very popular, and Pitt Krüger was sure he had denounced him after their argument over sending children to catechism. Pailler, aged forty-three in 1944, was a hardline Spanish Catholic, and had previously been curé of other parishes in the region; in Ansignan he was so disliked that the children threw stones at his window. He came to Mosset in February 1939, and in 1940 was also appointed curé of the parishes of the other Castellane villages, Molitg and Campôme, where he made more enemies. In Campôme they complained of being deprived of mass for three weeks, and that no offices at all had been celebrated at Christmas 1940. He had told them he wasn't coming back, and the good Christians of Campôme had said good riddance.

Pailler also fell out with the schoolteacher in Mosset, Madame Lambert. He wrote to the Prefect of the Pyrénées-Orientales complaining that she refused to send the children to catechism and had told them: 'If he wants to teach them catechism and transform them into bigots, he can do it on Thursdays and Sundays.' She had also failed to bring the children to the *Monument aux Morts* on 14 July as ordained by Pétain (a replacement for the traditional Bastille Day celebrations). The Prefect replied that the curé seemed to be rather hot-headed and vindictive, called for moderation on both sides and issued a warning to Pailler.

According to the account pieced together by the historian Jean Larrieu, on 9 August a group of Maquis, apparently Spanish guerrilleros who had retreated to the Col de Jau after the burning of the village of Valmanya on 1 and 2 August, had come down to Mosset for supplies. The villagers brought them food, and apparently the abbé was seen behind the curtains of the presbytery, taking notes. Then two of the Maquis entered his house and discovered that he was noting the names of those who provided the supplies. He was dragged outside and taken up to La Molinassa, the Maquis encampment on the other side of the Col de Jau.

Yvette, the *épicière*, was only five years old at the time, but she can still remember it. 'The forge was right next door to the church and the presbytery,' she told me. 'I can remember them taking the priest away.' They heard the banging on the door, saw the group of Maquis brandishing newly acquired weapons and watched fearfully from their doorway as the priest was bundled into a truck and driven away. 'They've taken the curé!' must have reverberated round the village. Then I remembered one of the local farmers, after his dog had bitten someone, saying: 'I took him up the mountain,' meaning he had shot him.

The priest was tried and condemned to death, but was killed only the following day, apparently shot in the back when he tried to escape, 'his soutane tucked into his socks'. His soutane was left hanging from a tree beside the road for several weeks. He was finally buried at Counozouls, the first village on the Aude side of the col, though years later he was taken to the village of Joch, where there is a mausoleum for the Pailler family, though no mention of Abbé Pailler.

There is still disagreement about the fate of the priest, and there are those who deny that he was really a traitor, and claim that the list he was making was never intended to be seen. Some accounts say he was left hanging naked from a tree. Some say they had not intended to kill him, it was only when he tried to run away that he was shot. Some of those involved in his death are still alive, but nobody is telling. It is still a village secret.

# CHAPTER 14

# REPRISAL

On a clear sunny June day in 2006 I climbed a steep stony path threading its way through the shady woodland of scrub oak and chestnuts that covers the western flank of Canigou. Sunlight pierced through the branches of the trees, highlighting mossy boulders, gnarled roots and dry leaves, glinting off the stream that trickles slowly down the mountainside. With me were seven men. One of them, Roger Chanal, an elderly silver-haired gentleman in a jaunty red cap and sunglasses, rested often on his walking stick looking upwards and shaking his head. 'I begin to remember it all now. But the trees have grown so much since then!'

He was eighty-five years old and it was the first time he had returned to this place since 1944, when he had played his part in the worst and most dramatic event of the war in this region. André Soucarrat, loaded down with cameras and clad in a khaki jacket with innumerable pockets, was filming him, determined this time to get the full story of what happened in Valmanya on 1, 2, and 3 August 1944. The ancestral village of Mosset poet Michel Perpigna, of which he wrote with such passion, was burnt to the ground in a vicious German reprisal operation only a few days before the liberation of the region, and two months after the Normandy landings.

Soucarrat had already made a film about Valmanya, and I had been to the first showing in Prades in 2003. The cinema had been packed, and an extra screening was already fully booked. At the end of the film Soucarrat and the three historians who had advised him, Jean Larrieu, Ramon Gual and Christian Xancho, stood in front of the red velvet curtain to answer questions. There was a palpable feeling of tension in the small cinema. As the film unfolded, with contemporary witnesses and combatants speaking often for the first time, it had become agonisingly clear that the tragedy was not only the burning of Valmanya but the revelation that the memory of it had been kept so long repressed. So much remained unexplored, buried but not forgotten, not only because of the horror of it, but also due to a deep unwillingness to acknowledge the event, or even to agree what really happened.

This despite the fact that a ceremony is held in Valmanya every year in memory of the tragedy. The year I attended there was a marching band, representatives of numerous Resistance groups carrying flags in white-gloved hands, and soldiers in battledress. (There was audible muttering about the fact that the soldier who barked out the orders was a woman.) The gendarmerie were represented, the Prefect of the region, the President of the Conseil Général, several mayors and a colonel in full uniform. Many of those who took part, including women, wore their medals. Speeches evoked the events of the tragedy and extolled the bravery of the Resistance. Then everyone followed the band, playing the Marseillaise, the *Chant des Partisans* and Spanish Revolutionary songs, to the cave in the rock outside Valmanya where there are memorial plaques to the Resistance fighters and those who died. Eventually the gathering went off for a good French Sunday lunch, and enough pourrons traditional Catalan drinking vessels with a long spout from which the wine is poured from a height into the mouth) of muscat to forget about it all for another year.

In the cinema in Prades that evening some of the audience spoke in favour of the film, but others asked what was the point in raking over the past. 'Why should the grandchildren of collaborators be made to feel guilty now?' asked one. Another demanded to know their reasons for making the film. One of the historians, Ramon Gual, the son of Spanish refugees, responded with a passionate speech. He declared the necessity of finally speaking about the war. Valmanya was only a symbol, and their film was intended as a catalyst. The time had come for people to talk about what had happened. There was a murmured response and finally applause. It seemed at that moment that people were ready at last.

The film was shown in cinemas throughout the region and proved intensely controversial. One scene showed a group of surviving members of the Resistance meeting for the first time, sitting round a table, arguing bitterly over what happened. And seeing the film prompted others to talk, to offer their own version of those fateful days. Soucarrat decided to remake and expand the film. He is a tenacious researcher and began burrowing deeper into the archives, some of which had only been opened in 2005, sixty years on, interviewing and questioning until he believed he was closer to the truth of what happened.

I went to see him at his home in a small village near Perpignan, a spacious modern house with a swimming pool and palm trees, and an

entire room devoted to his research material. Soucarrat, a big affable
fellow with a Beatle haircut, round glasses and a beaming smile,
seemed on the one hand delighted to have discovered a subject of
such intense interest and on the other slightly nonplussed by the ants'
nest he had disturbed. He generously shared his research, showing me
boxes and boxes of letters and documents he had retrieved from the
official archives.

There were testimonies from Resistants, correspondence by the
Milice, official reports of battles and skirmishes from both the French
and the German authorities. Some were stamped 'secret', others he
had copied out by hand, forbidden to photocopy them. As we talked he
sat at the table with a large calendar in front of him, diligently spelling
out key events day by day as they occurred.

Soucarrat is not a Catalan, and arrived in the region only a few
years ago after working as an independent commercial film-maker
in Paris for most of his career. He had no particular axe to grind
(except perhaps for a certain scepticism about communists) but was
determined to discover what he could establish as the truth of what
happened here in July and August 1944. If anything he seemed to be
most inspired by a sense of justice, wishing to pay proper tribute to
those who had defended Valmanya, many of them Spanish guerrilleros whose contribution to the Resistance was never as highly rated
as the French after the war. As he explained it: 'The communists
took credit for the actions of the guerrilleros. They say they did it
all. Even when it came to compensation, the distribution was often
unfair.'

I asked what he considered to be the main problem with the film.

'One of the main errors in my first film was the reason for the
Resistance attack on Prades. It always seemed a rather feeble pretext
when I read the first account – stealing cigarettes and attacking the
Gestapo. In fact the main reason was for money, but no one ever
mentions that. I wanted to find out what had happened to it.'

He had decided to revisit Valmanya, and in particular the Resistance
hideout at La Pinouse, the old iron mines high above the village, and
agreed that I could come along. Even today it is a long and winding
road up to Valmanya, and in a half-hour's drive I met only one other
car, even when passing through the one other village on the way,
Baillestavy. The road these days is highlighted in green on the map, a
Michelin scenic drive for tourists. It curves around the contours of the
valley, following the path of the river in the gorge below. To one side is
a wall of rocks and trees, to the other a steep drop, one you would be

unlikely to survive in a car or even a battle tank. There is no sound other than birdsong and the distant roar of the river in the gorge below. Hugging the bends of the road you slip back and forth from shadow to sunlight. Sometimes the peak of Canigou is visible in the distance, still with a patch of snow here and there, sometimes it vanishes beyond a fold in the hillside.

You never know what might face you around the next corner, a big truck loaded with wood perhaps, or maybe a Maquis ambush. Certain vantage points offer a view right down the valley, but on the road you would have no idea if anyone was watching from the dense cover provided by rocks and trees. Once spotted though, it would be hard to escape: the valley sides are so steep, and covered in slippery shale, scrub oak and gorse, which is tough and prickly to negotiate.

Today the village of Valmanya is oddly spruce, rebuilt houses with newly pointed stones, smart slate roofs, freshly varnished brown shutters and bright geraniums, sharply in contrast to the more shabby and weathered stone villages hereabouts. There had not been much left by the time that the Germans had finished with it. Only the church at the top of the village remained untouched and stands now, a bastion of ancient times, its graveyard full of local names, its bell still tolling hours and deaths. There is little to remind a visitor of the past: a war memorial in front of the *mairie*, and a small museum that devotes more time to the history of iron mining on Canigou, long the main employment of the village, than to its wartime history. A few black and white photos, shells, and a lone German helmet are all that remains.

Soucarrat arrived, accompanied by Christian Xancho, a young Catalan historian, small and sturdy, with close-cropped dark hair, neat blue jeans and walking boots. He is a specialist in the history of the Germans of the region and the wartime history of the coast. A small spade swung from his backpack and a metal detector stuck out of the top. We met up with the two sons of Sébastien Rius, a member of the communist Resistance, whose handwritten account of events had provided Soucarrat with much of his material. Both his sons, Gérard and Daniel, were nurses, and both had the deeply lined, tanned faces of Pyrenean *montagnards*.

When the sons of Rius were introduced to Roger Chanal, he looked blank.

'Sébastien Rius?'

'Constantin!'

'*Ah oui, Ah oui.* Constantin.' He had only ever known Rius by his Maquis name.

Finally there was Dr Mary, a retired doctor, dressed in smart blue overalls, braces and a faded blue peaked cap, whose father and grandfather had both been mayors of Valmanya. He owned the land where the mines of La Pinouse were situated and had given his permission for the filming. I clambered up into his old green Land Rover and we set off to drive partway up the mountain track, followed by the two civilian cars, which baulked only briefly at the river they had to ford. On the way Dr Mary stopped to rearrange the plastic pipes that were watering one of his meadows and to say *bonjour* to his young daughter who, he announced proudly, was tending a herd of sheep. Dr Mary had been only eleven when Valmanya was burnt but he remembered it well. He too had his version of the tale.

Soon the vehicle track petered out and we set out on foot, shouldering packs and adjusting bootlaces. After about half an hour we could see our destination, the jagged ruins of the old iron mines. At first they were highly visible but soon lost to sight again as we wound our way along the forest path. While Roger Chanal stopped to catch his breath André Soucarrat began to question him about his memories of the period. He'd been only eighteen, assigned to a Compagnons de France (youth work camp) in Prades, when he was drafted for forced labour in Germany in June 1944. He was sent for a medical check-up in Perpignan and from there managed to escape and join the Maquis in Fillols, the highest village on the side of Canigou, one of the first centres of Resistance in the area.

Valmanya too had been an early focus of resistance, with a Gaullist group founded in February 1941 by Abdon Casso. He had been an officer in the engineers corps, who had been taken prisoner after the fall of France but had escaped from Germany and returned to the *Zone Libre* in September 1940. An early photo shows a man with a thick handlebar moustache and kindly shining eyes. He had reported to the Vichy military authorities in Perpignan, offering to store weapons in his family farm in the mountains, but had been quickly dissuaded from any ideas of resistance. He soon found something else to do when the region was flooded in October 1940, and worked with the Spanish refugee labourers to help the work of reconstruction in the devastated valleys. Thus he met other like-minded Resistants and soon a network had been established, known as the Réseau Sainte-Jeanne. They made contact with London by means of a message hidden in a tube of shaving cream, and became a key link in the escape network, smuggling refugees across the border into Spain with the help of local smugglers and mountaineers who knew the paths.

The network was supported by several families in Valmanya and notably by the discreet assistance of the commune and even of the *Délégation Spéciale* which had been installed by Vichy to replace the left-wing elected council of the village. (This included Casso as mayor, an indication of how out of touch the Vichy administration was.) They harboured the escapees, provided them with official stamps and papers, then guided them over the frontier. One of them was Louise Horte, wife of the village schoolteacher, René Horte, who was a prisoner of war in Germany. Horte himself returned from Germany in March 1941 and joined the network. They were responsible for saving many refugees, as well as escaped soldiers and airmen who found their way through Spain to Morocco or Britain to continue the fight.

Things got much tougher after the Germans occupied the southern zone in November 1942. German frontier police established a lookout post at La Tour de Batère on the ridge overlooking Valmanya, a key strategic point – on one side the valley of the Têt, to the other the Vallespir. The Germans were kept regularly informed by collaborators and later by members of the Milice.

In early June 1943 the German police arrived at René Horte's home, the Valmanya school, to arrest him for sheltering two young men who had been discovered by the Spanish police after crossing the frontier. They had been handed over to the Germans, and persuaded to confess who had helped them. That summer evening Horte had been sitting round the family table with a small group of men he was arranging to have taken to Spain. The German police tried to surround the school but Horte, his son Jean-Claude, aged ten, and the rest of the group managed to escape. The Germans stayed all night and finally arrested Louise instead. She was deported to Ravensbrück. There she met Josephine and Francine Sabaté and was later to recount their fate to Odette.

Horte was suspended from his post as teacher, and he took to the woods, hiding out for several months through the summer with his young son. Jean-Claude was soon taken to a safe place outside the region, not knowing what had happened to his mother or what would happen to his father. He has never talked about it.

Horte took refuge in the Mas des Cabanats, a remote farm belonging to Casso and looked after by the Bartolis, a Spanish family who had arrived before the war to work in the iron mine. Horte was again denounced and in August 1943 the German police came to the Mas to arrest him. He shot at them from the window, and escaped with several other maquisards, having mortally wounded one of the Germans. Three days later the German police arrested Casso.

They also took away Sabine Bartoli Gonzalez, wife of one of the escaped Spanish Maquis Jovino Gonzalez who was Horte's right-hand man, and her mother, Carmen Bartoli, who died in Ravensbrück. Sabine returned only at the end of the war in 1945. Casso was deported to Buchenwald, from where he returned in 1945 to die two weeks later on his native soil. It was only later that I discovered that Sabine Bartoli had left behind her twenty-month-old baby. None of the other accounts had mentioned it.

At the Valmanya ceremony I attended I talked to Sabine's sister, Hermine Gource, a small plump woman with a cloud of fluffy hair, her black outfit enlivened by a string of green beads. She remembered: 'They were looking for Horte and the others. It was because of them they were deported. They held a gun to my head so I didn't talk, while they took them away. Then I was left with the baby.'

Like so many of the men of the village her father was up on the summer pastures with the cows. There are photos of her parents from before the war, both of them unusually unposed. They look unspeakably weary, old before their years. Carmen, in pinafore, with her hair pulled back and sleeves rolled up, stands in front of the Mas as if she has been caught feeding the chickens. Joan Bartoli, in checked shirt and beret, looks down as if he has just came to a stop in exhaustion after bringing down the cows from the mountain.

They did not hear about Carmen's death until the end of the war, when her wedding ring and a letter arrived in the post. Hermine twisted her own wedding ring and wiped her eyes, the memories still close to the surface. 'They'd been sent by a survivor of the camp. My mother had given them to her before she died – she must have known.' They went to see the survivor in a hospital in Bordeaux. 'They'd been put in wagons like animals, with no food or water, then my sister was sent to Czechoslovakia to work . . .' Again she insisted: 'It was because of the Maquis they were taken.'

Fuelled by anger and sorrow at the unknown fate of his wife, as well as his determination to resist at all costs, René Horte did not give up. Only six days after escaping the Mas, his small group of five, including Sabine's husband, Jovino Gonzalez, attacked a patrol of eight German soldiers near the frontier, killing four of them. With his Maquis of

Spanish guerrilleros Horte continued to harass the German frontier police. He is reputed to have killed more Germans than any other single person in the department.

From March 1943, after the forced labour laws were introduced, many young men had taken to the hills to avoid being sent to Germany. More Resistance groups were organised in the region, and attempts made to liaise between the various factions – Gaullists, communists, Spanish – though all kept their organisations separate and it was mostly the Gaullists who benefited from Allied parachute drops of weapons and supplies.

By the end of 1943 a new Maquis group was active on Canigou. They were assembled by Simon Battle, known as *Le Manchot*, 'the one-armed', Battle had grown up in Céret, working in a sawmill, which was where he lost his arm. Despite his handicap he had volunteered for the International Brigade in the Spanish Civil War, and when France fell to the Germans he was a Resistant *depuis le premier jour*. Soon he was an outlaw, hiding out in refuges all around Canigou and the Conflent valley. He was passionately committed, tireless in his efforts to regroup a fighting force after the attacks that had dispersed them. A photo taken in happier times shows him in Céret in 1940 sitting under a tree, with two friends, a girl in a flowery dress and another man. Battle is smiling, relaxed, and tanned, one arm covered with a sleeve tucked into his pocket, with the other nonchalantly smoking a cigarette.

This time the Maquis hid out in a ruined barn on the Col de Cogollo, between the villages of Taurinya and Fillols, on the north side of Canigou a few lateral ridges round the mountain from Valmanya. They took the name Henri Barbusse, after the socialist and pacifist writer whose bestselling novel *Le Feu* had exposed the brutal reality of war in the trenches in the 1914–18 war. (Actually I am told that not all the *maquisards* were even in agreement about their name, since they were Stalinists and Barbusse had been a Marxist-Leninist . . .) The communist core of the group were joined by several young Compagnons de France – the Vichy youth movement – from Prades, fleeing the forced labour laws. Even in photos taken in 1944 all still look terribly young, in their shorts, boots, and army shirts, wearing jaunty scout caps above smooth-skinned faces that look as if they hardly need to shave.

By 1944 the Germans were more determined than ever to crush any rebellion, and the Milice became more vicious in their attacks on Resistants and especially communists. As events came to a head, the

Resistance too had stepped up their battle. In Perpignan in February the deputy head of the Milice was killed on Place Arago. In March the Germans and Milice retaliated with the attack on the Maquis of Pleus, which had been described to me by M. Cabrie when I met him in the village of Cassagnes, when the Maquis were surrounded by 800 Germans and Milice, betrayed by the fifteen-year-old Jean Martinez.

In March the Canigou Maquis received a parachute delivery originally intended for the Gaullist Resistance, dropped on Pla Valenson above Prades. Thirteen containers of arms, munitions, food and cigarettes were shared between the communists and the Spanish. The weapons were hidden in a cave near Ria. Now they were armed.

The sequence of events over the next few months was critical, and I tried to piece together the story from the accounts of various survivors, and the historians who had laboured to reconstruct what happened. Inevitably the versions vary, and often there are key contradictions. André Soucarrat was convinced he had got closer to the truth than anyone. He explained to me with the help of his large calendar. 'To understand what happened in Valmanya you have to go back to May 1944,' he said. 'The Resistance desperately needed money to continue the struggle, and the communists tried to organise the theft of funds from the Trésor Générale in Perpignan.' They tried to attack the security agent who was carrying the funds to the Banque de France, but the attempt was bungled. The agent fired at his attackers, one was wounded and one escaped, but five others were caught and interned in the Citadelle in Perpignan. They were taken to Montpellier, where they were tortured and finally shot, going to their deaths, so it was said, singing the Marseillaise.

As the Allied invasion began in Normandy on 10 June 1944, two young brothers, Julien and Barthélemy Panchot, originally from the village of Canohès, near Perpignan, arrived in Prades. They were wanted by the Germans for communist activity and had fled to join the Maquis in the hills. The brothers looked very alike, with thick dark hair and eyebrows, sharp dark eyes and small moustaches. They were met by Sébastien Rius in the Café Salettes in Prades, and joined the growing group on Pic Cogollo above the village of Fillols. On 27 June Roger Chanal arrived after his narrow escape from deportation to Germany. For him it was to be a baptism of fire.

The Canigou Maquis had been denounced, and early the next morning the group of twenty men and inexperienced youths were attacked by eighty Milice. Roger Chanal remembers: 'It was terrible, I had just arrived, I knew nothing, not even how to use the weapons. All I could do was keep the machine-gunner supplied!'

At first the Maquis held them off, armed with the weapons from the parachute drop, and they mortally wounded one of the Milice. But reinforcements arrived in the shape of forty-five more German border police armed with grenades and machine guns. To this day it is hard to tell who came off worst in the shoot-out. The Milice report to Vichy claimed that six 'terrorists' were killed, one *milicien* fatally wounded and two Germans injured. According to historian Jean Larrieu only one of the Maquis had been wounded, Célestin Arnaud, one of the young men who had escaped forced labour deportation. The Germans burnt the barn to the ground.

I wanted to hear more about the attack, and went up to Fillols one day in the late autumn when the clouds were low on the mountain, the air damp, the falling leaves slippery under foot. It too was a mining village and looks today much as Valmanya would have done, houses with ancient stone walls and slate roofs clustered round the Romanesque church with its iron bell tower. I was introduced to one of the oldest inhabitants, Merce Bigorre, aged ninety, who still lives in the house on the square which she used to run as a café – in her ground floor kitchen there are still two dining tables. Several villagers wandered in as we talked, for her to cuddle the children, and help with some knitting. She is everyone's grandmother, tiny and hunched, but still active and bright eyed, in a sweater of many colours that, of course, she knitted herself. She still goes to feed her chickens twice a day at the top of the village.

She remembered the war years, '*Ah, oui*.' She crossed the border from Spain after the Retirada; as a trained nurse and midwife, 'I had seen enough,' she sighed. She found refuge with an uncle in Fillols, and after the war married Roger Bigorre, one of the key Resistants in the village and a close comrade of Sébastien Rius. Fillols had been one of the first centres of Resistance in the area. Unlike Valmanya, the Fillols iron mine was still in operation, and thus had a population of immigrant workers who were more inclined to resistance than most. 'Of course we were in the Resistance,' said Merce briskly. 'We were Spanish.' There had been an escape line through the village, and the iron mine itself provided hiding places. 'People were afraid – the Germans came up here to look for Roger several times,' she said. 'But we always knew it was them, you could hear them coming – they were the only ones who had a car!'

She shuddered as she remembered the battle. In the village they could hear the shooting and grenades exploding, 'They had only one machine gun. We knew when it stopped that it was all over. Poor things! . . . we really thought they would kill them all.'

But that summer day in July 1944 the Maquis did escape, arranging to meet again high up on Canigou. 'The climb up there usually took three and a half hours.' Merce laughed grimly. 'They just went straight up – they made it up there in only two hours!' Roger Chanal could also remember it all too well. 'I just remember climbing,' he says, 'and hiding all my papers under a stone, I was so worried they would catch me. I never found them again!' They arrived, exhausted by the fight and the gruelling climb, and hid below Pic Joffre, the lower peak of Canigou. There is something primitive, a deeply atavistic impulse, in the idea of seeking sanctuary high on Canigou, the mountain that dominated their lives. It was only safe if you knew it well and knew where to hide, otherwise why spiral ever upwards, almost to the topmost peak, not much bigger than a couple of parking spaces – a dead end? Sixteen of them were found there, shivering and hungry, by Sébastien Rius. He took them to shelter in the Alpine Club chalet at Cortalets, just below the peak.

All were there except Julien Panchot's small contingent. They made a meal of the supplies brought by Rius – potatoes, eggs, rabbits and a few litres of wine – and he advised them how to feed themselves. 'We told them how to recognise the sheep and cattle of suspected collaborators, from the initials branded on their necks.' Then Rius and his companions went to look for the missing group who had retreated to the village of Fillols with Célestin, who was in dire need of medical aid.

After finding a nurse who said that the wound was infected and needed proper medical attention they trudged all the way down to Prades with the injured boy, to find a doctor they trusted. The doctor was attending a birth, so they went to wait at the house of another trusted *maquisard*. By one in the morning there was still no doctor. Finally they went to knock up a surgeon who lived only 25 metres from the Gestapo headquarters, in a row of elegant villas on the road leading down to the Têt River and on to Catllar, Molitg and Mosset. Leaving two men on guard, they climbed over the garden wall and rang the bell. Finally the surgeon appeared at the window. In his handwritten account, given to me by his son Daniel, Rius recalls: 'I told him there had been an accident on the road, "You must come, there are two people injured." ' Reluctantly the doctor came down, and they told him the truth about the Maquis battle. Without letting them finish the doctor refused, indicating the Gestapo only a few houses away. 'But I talked to him about our struggle for liberty, and convinced him.'

In the end he changed his mind, opened the door and took care of their wounded comrade. 'I must take my hat off to that surgeon; after that he took care of many wounded, without regard for the danger despite living so close to the Gestapo, and never asking for payment.'

They returned to Fillols, another 6-kilometre slog back up the mountain, and the remaining small group of Maquis decided to join their comrades in the apparent safety of the Cortalets chalet near the peak. Rius, exhausted from two days of walking, decided to risk a night at his parents' house in Fillols, but at seven that evening his mother woke him, crying: 'Wake up, the Germans have occupied the village.' Bare-chested, with his trousers in his hand, Rius leapt out of the window, ran through the apple orchard and hid in the oak wood, where he dressed. 'I heard a shot. Now it begins, I thought, they will massacre everyone. I was so afraid for the inhabitants, for my parents, my sister and her daughter who had taken refuge in Fillols. They'd assembled them all in the village square, but no one spoke, even those suspected of being *petits collabos*.' After an hour or so the Germans left, having failed to find the wounded men they sought. The Maquis had slipped through their fingers again.

But not for long. For a few days the Maquis stayed at the Cortalets chalet, with Simon Battle hiding out below to tell them when supplies had been left in one of the shepherd's shelters up on the mountain. However, early on the morning of 7 July four *maquisards* arrived from Céret on the other side of Canigou to warn them that a squad of parachutists with dogs, dropped by a silent glider, was heading towards the chalet. Panchot ordered them all to evacuate and they fled down the mountain tracks, scattering pepper behind them to put the dogs off the scent. 'We'll meet again in Valmanya!'

The Germans and Milice encircled Cortalets, but to their frustration it was already empty. They burnt the chalet to the ground. It had been built in the 1890s close enough to the peak to enable keen climbers to spend the night there, and wake before dawn to make the final climb to see the sunrise. Now it was totally destroyed. The chalet de Cortalets was reconstructed after the war and you can still spend the night there to be ready for a sunrise climb to the peak. But you will see on the walls of the dining room photographs of the burnt-out hulk of the building after the Germans' pointless vicious destruction.

It was the sight that greeted Simon Battle, on his way to the chalet, completely unaware of what had happened. He was captured by the

Germans and taken to Perpignan, then Carcassonne. There he was tortured and finally killed when the Germans retreated, with a stick of dynamite shoved in his mouth and set alight. In Prades five young women had also been arrested on suspicion of supplying the Canigou Maquis. Two were released at once but two of them were sent to Carcassonne, where they saw poor Simon Battle. They escaped deportation and were liberated by the Aude Maquis on 20 August. When the escaped Maquis arrived at Valmanya they were warmly welcomed by the villagers, given food, a celebration drink and even a free haircut. René Horte took them up to the disused mine of La Pinouse, their new hideout.

When we all arrived at the mine, we paused while Dr Mary explained the process. We saw the galleries driven deep into the earth from which the iron ore was dug and trucked out on low wagons, and the counterweighted pulley system that swung the ore down the mountainside to the railway below. Until the mine closed in 1936 there had been accommodation here for 500 miners. They would spend all week up here, only returning to their villages and families on Sundays. 'It was like a small town,' Mary gestured. 'They had a grocer, a baker, an electricity generator.' It made a perfect refuge for the Maquis, except perhaps for its vulnerable location.

Several large stone buildings had housed the workers and then the Maquis, but all now were roofless and overgrown, crumbling ruins with empty windows framing blue rectangles of sky.

'Did the Germans blow them up?' Soucarrat asked.

Dr Mary tapped his nose twice with his finger. 'That's something we don't talk about,' he said with a complicit smile. Perhaps the village had helped in the destruction to increase the postwar compensation.

Inside the buildings there was little to see. They were clogged with rubble from the collapsed roofs, and overgrown with a tangle of brambles and ivy. A few twisted iron bedsteads were all that remained as evidence of habitation. It was as if the earth itself preferred to swallow up the story.

Soucarrat produced a plan drawn for him on a sheet of white paper by one of the surviving Maquis he had interviewed. The hillside was sketched in, with directions indicating the descent to Valmanya, the col to the west and the tracks up to the ridge above, a windswept scrubby spur which divided the valleys of the Têt and the Tech. Several dormitories were numbered. Neatly indicated on the map were the grocer-tobacconist, the kitchen, the electricity post, and even a telephone cable to the village. Number 7 was the '*école politique*' where the communists instructed the green youths who had joined them in the correct attitude to Resistance. Also labelled was the 'place of judgement', the 'place of execution' and 'graves'.

By June 1944, as Soucarrat explained, the communists had decided it was time to make another attempt to get funds, and to avenge their comrades shot in Montpellier. The town to be attacked was Prades. Instructions went out for the group to assemble. They wanted to strike hard against the occupiers, 'to inspire the population', and the sixteen men then at Valmanya would not be enough. For some this was their main objective, but others, in particular the communists, had grander schemes, and were determined to establish a force capable of effective intervention during the liberation of the department, and thus a future political role.

More and more Resistants assembled at La Pinouse. They came from various locations around the Conflent valley, and a large group of Spanish guerrilleros arrived from Céret, armed with a precious machine gun. There were also several more young *compagnons*, choosing the uncertain life of the Maquis over deportation, but mostly both frightened and inexperienced, like Roger Chanal himself. They were joined by a man named Nessim Eskenazy, who claimed to have escaped from Haute-Savoie. They agreed to hide him, and he made himself useful, giving shooting lessons and gaining everyone's confidence. Three days after he arrived, on 25 July, he disappeared. According to one account, they watched him walk away in the direction of La Tour de Batère, where there was a German guard post. One of the Maquis had even said: 'We should kill him, he knows everything.' He later turned out to have been a Romanian Jew, a spy in the service of the SS. When he was tried in Perpignan after the war, several of the Canigou Maquis volunteered to be his executioners. By 21 July there were 150 men stationed on the side of Canigou, about 50 French and 100 Spanish guerrilleros. Their hideout was remote but it was also very vulnerable to attack from all around the mountain. None of them were told their precise objective. Chanal recalled: 'We didn't know exactly what was planned, but when I saw the machine gun on the table, I knew something was up.'

Each of the Maquis groups remained in its own quarters. No doubt their different languages sometimes made it hard to communicate. Each had its own commander, Julien Panchot (code name Prosper) for the communists, Dédé Sabatier for the Spanish guerrilleros. Another group was led by René Horte, though they seem not to have been based at La Pinouse. They were relatively well organised, with a warning system established below the village of Valmanya; a flag flown from one of the farms along the way, green if the road was safe and red for danger. A special team was set up to get supplies of food and clothing, and many of the villagers provided food. Their basic diet was meat, beef and mutton, in particular the livestock of known collaborators. 'The Resistance ate the cows of the Pétainists,' Chanal laughed.

Their numbers did not go unnoticed, and the Sub-prefect of Prades was informed. He wrote to the Prefect of the Pyrénées-Orientales: 'The Maquis at Valmanya is growing and is made up mainly of Spaniards. It is no longer possible for the gendarmerie to go to Valmanya because all communication with the village has been cut by the Maquis.'

From 27 July events snowballed. A group of *maquisards* went down to collect a consignment of bread baked specially for them by the baker at Marquixanes, a small village on the main road into Prades from Perpignan. Again even eyewitness accounts differ, but it seems that once they had loaded up the loaves in the requisitioned truck, powered by the gazogene charcoal-burning engine they had to rely on instead of petrol, the vehicle would not start. They were spotted by a German detachment of twenty soldiers. (Other reports suggest the Maquis had been less than discreet, and had flaunted their presence in the village.)

As the Germans began shooting, the *maquisards* scrambled desperately out of the truck and hid in the ditches beside the road. One of them, Roger Roquefort, alias Raoul, from the nearby village of Millas, was badly wounded. He managed to crawl out of the ditch and into a nearby garden, begging for help. The Germans found him there and dragged him out. When he asked for a drink, he was shot between the eyes by Walter Wiese, chief of the German police in Prades. 'Here, I'll give you something to drink,' he is reported to have snarled. Roger Roquefort's funeral took place in Millas the same day Prades was attacked. There is a plaque today in his honour on the road through Marquixanes, opposite the old railway station. He was twenty-one when he died.

It was the symbolic moment the Maquis had been chafing for. As revenge for the killing of Raoul, as well as to impress public opinion and demoralise Vichy and the Milice, the Maquis Henri Barbusse organised a dramatic operation in Prades.

'Were you involved in that attack?' Chanal was asked.

'*Mais non!* Anyone with a connection in Prades – I had been living there for some time – was not involved, in case of reprisals.'

Instead he and another group were sent to the mine at La Batère to get dynamite. They staged a successful hold-up and carried several kilos of dynamite on their backs over the mountain.

On 29 July at 10.45, 200 Maquis attacked Prades. Access to the town was blocked, and the telephone lines were cut. The station, the post office and the gendarmerie were invaded and their tills and drawers emptied. According to the report from the post office, at 11 a.m. they heard shots outside.

'French forces, hands up!' Two people, one with a machine gun, the other a revolver, broke the windows of the door. One of the employees cried: 'The Maquis!' I ran to sound the alarm, then fixed the combination of the safe and locked myself in my apartment. Two men banged on my door demanding to be let in. I opened it, they made me open the safe and took 214,500 francs and put it into a sack. They took another 1,500 francs in coins.

Then, a bureaucratic postcript: 'When they left I asked for a receipt, which they gave me.'

Another group of Spanish guerrilleros attacked the gendarmerie, where there was one French gendarme on the ground floor, and three others upstairs. Here Soucarrat adds more details as we study his calendar and chronology of events, gleaned from the family of the gendarme, who came from Belfort, in eastern France. 'The whole thing was a farce! The guerrilleros, waving their machine gun shouted: "Open the door or we'll bomb the gendarmerie!" but the gendarme, named Beneux, did not understand Catalan, and the guerrilleros spoke no French. He had his orders, not to open to anyone, so he refused and closed the shutters.'

The other gendarmes got the message, came down and opened the door, and finally Beneux understood that they were looking for weapons and climbed on a chair to take down the repeating rifle he kept on top of a cupboard. All their other weapons had already been requisitioned by the Milice. Beneux himself was taken hostage – it is claimed he was carrying a list of people who had supplied potatoes to the Maquis.

Meanwhile another group attacked the Gestapo in the elegant Villa Lafabrègue. Soucarrat explained: 'They knew that between eleven and twelve only four people would be there. That was why the attack took place at that time of day. The whole thing was over in about an hour and a half.'

The Gestapo were attacked by a hail of bullets and grenades. Three of them, including the police chief Walter Wiese, were wounded and one was taken hostage. When my Dutch friend Hans, a gardener, worked in the garden of the villa sixty years later, pruning the plane trees, he found his chainsaw kept hitting bullets still lodged in the tree trunks.

A select group also attacked the bank, stealing typewriters and a considerable amount of money, which historian Jean Larrieu estimates at 1,560,000 francs. To this day, according to Soucarrat, many of the surviving attackers do not know what other groups were doing, and most did not understand that the main objective of the attack was to get money. One told him: 'We thought we were going to Prades to attack the Gestapo, to kill Walter Wiese and avenge the death of Roger Roquefort! Later when I discovered that the post office and the bank had been robbed, I realised they had succeeded, but we never saw a centime, nothing.' The Maquis left in triumph with about 2 million francs, 34 kilos of cigarettes and a supply of new boots and espadrilles. The Resistance was hard on shoes.

They took with them three hostages: the gendarme Beneux, a German customs officer, Ludwig Buttner, age thirty-nine and a *milicien*, Jean Durand Coulanjon, who had been pointed out to them in one of the cafés in Prades. The prisoners were slung into a truck along with the tobacco and shoes, and three hours later were in Valmanya. They were marched up the rough track to La Pinouse. The bags of money were hidden in the cellar beneath the café in Valmanya.

At La Pinouse a trial took place. The sketched plan showed the spot, and we all stood sombrely round a large flat area of grass near the entrance of one of the mine galleries, now overgrown with a tangle of wild raspberries and yarrow.

Sébastien Rius was there. 'A Jew served as interpreter with the German,' he states baldly in his handwritten account. 'The prisoners were condemned to death.' Everybody voted on the sentence, as was the Maquis tradition. The German and the gendarme were killed then and there with a bullet in the back of the neck. The suspected *milicien*, Coulanjon, was held prisoner till the next day in the hope of obtaining information, then he too was shot. According to the sketch plan, the bodies were buried close by. Even now there seems to be a suspiciously green patch of nettles marking the spot.

As we sat on a grassy bank outside the ruins of La Pinouse, each eating our own provisions (the *montagnards* were properly equipped with sausage, cheese, bread and a flask of wine), Daniel Rius talked a little about his father. 'He just sat down one day, many years later, and wrote it all out in an old school exercise book. It took him about a week. He just wrote as he spoke.' But he would never talk to his children about what happened. 'Of course we asked him, had he killed anyone in the war? He would never say yes or no. He just said: "It was war, and it was hard." That's all.'

Apart from the German there was no real proof of the guilt of the other two victims, though both were termed collaborators. Chanal had not been there for the trial, but said he had known Beneux in Prades.

'Was he a collaborator? What was he like?' we asked.

Chanal hesitated a moment. 'He was a bit dry . . . he was a cop. He had arrested Jews . . . But he was not a *collabo*.'

Soucarrat saw his grave near where he lived. 'It is inscribed "*Mort pour la France*", but actually he was shot by the Resistance!' No one said anything to Beneux's wife and children, then in Prades, and they remained ignorant of his fate until late in 1944, when the bodies were discovered by a shepherd and his dog. The German was interred in a German graveyard near Lyon, and Soucarrat and Xancho had been there to try and trace his family. Xancho shook his head. 'It was so frustrating – we saw fresh flowers on his grave and yet we've never been able to find out any more about him.'

The alleged *milicien*, Coulanjon, was exonerated by a tribunal in 1960. There was no proof he had ever belonged to the Milice or been a collaborator, though he may have complained about the Maquis. His widow was finally awarded a pension.

After the trial, Rius records that he returned to Prades with two other Maquis, including the leader of the Spanish guerrilleros. They spent the night hiding out in a hut in the middle of a vineyard, and according to Soucarrat this was when they must have divided the money between the different groups. 'But when you ask them about it, they play dumb. What money? they ask!' Others still insist that the money disappeared while it was hidden in the café in Valmanya. It remains a mystery.

By the next morning Prades was surrounded by Germans. There is no doubt that the attack on Valmanya four days later was revenge for the Resistance raid on Prades. It is not known who gave the order. However in May 1941 the High Commander of the Wehrmacht had ordered that: 'All attacks and all Resistance to the German army of occupation will be punished by a system of terror.'

For a long time the Germans and Milice had wanted to finish off the Maquis Henri Barbusse and the village of Valmanya, a key point of the Catalan Resistance since 1941. They relished their chance.

During the afternoon of 31 July, a combined force of the Wehrmacht, the German frontier police, and the SS, numbering about 500 altogether, plus 120 Milice, began to assemble north and south of Canigou, in the town of Vinça, east of Prades, and in the Tech valley. They began to encircle La Pinouse and the Maquis.

One German column left from Vinça and climbed the valley of Lentilla up to Valmanya. To the south, a column left from Arles-sur-Tech in the Vallespir and climbed by way of Corsavy and La Batère over the Col de Cirère and down to La Pinouse. From the west, German patrols came from the burnt-out Cortalets chalet to the north around the peak of Canigou and through the forest of l'Estanyol. The Milice – three groups from the Pyrénées-Orientales and one from the neighbouring Aude department – took up a position in the forest of La Bastide to the east, ready to intercept the *maquisards* withdrawing from the German advance.

The Maquis were tricked into believing that an attack would come from the mountain heights on the morning of 1 August, and they concentrated all their forces there. A small group of ten Spanish guerrilleros waited 2 kilometres below Valmanya to defend the entry to the village and keep an eye on the road, and a handful of French Maquis were posted on the balcony of a villa at the entrance to the village, ready to help to evacuate the villagers if necessary. The villagers waited in vain for the attack that morning, and finally resumed their daily routine. The trap worked. While most of the Maquis waited on the ridge above for the Germans, the main body of troops set out from Vinça and Baillestavy in the valley below.

I imagined Germans climbing the same road to Valmanya, passing a few isolated little farms on the plain, the peasants watching as they tended their vines and fruit trees, before entering the valley, to twist and turn mile after mile with murder in their hearts. Their intention was to destroy the village, kill the inhabitants and wipe out the Maquis. By then they knew that the war was all over, and they wanted revenge. How much was known by then of the atrocities committed elsewhere in June? At Tulle, in retaliation for a Maquis attack, the SS seized 99 men at random, tore them from their families and hanged them publicly from the balconies of the town. And there was Oradour-sur-Glane, where 642 villagers were massacred in the church, and the whole village burnt down.

The Germans had cut the telephone lines to avoid anyone warning Valmanya of their approach, but when the head of the German column approached the outskirts of Valmanya about 5 p.m. that evening, the group of guerrilleros keeping watch below the village spotted them with binoculars. They opened fire as soon as the Germans were close enough. One story goes that they held off the German troops for two hours, but Soucarrat disagrees. The metal detector began to make sense. 'We investigated the whole area and found only a few bullets – the hunters with us could see that the marks on the bullets meant they had only three guns and a machine gun. There were only fifty-seven bullets, so they could only have been shooting for a few minutes.'

But there was enough time for one of the Milice to climb up to the village by another route, speak to his collaborator father-in-law there and tell him to reassure the villagers that there had been only one German motorbike and it had already gone away. Whatever the precise preliminaries at nightfall about 7 p.m. in late summer, the Germans swapped their boots for espadrilles and crept towards the village. (I confess that I puzzle over this detail. Did they change their shoes again in order to fight?)

It would have taken several hours for all the German tanks and troops to arrive there. One of the witnesses in the film, a child at the time, described hiding all night long behind a wall as the Germans passed a few feet away.

The six Maquis at the entrance to the village opened fire as the Germans approached and did hold them off with grenades and Sten guns for twenty-five minutes, just enough time for most of the villagers to escape. It is this action, according to Soucarrat, that was the most critical in saving lives, since most of the Maquis were up on the ridge above the village expecting the Germans from the other direction.

The village population of about a hundred inhabitants and sixty refugees fled to the woods and caves they knew so well, trembling with fear as their village was destroyed. Few had time to return to their homes to retrieve any of their possessions. One little girl was left crying in the middle of the square, both parents thinking she was with the other. When her mother realised she was missing, she insisted to the *maquisard* with them: 'Give me the gun and go and find my daughter!' He managed to rescue her and return her to her mother.

François Arquer, then the sixteen-year-old son of the café owner, remembers it well. I met him on the day of the Valmanya commemoration in August and arranged to talk to him later at his home in Baillestavy. There I had first stopped to visit my English-speaking French friend Renée Castellas, for a cup of tea, and while I was still there M. Arquer was already knocking on the door. He had fallen out with Soucarrat over his interpretation of events, and was anxious to give his version of the story. He believed Soucarrat was being unfair to the communist Resistants. 'He only talks to the Right. One of them even has a picture of Chirac on his wall!' Old political differences die hard.

He bent towards me, a tall, rangy man, with a fringe of grey hair framing his angular face. 'This is only the second time I've ever talked about it,' he said abruptly, and it became clear to me then just how raw these memories remained. A whole generation had been traumatised by what happened.

'My parents were in a field two kilometres outside the village, with my cousin. The Germans were really close before they saw them and they had to crouch down and hide behind a wall while they waited for them to pass.'

Arquer was persuaded to sit down at the table in the dim coolness of my friend's cottage. He dragged his hand over his face, the skin stretched taut.

'I ran away with the others and had no idea what had happened to them. Later I met someone on the path who said, Your parents are alive!' His voice broke. 'I still dream of it now, I see the house I was brought up in burning down, not knowing where my parents were . . .'

His grandmother also had a blessed escape. Sixty-five-year-old Madame Arquer found herself trapped in her house when they started the fires. With the aid of a bed sheet, she escaped from a first-floor window, 'Then she jumped a metre-high fence,' marvelled Arquer, settling in his chair at the table, 'and hid in a corn field. She played dead all night and all the following day. The German soldiers passed beside her, and kicked her body, but they were convinced she was dead.'

Arquer added a touching postscript to this story, which I had never heard before. 'The dog found my grandmother, and began licking her face. She was sure he would bark and give her away but he didn't. He went off to find my grandfather, who was up on the pasture with the cows. He usually carried the milk down every day. He only spoke Catalan, and knew nothing of what had happened to his wife or children. The dog tried to drag him to help his wife. The dog ran back and forth between the two of them . . .' Here Arquer chokes back his tears, overwhelmed with the memory. He paused, remembering his grandmother, and added bitterly: 'She said she heard mostly French voices, while they were destroying the village . . .'

Four of the inhabitants of Valmanya refused to leave, believing they would not be in danger. Both Jacques Romeu, aged eighty-one (Arquer's uncle), and Pierre Baux, seventy-one, thought they were too old. Two Spanish woodcutters, José Gimeno, fifty, and Emitiero Barrera, thirty-five, perhaps thought it was not their fight. But all were beaten and, it was said, savagely tortured before being executed. According to one account, the elderly Baux tried to return to his house, and when a *milicien* obstructed him he hit him with his walking stick. The action has an obstinately authentic ring to it. This provoked the massacre of them all.

Their corpses were left without burial by express instruction of the Germans. When the bodies were finally retrieved after eight days exposed to the August sun, they were in such a state of decomposition that they had to be burnt where they lay. When the inhabitants of Valmanya saw the blackened corpses they believed the Germans had burnt them alive. Either way, any evidence of torture was destroyed. They were buried in the church cemetery above the still blackened village later that month. Their tombs can be still be seen there.

There was one further atrocity. It was recorded by René Horte in his deposition as the new mayor of Valmanya in November 1944, a bitter, angry account written while his wife was still in Ravensbrück. According to Horte a young woman of thirty-one who was four months pregnant and had with her two other children, a girl of eight and a boy of eighteen months, was raped by fourteen soldiers. According to Soucarrat, who spoke to her daughter, the woman would have been killed had she not been able to show her *livret de famille*, the official booklet recording births and deaths, which proved she was a widow, and not hiding a man. Later Soucarrat pointed out the house on the edge of the village, one of the few old buildings still remaining, with battered old wooden shutters and weathered roof tiles. Presumably the Germans were too busy inside to burn it. It has remained empty, the garden is overgrown and two horses were grazing around the doorway. Nobody talks about the rape now, indeed no mention was made of it in any further reports. The daughter kept the *livret de famille*, a macabre souvenir.

Dr Mary was in Valmanya when the Germans came, then a small boy of eleven. 'Both my father and grandfather thought I was with the other, and when I realised I was on my own I ran to hide in one of the mine galleries.' He stayed there all night. 'I could hear everything' – he flicks his wrist as if to eliminate the memory. 'The Germans and Milice had a party [*Ils ont fait la fête*]. I could hear them shooting all the animals, and smashing up the houses.'

After looting everything they could, killing the domestic animals, smashing all the furniture and agricultural equipment with hammers, and drinking the contents of the cellars the invaders set fire to the houses. By midnight flames were leaping to the sky, the whole village was on fire. With the exception of the church the village was razed to the ground. By the light of a full moon, the villagers watched helplessly as the flames consumed the lives they had always known. Photos taken soon afterwards show almost total destruction, with only blackened walls left standing, roofs and doors and shutters gone and the contents obliterated.

After setting fire to the village the Germans set out at dawn to flush out the Maquis, still on guard on the ridge above. They attacked from all sides, with tanks and machine guns, a brutal, well-trained fighting force. By contrast many of the Maquis were young and untrained, and certainly poorly armed. They were hopelessly outnumbered. The daughter of the raped woman, talking to Soucarrat, described seeing the Germans swarming 'like ants' over the mountainside, climbing to the heights, and firing furiously. 'My ears hurt. I covered them with my hands. It was unbearable!'

According to one *maquisard* witness: 'The Germans and the Milice came from all directions. We were attacked on all sides, and we didn't have the weapons or the ammunition to keep up the fight for long. The young ones soon fled in panic, abandoning their arms.'

Soucarrat investigated the ridge with the metal detector. 'There were only German bullets there. The Maquis had no time to respond. There was no battle.' Others argue that this is not definitive proof, that the Maquis themselves might have been using German ammunition. The official website of the village insists that there were three hours of heavy fighting before the Maquis dispersed.

The Maquis fled through the German lines around the upper reaches of Canigou, guided by the few locals and seasoned fighters who knew the paths of their mountain. Some found a goat track down to the village of Estoher, where they were sheltered by one of the women of the village. Only two actually died, one of them sadly never accounted for; he was probably injured and hid out in a shepherd's shelter that was later put to the torch. Despite everything, the Germans and the Milice had failed to vanquish the Maquis. Some headed for the other side of the Têt valley, and headed for Mosset and the Col de Jau to join the Maquis group there.

Perhaps for that reason Valmanya was no more than a footnote for the Germans. According to the German specialist Xancho: 'For the Germans Valmanya was insignificant. The report written immediately after the attack on 4 August 1944 simply says: "A mission against the bandits between 1 and 3 August was carried out with 13 wounded." ' According to the report filed from the Préfecture, the losses of the 'terrorists' were five killed and ten captured, those of the Germans and Milice were about the same.

Accounts of the burning of Valmanya and the fighting between the Germans and the Maquis vary considerably. Every participant had their own particular viewpoint, and no attempt was made at the time to compile a true version, even had it been possible. Probably no one will ever know the true sequence of events.

After our brief lunch break (the *montagnards* even provided a flask of coffee) Xancho unpacked his metal detector and spade and we walked down to a corner at the end of the ruined buildings, the most sacred corner at La Pinouse. There on the stone wall a marble plaque was displayed:

> Ici est tombé Julien Panchot. Capitaine des 4101ième et 4102ème
> Compagnies FTPF Maquis Henri Barbusse
> Les Armes à la Main Face aux Hordes Nazies
> 2.8.1944

Panchot had been responsible for a group of eight men who were detailed to defend the approaches to the village from the east. According to the official Resistance accounts, when the Germans attacked the Maquis, Panchot was wounded in the legs. Unable to run, he took up a position facing the enemy, armed with the machine gun. He told his men to flee, and covered the retreat of his team, and kept firing until he had run out of ammunition. He was taken prisoner, left for a day with his wounds untended, then tortured (the usual practice was to tear out fingernails and hair, and gouge out the eyes) and killed. Unable to stand, he was shot sitting against the wall of one of the buildings at the mine of La Pinouse. From this point on the mountain there is a spectacular panoramic view northward to the Fenouillèdes and beyond. I found myself thinking what an amazing last view to see as you are being shot, but then I remembered they had gouged his eyes out.

Soucarrat wanted to know all the details. He turned to Roger Chanal, the last remaining witness of these events. Chanal had been sent down to investigate what was happening at La Pinouse. 'At first it seemed to be all over, but I could still hear some shooting, and then I was shot at.' He tumbled into the stream and pretended to be dead, then crept his way down the river bed, crawling from stone to stone. In desperation, the eighteen-year-old climbed into a tree to hide. It was then he saw a group of five or six German soldiers with Julien Panchot.

'You are sure it was Prosper?' asked Soucarrat.

'*Oui, oui, c'était lui.* He was obviously wounded and was being dragged back down to La Pinouse by the Germans. They passed right under my tree.' He shuddered at the memory.

Chanal stayed in his tree till nightfall, and then crept his way around the complex of buildings at La Pinouse, crossed to the other side of the river, climbed into another tree and went to sleep. He heard no more from the Germans or from poor Julien Panchot. No one will ever know the truth about Prosper's last stand.

The seven men gathered round the corner of the house below the plaque to Prosper. Daniel Rius produced one of the books about Valmanya with photographs of Panchot's body, a dark, broken corpse. 'The body was stretched out right here when it was found.' Daniel Rius demonstrates, lowering himself into position. He points out the bullet holes low in the wall carefully outlined in white paint. 'They are so low down, he must have been sitting, not standing, when he was shot.'

Soucarrat peers inside the building. 'This is where the Maquis lived, all their belongings would have been here. This is where the Germans would have stopped to go through everything. It's probably here that Panchot was tortured.' They started to dig at the spot, hoping to find more bullets, the proof that this was indeed where Panchot was shot. But it was difficult and they found nothing. Soucarrat was frustrated. 'There must be twenty centimetres of roof tiles and rubble here, before we get to the original ground level.'

Panchot's tortured body had been found two weeks later by his brother Barthélemy and René Brial, a fellow member of the Maquis. They had covered it with a temporary cairn of branches and stones, to protect it from wild animals. Later Brial wrote: 'He had been shot sitting down. The bullet marks were about 75 cm high on the wall. He had no eyes and his hands were mutilated. There were only two fingers left on his right hand.' There were fourteen bullet holes in his body. After the Liberation, on 29 August, a large group of people went up to reclaim the body, and a photo was taken of them all in front of the coffin. Panchot's mother, Marguerite, stands to one side of the group, dressed entirely in black, a shawl wrapped around her head, her face a mask of suffering acceptance. The body was brought down in a coffin roped on to the back of a mule and taken to his native village of Canohès, to be buried with due ceremony.

As we made our way back down the same stony path, I asked Daniel Rius what he thought of this literally digging up history. 'It's just another theory, that's all,' he said. 'It is impossible to know the truth.' So why was Soucarrat so determined to know what really happened? I asked him.

In his film script he writes:

when Panchot's funeral took place on 1 September in Canohès, the leader of the communist Front National gave a speech. 'Due to the sacrifice of Julien Panchot, the women, children and old people of Valmanya escaped torture, and being burnt to death.' But Panchot had nothing to do with saving the village. That was due to the actions of the Spanish guerrilleros and the Maquis who had defended the village and warned the inhabitants. Panchot is owed respect because he died for his ideals, and for freedom. But not because he saved Valmanya.

During August the Germans withdrew from Valmanya. René Horte and his group of Spanish guerrilleros attacked them on the way down, throwing home-made bombs, destroying one of the trucks and killing several Germans. The Germans took their loot from Valmanya – sheets, crockery, linen, and ornaments – and sold it cheap on the streets of Vinça. Everything was snapped up. One of the women of Valmanya said in the film: 'I still don't know which family is sleeping in my sheets, embroidered with my initials.'

Later the village of Valmanya was awarded the Croix de Guerre. Yet a thick veil has fallen over these events. All the archives had been burnt in the fire, and a collective amnesia took hold of the inhabitants who remained – only forty-four in 1946. They had no wish to remember.

A further twist emerged during the commemoration day I attended. One of the remaining Maquis had been forbidden by the mayor to make a speech, and it turned out that this was because André Soucarrat had discovered he was an impostor. There is a film, *Un Héros trés discret* (A self-made Hero) which tells the story of a man who invents his Resistance past, and here was a bizarre corollary.

'It was odd,' Soucarrat later recalled. 'He was the only one who knew what happened from beginning to end.' When Soucarrat arranged a round-table discussion for former *maquisards* at his home, another of the Maquis had looked at the man across the table and said: 'You were never one of us.' Soucarrat took notice. 'I began comparing his accounts in the two interviews I did. I set traps for him and it was obvious he was making it all up. He had studied it all and memorised the sequence of events, taking on the identity of another Maquis of the same surname.' He was apparently the only one who never returned his release form giving permission to be filmed. This new revelation was just emerging as I left the ceremony lunch, with worried whispering groups discussing this latest revelation. Somehow this one man's rather sad gesture, his desire for vicarious glory seemed emblematic.

The fact that his story had been largely accepted emphasised the general uneasiness with the past, a deep reluctance to ask too many questions. Anyone researching the history of a rural area so far removed from the mainstream of events, is likely to encounter a natural instinct to close ranks against curious outsiders. When those events took place over sixty years ago, and are compounded by the hatreds of not one but two viciously fought wars, it is not surprising that the truth is hard to find. The closed faces and unbroken silences of so many in this region conceal truths that will never be spoken.

# EPILOGUE

'It is more arduous to honour the memory of the nameless
than that of the renowned. Historical construction is devoted to the memory of the nameless.'

Walter Benjamin

As I lean out of the window at Corbiac for the last time, I find myself
wishing I was writing a novel. Then I could resolve what would happen
to everyone, decide the fate of my characters, tie up the ends neatly. But
for most of these people there were no tidy endings, indeed for most
the impact of the war is still unresolved. For those who suffered, who
were tortured, betrayed or killed, there was real pain, both for them and
their loved ones. Pain that has often lived on to the next generation.
And for those who themselves were guilty of betrayal and of inflicting
pain, it was terrible too. The shame too lives on. As perhaps it does for
those who did nothing. Now I could better understand why so many
were reluctant to talk, had never talked about it. There is a sweet irony
that honour is due most to those who quietly, often anonymously,
resisted in any way they could.

After Pierre died, Amélie moved to Mosset with her children. The
small rural community had become her home. There was milk to be
had in Mosset. Corbiac was sold, though the family kept some of the
land. Henri, the much-loved first child, came to tea with me there one
day not long before he died, the first time he had been back since he
was a child. He was clearly moved by the experience, remembering the
apples they stored in the old vaulted cellar, bringing up water from the
river when the well ran dry. Later I met his sister, Michèle, who gave
me her parents' letters and said how pleased she thought her father
would have been with the restoration work we had done. We had begun
to fulfil his dream.

At La Coûme too the dream lived on. Pitt Krüger did return after the
war, though his fate remained unknown for some years. His wife Yvès
used all the means in her power to find him, eventually tracking him
down with the aid of the Red Cross. After his initial imprisonment in
Perpignan he had been dispatched to a concentration camp in Germany. He was compelled to join the German army, and sent to fight

against the Russians as they encircled Berlin. 'We were dug in there for three days and nights without food or relief,' Krüger recalled. 'Behind us were the SS, in front of us the Russians.'

He was imprisoned by the Red Army and ended up in a Leningrad concentration camp. 'The camp was very hard, like those described by Solzhenitsyn,' Krüger said, but nevertheless, 'I don't regret my captivity in Russia. I'd been fourteen or fifteen when the Russian revolution happened, and it always represented a great hope to us. I wanted to see it with my own eyes.'

Eventually Krüger's anomalous situation became known. 'I accepted that German prisoners should work to rebuild Russia, but it was ironic for me to be there, one of the first victims of Nazism, an anti-fascist and French Resistant.' Eventually he was freed and returned to France in July 1948, utterly wasted by his ordeal. Denis Healey described visiting La Coûme again in 1970 and listening to the details of Pitt's ordeal in the Russian camps. 'I was moved to uncontrollable tears,' Healey wrote.

Meanwhile Hilda Clark had given the farm outright to Yvès, who struggled to hold it all together, even after a fire destroyed the farmhouse in 1945. Among the volunteers who arrived to help rebuild it was a young railwayman, Gérard Bétoin. He stayed, married and brought up his family there, and it is they who have helped to maintain the spirit of the place today.

After the war La Coûme became a charitable foundation, L'Ecole de Plein Air, the Open Air School, following the educational philosophy that had always inspired the Krügers. It was based on practical experience and outdoor life, teaching children independence and self-reliance. Conditions were spartan, and economic necessity demanded that the children should take part in the life and work of the community. When they were rebuilding each child had to carry a brick up the steep hill each time they returned. Two children were dispatched daily to pick up the milk churn from the lane at the bottom of the hill.

Pitt Krüger died in 1989, Yvès the year before; both are buried at La Coûme. It was the year we came to Mosset, and although I never met them I was glad to have been living in the same village even for a short time.

A few years ago a conference at La Coûme gathered children from Germany, Spain and France to research the history of refugees in the region; the camps at Rivesaltes, St-Cyprien and Argelès, and the refugees at La Coûme. The memorial museum that the children proposed on the site of one of the old camps is at last being established at Rivesaltes.

Another year Dutch members of the community in Mosset organised a German writers' conference about the war. It was a truly international moment; one of the children of Spanish exiles, Serge Barda, described the experience of his parents on the beaches of Argelès. Though Spanish, he spoke in French; Margriet, a Dutchwoman living in Mosset, translated his words into German for the visiting writers.

The spirit of Pablo Casals lives on here too. He continued to live in Prades after the war, and remained involved in the welfare of the refugees. He was bitterly disappointed at the reluctance of the West to liberate Spain, and as a protest refused to play in public any more. It was, he said, 'the greatest sacrifice of my life'. Many attempts were made to persuade him to perform in the USA, for which he was offered large sums of money, but he always refused. Eventually the Americans decided to come to him, and suggested a music festival in Prades, this shabby little town with few hotels and no auditorium. But it happened, and evolved into the Prades Bach Festival, now a key date in the European musical calendar. The ancient abbey of St Michel de Cuxa is the main performing space, its high Romanesque vault providing fine acoustics, best of all for the haunting notes of a single cello. All over the area music concerts are played in small churches throughout the summer months, a legacy of art and beauty directly attributable to Casals's exile here.

In 1960 in Puerto Rico he finally completed the oratorio of the *Pessebre*, the poem he had begun to set to music in the dark days of 1943. It became the focus of a peace campaign which preoccupied Casals for the rest of his life. He said: 'Through this music I have sought to draw attention to the suffering that afflicts humanity, to the fearful danger of nuclear war, and to the happiness man can attain if all men work together as brothers and in peace.'

For the Spanish the war was not over. Pierre Solanes described to me the day, 25 August 1944, when they finally came down from the mountain.

'I'll never forget it – it was my birthday – the sense of rejoicing as we all piled into the truck, and headed down the road to Perpignan to join in the celebrations. It was such a big day! There were two Spaniards in our Maquis group, and about halfway to Perpignan they suddenly stopped the truck and jumped out. They simply disappeared. I never understood why . . .'

They still had their own war to fight. They had continued the war against fascism in France believing that once the Allies had defeated Hitler, they would turn to Franco. They waited, while negotiations went on amongst the great powers. They had to wait a long time. Franco remained in power until he died in 1975. Many of the Spanish exiles remained imprisoned in the camps, some eventually returned to Spain, but large numbers were absorbed into the local population, another emotional thread through this frontier land.

Certainly one of the key elements I came to understand in writing this book was the role of the Spanish. I realised I could not fully comprehend what happened in this region of France without going beyond its borders, and learning more about the Spanish Civil War helped in understanding what happened in France, which as a result of defeat and occupation was reduced to its own civil war as the politics of left and right polarised inexorably.

It is this that makes the French experience of the war so different from the British. We fought and won the war together, not without dissension naturally, but resulting in a communal feeling of pride, untainted by compromise. We don't know what we would have done had the Germans invaded Britain – though in the Channel island of Guernsey, the nearest we got to occupation, the population gave up its Jews as soon as the Germans arrived. The French have had to live with a sense of shame, and perhaps worse, a loss of trust in others. Even now there are those who are ostracised for their perceived collaboration, village cafés which are still earmarked for one side or the other.

They were presented with moral choices that we never had to make. Jean-Paul Sartre said that being in the Occupied zone with the Germans as a daily presence made the choices more acute. Unlike my Spanish friend, we do not weep for our poets.

I have wanted most of all to pay tribute to those who did choose on principle to resist, those who made that moral choice: to the Germans who stood against the Nazis, the Resistance who risked their lives, the brave Spanish partisans, the Quakers and other aid organisations, the nurses in the camps, the priests who defied the Church hierarchy, the gendarmes who warned Jews about the round-ups, the garage owner who put sugar cubes in the Germans' petrol tanks. All the candles in the darkness. It is important to remember them. The classic quotation from George Santayana bears repeating – 'Those who forget history are doomed to repeat it.'

In getting to know my adopted country better, I have grown to love it more, to feel more emotionally involved. Every love does have its landscape. More than ever I enjoy returning there, savour my first sight of the mountains, the first glimpse of the peak of Canigou. Some of that profound French attachment to their own little corner has rubbed off on me.

As I finish writing this book I can hear church bells chiming, the bells of another village. We too have sold Corbiac, passed the baton on to others who want to establish a retreat there and use the chapel for music once again – the closest we could get to the monks. We have moved further down the Castellane valley, closer to Canigou. We see the mountain from another angle now. Sometimes it seems such an implacable presence, with a serenity and permanence that is immensely reassuring. But mountains do not remember. It is people who must remember.

# SELECT BIBLIOGRAPHY

Appelfeld, Aaron, *The Story of a Life*, Hamish Hamilton, London, 2005.

Baldock, Robert, *Pablo Casals*, Victor Gollancz, London, 1992.

Barber, Noel, *The Week France Fell*, Macmillan, London, 1976.

Barlone. D. A., *French Officer's Diary*, Cambridge University Press, 1942.

Beevor, Antony, *The Battle for Spain*, Weidenfeld & Nicolson, London, 2006.

Benassar, Bartolome, *La Guerre d'Espagne et ses lendemains*, Perrin, Paris, 2004.

Bohny-Reiter, Friedel, *Journal de Rivesaltes*, Editions Zoé, Geneva, 1993.

Boitel, Anne, *Le Camp de Rivesaltes*, Mare Nostrum, Perpignan, 2001.

Bonet, Gérard, *Les Pyrénées Oriéntales dans la Guerre 1939–1944*, Horvath, Ecully, 1992.

Bousquet, Jean, *Mosset*, Ciais, Nice, 1999.

Brenan, Gerald, *The Spanish Labyrinth*, Cambridge University Press, 1960.

Brodersen, Momme, *Walter Benjamin: a Biography*, Verso, London, 1996.

Brome, Vincent, *The Way Back*, O'Leary Cassell, London, 1957.

Burrin, Philippe, *Living with Defeat. France under the Germans*, The New Press, New York, 1996.

Callil, Carmen, *Bad Faith. A Story of Family and Fatherland*, Jonathan Cape, London, 2006.

Casals, Pablo, *Joys and Sorrows*, Simon & Schuster, New York, 1970.

Caskie, Donald, *The Tartan Pimpernel*, Oldbourne Press, London, 1957.

Chaix-Durand, Gemma, *Un poéme en terre étrangère*, Domens, Pezenas, 1997.

Cobb, Richard, *French and Germans. Germans and French*, Brandeis University Press, London, 1983.

Collier, Basil, *Catalan France*, J.M. Dent, London, 1939.

Cros, Pierre, *Saint Cyprien de 1939–1945*, Trabucaire, Canet, 2001.

Curtis, Jean-Louis, *The Forests of the Night (Les Forêts de la nuit)*, John Lehmann, London, 1950.

Eychenne, Emilienne, *Pyrénées de la Liberté*, Editions Privat, Toulouse, 1983.

Fittko, Lisa, *Escape through the Pyrenees*, Northwestern University Press, Illinois, 1991.

Folcher, Gustave, *Marching to Captivity, The War Diaries of a French Peasant. 1939–45*, Brasseys, London, 1996 (François Maspero, Paris, 1981).

Forty, George, and Duncan, John, *The Fall of France*, Guild Publishing, London, 1990.

Foot, M.R.D., *SOE in France*, Frank Cass, London, 2004.

Foulkes, Peter, *Tales from French Catalonia*, Xlibris, USA, 2000.

Fry, Varian, *Surrender on Demand*, Johnson Publishing, Colorado, 1977.

Grando, René, Querault, Jacques, Febrés, Xavier, *Camps du Mepris*, Editions Trabucaire, Perpignan, 1999.

Healey, Denis, *The Time of My Life*, Michael Joseph, London, 1989.

Jackson, Julian, *France. The Dark Years, 1940–1944*, Oxford University Press, 2001.

Janes, Peter Scott, *Conscript Heroes*, Paul Mould Publishers, 2004.

Kedward, Roderick, *In Search of the Maquis*, Clarendon Press, Oxford, 1993.

Koestler, Arthur, *Scum of the Earth*, Eland, London, 1991.

Laharie, Claude, *Le Camp de Gurs*, J & D Editions, Pau, 1993.

Larrieu, Jean, Gual, Ramon, *Vichy, l'Occupation Nazie et la Résistance Catalane*, 4 vols, Terra Nostra, Codalet, 1994–1998.

Lazare, Lucien, *Rescue as Resistance. How Jewish Organizations Fought the Holocaust in France*, Columbia University Press, New York, 1996.

Levi, Primo, *If this is a Man/ The Truce*, Abacus, London, 1991.

Long, Helen, *Safe Houses are Dangerous*, William Kimber, London, 1985.

Lowrie, Donald, *The Hunted Children*, W.W. Norton, New York, 1963.

Marin, Progreso, *Exil. Temoignages sur la Guerre d'Espagnol les Camps et la Resistance au Franquisme*, Editions Loubatières, Portet-sur-Garonne, 2005.

Marriott, Edward, *Claude and Madeleine, A True Story*, Picador, London, 2005.

Maury, Lucien, *La Résistance Audoise*, Comité d'Histoire de la Résistance, Aude, 1980.

Mercer, Catherine, *Revenge and Regret*, Camdale Press, Bristol, 2000.

Mettay, Joel, *L'Archipel du Mepris, Histoire du Camp de Rivesaltes de 1939 à nos jours*, Editions Trabucaire, Canet, 2001.

Neave, Airey, *Saturday at M19, Underground Escape Lines*, Hodder and Stoughton, London, 1969.

Orwell, George, *Homage to Catalonia*, Penguin Books, London, 1964.

Parens, Henri, *Renewal of Life*, Schreiber Publishing, Rockville, Maryland, 2004.

Paxton, Robert, *Vichy France*, Barrie & Jenkins, London, 1972.

Perpigna, Michel, *Les Mossetans*, Les Presses Litteraires, Saint-Esteve, 2005.

Rousso, Henry, *The Vichy Syndrome*, Harvard University Press, 1991.

Ruffiandis, Jean-Jacques, *Mosset, Vieille Cité*, Tramontane, Perpignan, 1970.

Stein, Louis, *Beyond Death and Exile*, Harvard University Press, 1979.

Synessvedt, Alice Resch, *Over the Highest Mountains*, Intentional Productions, California, 2005.

Teissier de Cros, Janet, *Divided Loyalties*, Canongate, Edinburgh, 1992.

Thomas, Hugh, *The Spanish Civil War*, Eyre & Spottiswoode, London, 1961.

Vercors, Michel, *Le Silence de la Mer*, Editions Albin, Paris, 1951.

Vinen, Richard, *The Unfree French. Life under the Occupation*, Penguin, London, 2007.

Webster, Paul, *Pétain's Crime*, Macmillan, London, 1990.

Wriggins, Howard, *Picking up the Pieces from Portugal to Palestine: Quaker Refugee Relief in World War II*, University Press of America, New York, 2004.

Xancho, Christian, *La Wehrmacht à Port Vendres*, Mare Nostrum, Perpignan, 2004.

*Exilés en France – Souvenirs d'antifascistes allemands émigrés (1933–1945) (Interview with Pitt Krüger)*. Actes et Mémoires du peuple – Françis Maspéro, 1982.

# ACKNOWLEDGEMENTS

I would like to thank the libraries and individuals who have helped in the research for this book. The London Library was a rich source of material on wartime history. The Library of the Society of Friends at Friends House provided books and unpublished material on the Quakers, the Imperial War Museum gave advice on contacting military personnel, and the Royal Escaping Society supplied contacts; the Institut Français was an excellent source of French material, and the French Resistance Archive at Anglia Ruskin University, Cambridge yielded several elusive books. The library of Mosset has been as helpful as ever and has waited patiently for my long overdue books. The Municipal Archives in Perpignan located key information. A big thank-you to historian Jean Larrieu for his initial encouragement and his own in-depth research.

I am very grateful to all those I have interviewed for sharing their memories and information, Montserrat Alavedra, François Arquer, Marc Belli, Olivier Bétoin, Pierre Bétoin, Merce Bigorre, Willem Brederode, Roger Chanal, Martha Casulleras, Narcisse Falguera, Henri Goujon, Hermine Gource, Elvira Grau, Louisette Grau, Denis Healey, Gordon Laming, Reg Lewis, Madame Marty, Dr Francis Mary, Sonia Marzo, José Molina, Jamine Noack, Yvette Querol, Jean and Marcelle Rostand, Roger Rull, Pierre Solanes, Odette Sabaté-Loiseau. And to Jean Sanchez (Jonquille) and all the members of the Maquis de Salvezines for sharing their lunch and wartime memories with me.

Special acknowledgement is due to Henri Melich, José Sangenis, Michel Perpigna and Jean Kohn for allowing me to quote from their own writings, published and unpublished, to Gerard and Daniel Rius, the sons of Sébastien Rius for giving me his account, and to André Soucarrat and Christian Xancho for generously sharing their research.

I am grateful to everyone who has helped me with advice and assistance; Jacqueline Bergès, Pierre Bétoin, Renée Castellas, Marie-Jo Delattre, Monique Didier-Mereau, Gemma Durand, Robin Eggar, Peter Foulkes, Annick Four, Keith Janes, Christopher Long, Paul Mirat, Pierre Noack, Gabriel Pages, Jean Parès, Log Pareathumby, Hans Peters, Marianne Petit, Paulette Puig, Henri Sentenac, Paul Timberlake, Lettie Uilerwijk and Clara Villaneuva, and especially to Ginette Vincendeau, for incisive editorial criticism.

A heartfelt thanks to the Society of Authors who awarded me a grant from the Francis Head Bequest when it was most needed. A very special thank-you to Martha Stevns – much of this book was written in her house in

Mosset, where the peace of the swimming pond provided a blessed respite from stories of war.

Thanks to my agent, Julian Alexander, for his confidence in the project, and to my editors, Alan Samson, Lucinda McNeile and Steve Cox, for all their work. To my son Theo whose school studies on the Second World War provided a wider context for my story, to my mother, Irene Bailey, for her memories of the war in Britain, and her loving support, and to my husband Barry Miles as ever for his love, loyalty and patience, his editorial skill, and for all those morning cups of tea.

The translations are my own as are any mistakes. I have changed a few names in order to protect the privacy of some individuals. I have not included footnotes but anyone wishing for further information or background is welcome to contact me via my website www.rosemarybailey.com

# INDEX